P9-DXM-483

DISCARD

Silver Poets
of the
Seventeenth Century

Edited, with an introduction, by
G. A. E. Parfitt
School of English Studies,
University of Nottingham

Dent, London
Rowman and Littlefield, Totowa, N.J.

This book is set in 9 point Baskerville 169

Dent edition
Hardback ISBN 0 460 10369 5
Paperback ISBN 0 460 11369 0

Rowman and Littlefield edition
Library of Congress Cataloging in Publication Data

Parfitt, George A E comp.
Silver poets of the seventeenth century.

(Rowman and Littlefield university library series)
Includes bibliographical references.
1. English poetry—Early modern (to 1700)
I. Title
PR1209.P27 821¹.008 74–1167
ISBN 0–87471–517–2 (HARDBACK)
ISBN 0–87471–534–2 (PAPERBACK)

Contents

[v]

SIR JOHN DENHAM

RICHARD CRASHAW

ABRAHAM COWLEY

Note on the text

The text of the poems printed in this volume are based on the first
published editions, unless otherwise specified in the notes. The editor
has checked texts against standard modern editions where relevant;
the modern texts used are given in the bibliography.

Introduction

The term 'silver' in the title of this volume should suggest two associated ideas—that of value and that of the second of the traditional four ages of human history, the silver age being inferior to that of gold but superior to those of bronze and iron. In reference to the poets represented here the term should thus suggest that each has value but that none belongs to the seventeenth-century first division. However, since that first division contains Donne, Jonson, Milton, George Herbert, Marvell and Dryden, 'silver' is in no way disrespectful of Vaughan, Crashaw, Denham, Waller and Cowley. Each contributes something to the English poetic tradition, none is wholly without individuality, yet none is consistently good enough to be a major poet, although Vaughan is in flashes a great one.

It is perhaps necessary to say a little about the selection of poets and poems for this book. The five chosen poets are not the only 'silver' poets of the seventeenth century, but none of them is available in bulk in annotated and reasonably inexpensive form while most of the other candidates (for example Herrick, Lovelace, Carew) are. Another reason for choosing the three secular poets that have been included is that their kind of public poetry has been neglected for too long and it is hoped that this book may encourage renewed interest in this type of writing. The only poet whom I should have liked to include and cannot (for reasons of space) is Charles Cotton, who deserves to be more widely read than he is.

Every poem printed here is printed whole, although it has not been possible to print more than one version of poems (like 'Cooper's Hill' and several of Crashaw's) which exist in two or more forms. With each poet I have tried to achieve a balanced selection rather than simply choosing what I consider the poet's best poems. Thus I have included selections from the secular verse of Vaughan and Crashaw to help make the point that both were competent verse-technicians rather than merely devotional versifiers. With Crashaw it is also important to show something of his 'baroque' manner as well as of the more successful style he evolved with his best poems. Cowley and Waller were both highly professional writers, willing to attempt a wide range of genres, and both need to be presented in a way which indicates that range. Denham presents little problem since his output was comparatively small.

I

As already said, Henry Vaughan is technically competent in his secular verse: his occasional and amatory poems have life and considerable control and are the work of a man writing in the shadows of others, but not contemptibly. If Vaughan's secular poems had been all that survived he would be remembered as a poet of, say, the calibre of Habington or Stanley. But, of course, he is largely a religious poet, remembered as one of the metaphysicals, as operating in the tradition of Donne and Herbert.

Vaughan made perfectly clear the debt he felt to Herbert, and even if he had not done so the links between *Silex Scintillans* and *The Temple* could scarcely be missed: Vaughan borrows some of Herbert's titles, echoes him verbally and is influenced by his verse forms. But while Vaughan may often remind us of Herbert in particular details he is seldom really like him, and in the difference lies Vaughan's particular value. Herbert is usually concerned with the operation of God's grace on earth and, characteristically, conceives of reconciliation with God as something which transforms man's earthly life or as a heavenly existence presented in earthly terms. Vaughan is more truly visionary; he has glimpses of the afterlife and is consequently impatient of earthbound existence. His impetus is towards getting beyond this life into a state of union with God, a union thought of in terms of radiance, a state free of earthly dross.

As a result Vaughan's poetry is much less concrete than Herbert's. The world of 'Regeneration', for example, is an allegorical world which lacks any specific sense of time and place. By contrast, the allegory of Herbert's 'Redemption' is imaged in terms of a mundane environment. This basic contrast is reflected at the technical level. On Herbert's terms Vaughan is clearly the inferior poet, for where Herbert generally makes individual words, line breaks and variations in line length locally significant this is often not the case with Vaughan, who operates far more with the stanza as dominant unit and often neglects detail. But this difference mirrors different concerns, for while Herbert's careful craftsmanship reflects his desire for harmony in the sublunary world and captures the spiritual serenity which is his particular tone, Vaughan—seeking to trap visionary moments—operates in more general, less predictable ways and his vision is scarcely to be apprehended by Herbert's kind of precision.

This leads directly to the question of Vaughan's individual contribution to English religious verse. A full discussion would have to take account of his use of hermetic material (although the *poetic* importance of this has been overestimated) but a brief account can more usefully concern itself with Vaughan's use of imagery, for it is in this and the vision it contains that Vaughan's importance lies.

One is soon struck by his reliance upon a few pairs of images, and upon one particular pair whereby heaven is associated with light and its attributes and earth with darkness and its attributes. Throughout his religious verse Vaughan's controlling purpose is to communicate his sense of God and heaven and his desire to be assimilated with them. His association of light with God is advantageous in that it allows him to draw upon a host of mythical, religious and literary allusions and to set this world of light against that produced by the associations of darkness with death, the devil, evil, fear. In poem after poem Vaughan utilizes this dichotomy, either directly or in one of its variants (day/ night; sun/cloud; fire/ashes), and at his best is able to catch the ineffable sense of the heaven he is always seeking. His images of darkness, on the other hand, pin down the light-vision and the poet's joy in it because they exploit our fear of darkness and death and communicate the poet's sense of the gloom of this earthly life. Often, as in 'They are all gone into the world of light', this basic contrast becomes the poem's fundamental principle of organization.

One could go on to talk of other recurrent images, those of hatching, for instance, or those of flowers and vegetable growth, but the importance lies in how the poet uses his small range of imagery. Vaughan is seldom intellectually demanding: instead the images work by their emotional and psychological appeal, and it is this that singles Vaughan out from Donne and Herbert, where the intellectual content is much higher. Vaughan shows little desire to draw recondite images into his poetry and little desire to shock by abrupt transitions or startling collisions between referee and referent. The value of Vaughan's way of working lies in the fact that his variations on a small stock of images can, intermittently, communicate his vision, less by argument than by repetition. His achievement is patchy but at best it is unique—the embodiment of *his* vision and *his* joy in that vision.

There are some points of contact between Vaughan and Crashaw in that both are emotional rather than intellectual poets who rely heavily on repetition to communicate vision; but the differences are more important than the similarities. Crashaw often seems to ask to be discounted as any kind of poet at all. In the light of this, his secular verse is important because it shows an ability to write with orthodox control and accuracy, sufficiently to make it clear that he was not technically incompetent, although his religious verse often seems to say that he was. Certainly the style is often challenging, as in the famous description of Mary Magdalene's eyes as

> Two walking baths, two weeping motions;
> Portable and compendious oceans.
>> (' *The Weeper*', *1648 version*)

—or in this epigram, 'Blessed be the paps which Thou hast sucked':

> Suppose he had been tabled at thy teats,
> Thy hunger feels not what he eats:
> He'll have his teat ere long (a bloody one)
> The mother then must suck the son.

There are various possible influences that may help to explain this sort of writing, but excusing it is another matter; and not so much one of taste as of technique. For Crashaw often seems to lack self-control, self-criticism and intelligence, deficiencies which emerge as weak anti-climaxes of sense and rhythm in epigrams like this:

He scorns them now, but O they'll suit full well
With the purple he must wear in hell.

('*Upon Lazarus his tears*')

and also in more ambitious poems such as 'The Weeper' and 'In
memory of the virtuous and learnèd lady. . . .'

Chronology is tricky with Crashaw but there is some reason to
believe that the poems in *Carmen Deo Nostro* which are not revisions
were his last poems, and these show him moving away from his earlier
witty style towards a manner which is altogether more valuable.
Perhaps the best example of this style comes in 'To the name above
every name. . . .'

The poem is not one of detailed argument or intellectual density.
Instead it takes a fairly simple 'plot' and drenches it with synonyms so
that words as individual particles of meaning seem of little concern
when compared with the stress on sound and repetition. Here the
rhyme-pattern is revealing as the poem moves progressively away from
its couplet-base to a kind of joyful anarchy (there are only five straight-
forward couplets in the last thirty-nine lines)—but the technique is
functional, miming the increasing excitement as the poem moves to its
climax. 'To the name . . .' has great rhythmical variety and no single
pattern dominates. A reader's mind is drawn away from individual
words towards the total complex of sound, an effect increased by a
syntax which is rhetorical rather than logical, embodying an emotional
response to a metaphysical experience.

This might suggest that Crashaw is seeking to write a poem in which
words have value only as sounds, but this would be a misleading
impression and it is more accurate to say that he is creating a kind of
contemplative verbal meaning. His adjectives are commonplace and
often used in pairs which become motifs whereby earth is dull, dark,
sad, humble, while heaven is presented through adjectives of size,
scope and power. Nouns and verbs are chosen from a narrow range
and, through repetition, particular words come to have solidity,
become the poem's basic 'facts'. So, in a real sense, 'To the name . . .'
is beyond paraphrase: its meaning is its whole, the presentation and
definition of the name of Jesus by all the words and rhythms of the
poem.

In poems like this Crashaw is unlike Donne or Herbert. They both
use imagery to suggest that aspects of their religious experience are like
particular features of secular life—that is, their method is that of simile.
Crashaw, on the other hand, operates by drawing the reader into a
melodic experience which is an enactment of his sense of being in God's
presence. He neglects simile for he is not saying that this experience is
like anything secular: instead he reënacts the experience itself. The
normal relative contributions of sense and sound have been redistri-
buted but as a result a vision is conveyed which would not otherwise be
apprehensible at all. The nature and reality of this vision are in the
unity and harmony of the poem.

I suggest, then, that the best-known Crashaw poems are the wrong ones to concentrate on. As a poet of wit Crashaw is usually disastrous, and in so far as the term 'baroque' is used to include that element of his work which celebrates blood and martyrdom at the expense of life it describes an aspect of Crashaw which can appeal only to the type of morbidity which sees denial of life as the only approach to God. The important Crashaw lies in a few poems, in poems like 'To the name . . .', 'To the noblest and best of ladies . . .' and 'In the glorious epiphany of our Lord . . .'. At his best and most important Crashaw creates an arte-fact which *is* his experience of God and which is unlike Donne's self-analysis, Herbert's concern with God-in-life and Vaughan's flashes of insight.

II

Waller, Denham and Cowley have already been referred to as 'public' poets. I do not want to suggest that they are copies of each other, for they are not, but each can usefully be approached *via* the general term, which therefore calls for some definition.

'Public' poetry is not simply a type of verse which presupposes an audience, or even a kind of poetry which concerns itself with matters extrinsic to the private life or psychology of the poet. It does require a sense of a public which is both sizeable and reasonably homogeneous; but, more importantly, it is a poetry which grows from the writer's sense of himself as fulfilling a distinct rôle in society, a rôle defined less by the quiddities of personality than by some concept of 'the poet' as having a special task or tasks in the society to which he belongs. The task may be to expose folly and vice, to praise virtue or great achieve-ment, to celebrate a birth, a death, a war, a marriage. The union of a strong sense of definable audience and definable 'impersonal' rôle leads naturally to a style which will reach the audience in a way with which they will readily identify and to which—hopefully—they will respond by accepting the poet's assessment as that proper to the society in question (this society need not be, indeed seldom is, coter-minous with society as a whole). For the three poets with whom I am concerned here the relevant influence is Ben Jonson, who—more, perhaps, than any earlier poet—shows the sense of audience and rôle described above.

Abraham Cowley was certainly conscious of his rôle and seems to have thought of himself as poet and of the poet's function with a great deal of seriousness. This lies behind his attempt at epic (*Davideis*) and his Pindaric odes—it being part of the public poet's duty to match in his own tongue the achievements of other languages—and there is evidence that even *The Mistress* was a self-conscious attempt, during his exile in France, to conform to the erotic lyricism wanted by the court with which he was then involved. This sort of self-consciousness makes Cowley a thoroughly professional poet, and like most others of this kind he is at times boring, merely giving the impression of an unin-

volved mind going through metrical mechanics. Yet usually Cowley's
professionalism is such that reading him is a rewarding experience, as
it is in these lines from 'To the Lord Falkland':

> And this great prince of knowledge is by fate
> Thrust into the noise and business of a state.
> All virtues and some customs of the court,
> Other men's labour, are at least his sport;
> Whilst we who can no action undertake,
> Whom idleness itself might learnèd make,
> Who hear of nothing, and as yet scarce know
> Whether the Scots in England be or no,
> Pace dully on, oft tire, and often stay,
> Yet see his nimble Pegasus fly away . . .

The clarity and continuity of sense here, together with the quality of
the enactment in the last couplet, are the features which make Cowley
an intelligent and, in the best sense, entertaining poet. He is a neat and
witty translator of Anacreontics and can write celebratory verse which
has wit, verbal precision and technical dexterity, even where it lacks
the moderate tone and sense of ethical awareness that mark Jonson's
best verse.

I have, however, deliberately chosen to stress Cowley's love lyrics in
this selection because in *The Mistress*, despite all its limitations, he
achieves a lyric voice which shows intelligent awareness of Donne,
modifying that poet's manner towards a more public voice. Cowley is
closest to Donne when he imitates the insolent poise of the latter's
elegies and 'witty' songs. In poems such as 'Inconstancy', 'Answer to
the Platonics' and 'Written in juice of lemon' Cowley resembles
Suckling in his ability to catch the clever, detached note of insult which
is one of Donne's voices; but this is a matter of following where Donne
is most easily followed and it gives Cowley no individual voice. Else-
where Cowley seems to be taking on a more difficult Donne, but in
poems like 'All over love' he fails to match the urgency of Donne's
finest lyrics: by comparison he seems to be *pretending* to analyse himself
and because of this there is little of that sense of unstable complexity
which Donne's best poems convey. Clarity, ease, neatness and plain-
ness are admirable features in certain kinds of poetry but they are not
the tools with which to seek to match John Donne.

These features, however, provide a clue to what happens in Cowley's
best love poems for they are characteristics which suit the national or
public poet. Occasionally outside *The Mistress* Cowley achieves a
Jonsonian sense of concern for social values and at times also, within
that collection, he creates something which is his own and not faded
Donne. This can happen even where the poem seems close to Donne,
as in 'Platonic love' with its echoes of Donne's 'Extasie'. In his poem
Cowley, as usual, fails to convey Donne's sense of urgency and the
poem is unconvincing if regarded as a re-creation of personal experience.
And yet the poem is not easily dismissed as sub-Donne. There is an

I-persona but not individualized as in Donne—instead it is a representative figure and the poem is generalized rather than particular. Writing of this type needs to be good if it is to hook the reader's mind at all, and here Cowley is good:

> Can that for true love pass
> When a fair woman courts her glass?
> Something unlike must in love's likeness be,
> His wonder is one and variety;
> For he, whose soul nought but a soul can move,
>   Does a new Narcissus prove
>   And his own image love.

Cowley is making distinctions about love and the manner is Elizabethan in its contentment with generalizations, social in its concern to state well generally accepted views of love. At his best Cowley is a poet who finds a smooth yet natural tone, the voice of a balanced and reasonable man. He pacifies Donne in his lyrics, making love a topic of conversation and reasonable discourse even where the material is basically wittily extreme:

> I little thought, thou fond ingrateful sin,
>   When first I let thee in,
>   And gave thee but a part
>   In my unwary heart,
>   That thou wouldst e'er have grown
> So false or strong to make it all thine own.
>
> ('*Love's ingratitude*')

What lies behind this, helping to explain the peculiar blend of extravagance of manner and moderation of matter, is the Horatian theme of *beatus vir*, to be found explicit in poems like 'The Wish'.

So Cowley is evasive and his achievement precarious. When the pull of Donne is too strong Cowley is made pale in Donne's orbit. When the pull to generalize is too strong neatness becomes emptiness and generality vagueness. But Cowley is capable of blending extravagance and generalization to produce poems which are poised and self-possessed, convincing not as self-analyses but as summaries of love attitudes and as artefacts. It is not an immediately striking achievement but fundamentally a civilized one, informed with an assurance reminiscent of the neglected Matthew Prior, a poetry to which we should respond if we have any taste for the moderate virtues.

Waller shares Cowley's sense of himself as poet but is remembered mainly for one lyric ('Go lovely rose . . .') and because the Augustans tell us that he was their predecessor. Dryden says in the Preface to *The Rival Ladies* (1664) that 'the excellence and dignity' of rhyme were 'never fully known till Mr. Waller; he first made writing easily an art . . .'. Much later, in the Preface to *Fables, Ancient and Modern* (1700), he is still offering the same kind of tribute: 'our numbers were in their nonage' until Waller and Denham appeared (*Selected Criticism*, ed. Kinsley and Parfitt, pp. 5, 293).

Thus Waller has an historical niche. He deserves better but his reputation has not been helped by his willingness to be professional to the point of praising whoever happened to be in power, be he Cromwell or Charles II. Yet it is arrogantly unsympathetic to make too much of this, for the pressures of the period were complex and considerable. Waller is, in any event, little read: even those who know the fine 'Go lovely rose' seldom look much beyond that piece, and yet even a casual glance at the complete poems suggest a real writer, even when his ideals and materials are not immediately appealing. Here are the closing lines from 'Of the last verses in the book':

> The soul's dark cottage, battered and decayed,
> Lets in new light through chinks that time has made:
> Stronger by weakness wiser men become
> As they draw near to their eternal home.
> Leaving the old, both worlds at once they view
> That stand upon the threshold of the new.

One can see what Dryden meant when he said that Waller made writing 'easily an art'. The couplets are confidently smooth and assured, the units clearly marked, the rhymes coming naturally and without shock, the language ordinary, rather plain, communicating a simple idea without fuss or obvious decoration. But we should see more than a technical achievement for technique is being used to convey emotion which is generalized but not spurious, a dignified sense of coming death and of how it may be faced. The quiet image of the soul as cottage grows in strength as we recognize its paradoxical aspect, which is drawn out in the third line and which leads to the technically and literally poised position of the close, an ending which conveys both regret and hope, a calm yet solid position, one which can be felt by a reader and felt to have worth.

It is not always easy to get beyond Waller's surface virtues and he is certainly not a poet of shocks and sudden illuminations. But he is intelligent and can work with a quiet assurance that makes his poetry, in the best sense, social and civilized. He extends Cowley's achievement in generalizing the love lyric, finding a delicate balance between conventionality of material and animation of it through careful phrasing and imagery. In the opening lines of 'To the mutable fair', for example, the confident control of the writing is sustained throughout and serves to distance the poet-figure from the subject, so that we as readers do not feel any urgent involvement: no genuine struggle is going on—love is not serious enough for that. But the lines are not empty. There is, slipping through in the very smoothness of the writing, a witty sense of situation and attitude:

> Here, Celia, for thy sake I part
> With all that grew so near my heart—

> The passion that I had for thee,
> The faith, the love, the constancy—
> And that I may successful prove
> Transform myself to what you love.

There are, Waller says, values which he has held for Celia's sake, but they have got him nowhere because of what she is. Yet success with her is still what he most desires and so he has resolved to abandon his standards to become 'what you love'. What this opening does is to set up a situation which acknowledges moral values but places them in a context where they will not work, and the poet goes on to develop this situation wittily and gracefully. The result is a typical Waller lyric—polished, readable, insidiously intelligent, attractive on the surface but with more substance than at first appears. It is silver lyric but the silver is genuine.

The occasional poems that make up much of Waller's output tend to have a more elevated manner and they move between description and panegyric, usually without the moral underlay that strengthens the occasional verse of Jonson and Carew. But even where the sentiments seem extravagant, almost sycophantic, there is usually a wit and cool self-knowingness which makes Waller better at this kind of poetry than Wordsworth and Tennyson when they put on their public robes. It would take a long digression to suggest why this is, but it is worth making the point in passing that Waller conveys the sense of writing to a definable audience, so that his allusions come confidently while the stylistic assurance produces a crispness of language and metre and a cool sense of distanced artifice. The poet knows his rôle and this allows him to entertain through wit and allusion, to be hyperbolic without becoming ridiculous.

John Denham is—as by Dryden—often linked with Waller; but the link depends mainly on 'Cooper's Hill' and Denham is not just a one poem man, good though 'Cooper's Hill' is and important though it is in the history of English 'local' poetry. Denham is the only one of the poets in this book who emerges as actively involved in the Civil War and its aftermath, and this makes him rather a different kind of public poet than either Cowley or Waller. The war put Englishmen under greater stress than perhaps any other event in our history. In recent years historians have begun to indicate the intricacies of loyalty which underlie the glib labels of Cavalier and Roundhead. The problem of what loyalty is and what it means was acute for thinking, caring men, including poets. Milton solved the problem by becoming a Parliamentary pamphleteer, so the real index of how difficult sensitive and responsible reaction to events was is found in Marvell. Apart from Milton, he was probably the most talented writer of the mid-century and he is repeatedly driven to evasions, ambiguities and perplexities as he tries to find out how a man can decently resolve the complexities of civil war. Other poets just took sides: some stuck to their chosen side with real loyalty (Lovelace, Cleveland) while others stuck with real effrontery to the winning side (Wither, Waller). This kind of side-taking may seem simple-minded but it is unfair to underestimate the temptation to simplify when the issues are as difficult and entwined as in the civil war.

Denham opted for the king. 'Cooper's Hill', with its strong sense of tradition and stability, provides the essential backcloth to Denham's choice, giving a context to his satirical propaganda poems. The satires of the civil war are usually, and inevitably, closely involved with detail, to the extent that many are almost incomprehensible without extensive glossing, and the effect is particularly daunting when, as with Cleveland, the detail is conveyed with a style borrowed from Elizabethan satire. Denham emerges from this situation better than most. In his propaganda poems he often achieves satire rather than mere lampoon, showing a wit and gusto that communicate ridicule without bitterness. It is not, I think, that Denham is a mindless, gay Cavalier but rather that he found a way of coping with the war by refusing to ignore the potentially ridiculous side of it. His technique is constantly to belittle his opponents and it is a good technique in that he refuses them the dignity of serious attack—something which comes across in the swing of his often ballad-based metres. Even where the detail of Denham's satire is obscure, the point and tone are usually conveyed through the straightforward vitality of his language and rhythms. He is not a great satirist but he is lively and entertaining, with a ready eye for pretension and hypocrisy, even though we may often feel that his targets and his shots are obvious rather than deeply perceptive.

In his non-satirical verse Denham is nearer to Waller than elsewhere and poems like 'Cooper's Hill' show quite clearly why the Augustans regarded Denham so favourably. In his hands the couplet becomes strongly the governing unit and more frequently antithetical than earlier; while his diction, in contrast to that of the satires, is lofty, allusive, and gives the impression of having been selected from a limited stock of words suitable for poetry rather than from the language's full resources. Clarity and elegance mark 'Cooper's Hill' but it is also a poem with a genuine concern for social values which the poet feels to be threatened; and, despite what has been said about the range of language, it is a real poem in the sense that a reader feels that Denham has chosen his words with care for the overall effect, that he is genuinely concerned to make something. This kind of professionalism links him again with Waller and Cowley and is a feature of the other non-satirical poems as well as of his translations. His elegy for Strafford may seem in historical terms culpably biased, but Denham has a confident manner which makes the poem a genuine challenge. A couplet like

> Crushed by imaginary treasons' weight
> Which too much merit did accumulate

runs smoothly, but the smoothness masks some real depth of response, an awareness that life is more complex than art may choose to pretend it is. Here Denham conveys the paradox whereby a man may be crushed by reasons which, in the poet's view, do not exist and where merit may accumulate not reward but punishment. It is a view of Strafford which we may not share, but what is important is that the world Denham touches in this couplet is recognizable in its evasiveness and baffling way of making white appear black. The view is steadily held too, as we can see in a line like 'Pretexts are into treason forged by law', with its neat pun on 'forged' and its recognition that a legal system which transforms pretexts into treason is perverted.

I have suggested some of the reasons why the poets in this volume still deserve to be read. Each of them has real talent and none is merely an imitator of some other writer. I have deliberately stressed their qualities as *poets* since I am claiming that each has intrinsic merit which transcends the purely historical (which, of course, is not to deny that they indicate important things to us about the societies from which they come). They are 'second division', but it will be a sad day when we have no time for artists who are genuine while falling short of genius.

1974   G. A. E. Parfitt

Select Bibliography

GENERAL REFERENCE

E. Miner, *The Cavalier Mode from Jonson to Cotton*, Princeton U.P., 1971; E. Miner, *The Metaphysical Mode from Donne to Cowley*, Princeton U.P., 1969; H. C. White, *The Metaphysical Poets*, Collier-Macmillan, 1962.

INDIVIDUAL POETS

COWLEY. WORKS: *English Writings*, ed. A. R. Waller, Cambridge U.P., 1905–6. BIOGRAPHICAL AND CRITICAL: R. B. Hinman, *Abraham Cowley's World of Order*, Oxford U.P., 1960; Samuel Johnson, 'Life' in *Lives of the Poets*, ed. G. Birkbeck Hill, 1905; A. Nethercot, *Abraham Cowley, the Muses' Hannibal*, Oxford U.P., 1931.

CRASHAW. WORKS: *Poetical Works*, ed. L. C. Martin, Oxford U.P., 1957; *Steps to the Temple 1646*, Scolar Press, 1970. BIOGRAPHICAL AND CRITICAL: R. Wallerstein, *Richard Crashaw*, Madison, 1935; A. Warren, *Richard Crashaw*, Louisiana U.P., 1939.

DENHAM. WORKS: *Poetical Works*, ed. T. W. Banks, Yale U.P., 1928. BIOGRAPHICAL AND CRITICAL: B. O Hehir, *Harmony from Discords*, California U.P., 1968; B. O Hehir, *Expans'd Hieroglyphicks*, California U.P., 1969; Samuel Johnson, 'Life' in *Lives of the Poets*.

VAUGHAN. WORKS: *Works*, ed. L. C. Martin, Oxford U.P., 1914; *Silex Scintillans*, Scolar Press, 1968. BIOGRAPHICAL AND CRITICAL: R. Durr, *On the mystical poetry of Henry Vaughan*, Oxford U.P., 1962; R. Garner, *Henry Vaughan: Experience and Tradition*, Chicago U.P., 1959; F. E. Hutchinson, *Henry Vaughan*, Clarendon Press, 1947; L. L. Martz, *The Paradise Within*, Yale U.P., 1964; E. Pettet, *Of Paradise and Light*, Cambridge U.P., 1960.

WALLER. WORKS: *Poems*, ed. G. Thorn Drury, Routledge, 1893; *Poems 1645*, Scolar Press, 1971. BIOGRAPHICAL AND CRITICAL: A. W. Alison, *Towards an Augustan Poetic*, Kentucky U.P., 1962; W. L. Chernaik, *The Poetry of Limitation*, Yale U.P., 1968; Samuel Johnson, 'Life' in *Lives of the Poets*.

Edmund Waller (1606–87)

SONG

Say lovely dream where couldst thou find
   Shades to counterfeit that face?
   Colours of this glorious kind
Come not from any mortal race.

5   In heaven itself thou sure wert dressed
   With that angel-like disguise;
   Thus deluded am I blessed
And see my joy with closèd eyes.

But, ah! this image is too kind
10   To be other than a dream;
   Cruel Sacharissa's mind
Never put on that sweet extreme.

Fair dream, if thou intend'st me grace,
   Change that heavenly face of thine;
15   Paint despised love in thy face
And make it to appear like mine.

Pale, wan, and meagre let it look,
   With a pity-moving shape,
   Such as wander by the brook
20   Of Lethe or from graves escape.

Then to that matchless nymph appear
   In whose shape thou shinest so;
   Softly in her sleeping ear
With humble words express my woe.

25   Perhaps from greatness, state, and pride,
   Thus surprisèd she may fall;
   Sleep does disproportion hide,
And death-resembling equals all.

[1]

TO AMORET

Fair, that you may truly know
What you unto Thyrsis owe,
I will tell you how I do
Sacharissa love and you.

5   Joy salutes me when I set
My blessèd eyes on Amoret:
But with wonder I am strook
When I on the other look.

If sweet Amoret complains
10   I have sense of all her pains:
But for Sacharissa, I
Do not only grieve, but die.

All that of myself is mine
Lovely Amoret is thine:
15   Sacharissa's captive fain
Would untie his iron chain;

And those scorching beams to shun
To thy gentle shadow run:
If the soul had free election
20   To dispose of her affection,

I would not thus long have borne
Haughty Sacharissa's scorn:
But 'tis some pure power above
Which controls our will in love.

25   If not love, a strong desire
To create and spread that fire
In my breast solicits me,
Beauteous Amoret, for thee.

'Tis amazement more than love
30   Which her radiant eyes do move:
If less splendour wait on thine
Yet they so benignly shine,

I would turn my dazzled sight
To behold their milder light:
35   But as hard 'tis to destroy
That hard flame as to enjoy;
Which how easily I may do
Heaven (as easily scaled) does know:

Amoret, as sweet and good
40   As the most delicious food,
Which, but tasted, doth impart
Life and goodness to the heart.
Sacharissa's beauty wine
Which to madness doth incline;
45   Such a liquor as no brain
That is mortal can sustain.
Scarce can I to Heaven excuse
That devotion which I use
Unto that adorèd dame;
50   For 'tis not unlike the same
Which I thither ought to send;
So that if it could take end
'Twould to Heaven itself be due
To succeed her and not you,
55   Who already have of me
All that's not idolatry:
Which, though not so fiercc a flamc,
Is longer like to be the same.

Then smile on me and I will prove
60   Wonder is shorter lived than love.

THE STORY OF PHOEBUS AND DAPHNE APPLIED

Thyrsis, a youth of the inspirèd train,
Fair Sacharissa loved, but loved in vain;
Like Phoebus sung the no less amorous boy,
Like Daphne she, as lovely and as coy.
5   With numbers he the flying nymph pursues,
With numbers such as Phoebus' self might use:
Such is the chase when love and fancy leads
O'er craggy mountains and through flowr'y meads,
Invoke to testify the lover's care
10   Or form some image of his cruel fair.
Urged with his fury, like a wounded deer
O'er these he fled, and none approaching near
Had reached the nymph with his harmonious lay,
Whom all his charms could not incline to stay.
15   Yet what he sung in his immortal strain,
Though unsuccessful, was not sung in vain:
All but the nymph that should redress his wrong
Attend his passion and approve his song.
    Like Phoebus thus acquiring unsought praise
20   He catched at love and filled his arms with bays.

Edmund Waller

TO A LADY IN RETIREMENT

Sees not my love how time resumes
The glory which he lent these flowers;
Though none should taste their sweet perfumes
    Yet must they live but some few hours:
5   Time what we forbear devours.

Had Helen or the Egyptian queen
Been ne'er so thrifty of their graces,
Those beauties must at length have been
    The spoil of age which finds out faces
10   In the most retiréd places.

Should some malignant planet bring
A barren drought or ceaseless shower
Upon the autumn or the spring,
    And spare us neither fruit nor flower,
15   Winter would not stay an hour.

Could the resolve of love's neglect
Preserve ye from the violation
Of coming years, then more respect
    Were due to so divine a fashion,
20   Nor would I divulge my passion.

THE SELF-BANISHED

It is not that I love you less
Than when before your feet I lay:
But to prevent the sad increase
Of hopeless love I keep away.

5   In vain, alas, for every thing
Which I have known belong to you,
Your form does to my fancy bring
And make my old wounds bleed anew.

Whom the spring from the new sun
10   Already has a fever got,
Too late begins those shafts to shun
Which Phoebus through his veins has shot.

Too late he would the pain assuage
And to thick shadows does retire,
15   About with him he bears the rage
And in his tainted blood the fire.

But vowed I have, and never must
Your banished servant trouble you,
For if I break you may mistrust
20   The vow I make to love you too.

SONG

Go lovely rose,
Tell her that wastes her time and me
   That now she knows
When I resemble her to thee
5   How sweet and fair she seems to be.

Tell her that's young
And shuns to have her graces spied,
   That hadst thou sprung
In deserts where no men abide
10   Thou must have uncommended died.

Small is the worth
Of beauty from the light retired;
   Bid her come forth,
Suffer herself to be desired,
15   And not blush so to be admired.

Then die that she
The common fate of all things rare
   May read in thee;
How small a part of time they share,
20   That are so wond'rous sweet and fair.

OF LOVE

Anger in hasty words or blows
Itself discharges on our foes;
And sorrow too finds some relief
In tears which wait upon our grief;

5   So every passion but fond love
     Unto its own redress does move.
     But that alone the wretch inclines
     To what prevents his own designs;
     Makes him lament and sigh and weep,
10   Disordered, tremble, fawn and creep;
     Postures which render him despised
     Where he endeavours to be prized:
     For women, born to be controlled,
     Stoop to the forward and the bold,
15   Affect the haughty and the proud,
     The gay and frolic, and the loud.
     Who first the generous steed oppressed
     Not kneeling did salute the beast,
     But with high courage, life and force
20   Approaching, tamed th'unruly horse.
     Unwisely we the wiser East
     Pity, supposing them oppressed
     With tyrants' force whose law is will,
     By which they govern, spoil and kill:
25   Each nymph but moderately fair
     Command with no less rigour here.
         Should some brave Turk that walks among
     His twenty lasses bright and young,
     And beckons to the willing dame
30   Preferred to quench his present flame,
     Behold as many gallants here,
     With modest guise and silent fear
     All to our female idol bend,
     Whilst her high pride does scarce descend
35   To mark their follies, he would swear
     That these her guard of eunuchs were,
     And that a more majestic queen
     Or humbler slaves he had not seen.
         All this with indignation spoke
40   In vain I struggled with the yoke
     Of mighty love, that conquering look,
     When next beheld like lightning struck
     My blasted soul and made me bow
     Lower than those I pitied now.
45   So the tall stag upon the brink
     Of some smooth stream about to drink,
     Surveying there his armèd head
     With shame remembers that he fled
     The scornèd dogs; resolves to try
50   The combats next; but if their cry
     Invades again his trembling ear
     He straight resumes his wonted fear;

Leaves the untasted spring behind
And winged with fear, outflies the wind.

TO THE MUTABLE FAIR

Here, Celia, for thy sake I part
With all that grew so near my heart—
The passion that I had for thee,
The faith, the love, the constancy—
5   And that I may successful prove
Transform myself to what you love.
    Fool that I was so much to prize
Those simple virtues you despise,
Fool that with such dull arrows strove
10   Or hoped to reach a flying dove;
For you that are in motion still
Decline our force and mock our skill,
Who like Don Quixote do advance
Against a windmill our vain lance.
15   Now will I wander through the air,
Mount, make a stoop at every fair,
And with a fancy unconfined
(As lawless as the sea or wind)
Pursue you wheresoe'er you fly,
20   And with your various thoughts comply.
    The formal stars do travel so
As we their names and courses know,
And he that on their changes looks
Would think they governed by our books;
25   But never were the clouds reduced
To any art: the motion used
By those free vapours are so light,
So frequent, that the conquered sight
Despairs to find the rules that guide
30   Those gilded shadows as they slide;
And therefore of the spacious air
Jove's royal consort had the care,
And by that power did once escape,
Declining bold Ixion's rape.
35   She with her own resemblance graced
A shining cloud which he embraced.
    Such was that image, so it smiled
With seeming kindness which beguiled
Your Thyrsis lately, when he thought
40   He had his fleeting Celia caught.

'Twas shaped like her, but for the fair
He filled his arms with yielding air:
   A fate for which he grieves the less
Because the gods had like success,
For in their story one (we see)
Pursues a nymph and takes a tree;
   A second with a lover's haste
Soon overtakes whom he had chased—
But she that did a virgin seem,
Possessed, appears a wand'ring stream;
For his supposèd love, a third
Lays greedy hands upon a bird—
And stands amazed to find his dear
A wild inhabitant of the air.
   To these old tales such nymphs as you
Give credit, and still make them new.
The am'rous now like wonders find
In the swift changes of your mind.
   But, Celia, if you apprehend
The muse of your incensèd friend,
Nor would that he record your blame
And make it live repeat the same,
Again deceive him and again,
And then he swears he'll not complain.
For still to be deceivèd so
Is all the pleasures lovers know:
Who, like good falc'ners, take delight
Not in the quarry, but the flight.

45
50
55
60
65

PUERPERIUM

You gods that have the power,
   To trouble and compose
  All that's beneath your bower,
Calm silence on the seas, on earth impose.

5

Fair Venus in thy soft arms
   The god of rage confine,
  For thy whispers are the charms
Which only can divert his fierce design.

What though he frown and to tumult do incline,
   Thou the flame
  Kindled in his breast canst tame,
With that snow which unmelted lies on thine!

10

Great goddess give this thy sacred island rest;
　　Make heaven smile,
15　　That no storm disturb us while
Thy chief care, our halcyon, builds her nest.

　　Great Gloriana, fair Gloriana,
Bright as high heaven is, and fertile as earth,
　　Whose beauty relieves us,
20　　Whose royal bed gives us
　　Both glory and peace,
Our present joy and our hopes increase.

TO PHYLLIS

Phyllis, why should we delay
Pleasures shorter than the day?
Could we (which we never can)
Stretch our lives beyond their span,
5　Beauty like a shadow flies
And our youth before us dies;
Or, would youth and beauty stay,
Love hath wings, and will away.
Love hath swifter wings than time;
10　Change in love to heaven does climb.
Gods that never change their state
Varied oft their love and hate.
Phyllis, to this truth we owe
All the love betwixt us two:
15　Let not you and I enquire
What has been our past desire;
On what shepherds you have smiled,
Or what nymphs I have beguiled.
Leave it to the planets too
20　What we shall hereafter do.
For the joys we now may prove,
Take advice of present love.

TO FLAVIA: SONG

'Tis not your beauty can engage
　　My wary heart;
The sun in all his pride and rage
　　Has not that art;
5　And yet he shines as bright as you
If brightness could our souls subdue.

'Tis not the pretty things you say,
 Nor those you write,
Which can make Thyrsis' heart your prey:
 For that delight,
10 The graces of a well-taught mind,
In some of our own we find.

No, Flavia, 'tis your love I fear,
 Love's surest darts:
Those which so seldom fail him are
15 Headed with hearts,
Their very shadows make us yield,
Dissemble well and win the field.

THE FALL

See how the willing earth gives way
To take the impression where she lay;
See how the mould, as loth to leave
So sweet a burden, still doth cleave
5 Close to the nymphs stained garment! Here
The coming spring would first appear,
And all this place with roses strow
If busy feet would let them grow.
Here Venus smiled to see blind chance
10 Itself before her son advance,
And a fair image to present
Of what the boy so long had meant:
'Twas such a chance as this made all
The world into this order fall.
15 Thus the first lovers, on the clay
Of which they were composèd, lay;
So in their prime, with equal grace
Met the first patterns of our race.
Then blush not, fair, or on him frown,
20 Or wonder how you both came down:
But touch him and he'll tremble straight:
How could he then support your weight?
How could the youth, alas, but bend
When his whole heaven upon him leaned?
25 If aught by him amiss were done,
'Twas that he let you rise so soon.

THE BUD

Lately on yonder swelling bush,
Big with many a coming rose,
This early bud began to blush,
And did but half itself disclose;
    And, plucked, it, though no better grown,
    Yet now you see how full 'tis blown.

Still as I did the leaves inspire,
With such a purple light they shone
As if they had been made of fire,
And, spreading so, would flame anon;
    All that was meant by air or sun
    To the young flower my breath has done.

If our loose breath so much can do,
What may the same in forms of love,
Of purest love and music too
When Flavia it aspires to move;
    When that which lifeless buds persuades
    To wax more soft her youth invades?

LOVE'S FAREWELL

Treading the path to nobler ends,
A long farewell to love I gave;
Resolved my country and my friends
All that remained of me should have;
And this resolve no mortal dame,
None but those eyes, could have o'erthrown.
The nymph I dare, nor need not name,
So high, so like herself alone.
Thus the tall oak which now aspires
Above the fears of private fires,
Grown and designed for nobler use,
Not to make warm, but build the house;
Though from our meaner flames secure,
Must that which falls from heaven endure.

TO CHLORIS

Chloris, what's eminent we know
Must for some cause be valued so;
Things without use, though they be good,
Are not by us so understood.
5   The early rose made to display
Her blushes to the youthful May
Doth yield her sweets, since she is fair
And courts her with a gentle air.
Our stars, to show their excellence,
10 Not by their light, but influence,
When brighter comets still are known,
Fatal to all, are liked by none:
So your admirèd beauty still
Is by effects made good or ill.

TO A FAIR LADY PLAYING WITH A SNAKE

Strange, that such horror and such grace
Should dwell together in one place;
A fury's arm, an angel's face!

'Tis innocence and youth which makes
5   In Chloris' fancy such mistakes,
To start at love and play with snakes.

By this and by her coldness barred,
Her servants have a task too hard:
The tyrant has a double guard.

10 Thrice happy snake, that in her sleeve
May boldly creep: we dare not give
Our thoughts so unconfined a leave.

Contented in that nest of snow
He lies, as he his bliss did know,
15 And to the wood no more would go.

Take heed, fair Eve, you do not make
Another tempter of this snake;
A marble one so warmed would speak.

THE NIGHT-PIECE

Darkness which fairest nymphs disarms
Defends us ill from Mira's charms:
Mira can lay her beauty by,
Take no advantage of the eye,
Quit all that Lely's art can take,
And yet a thousand captives make.

 Her speech is graced with sweeter sound
Than in another's song is found,
And all her well-placed words are darts
Which need no light to reach our hearts.

 As the bright stars and Milky Way,
Showed by the night, are hid by day,
So we, in that accomplished mind,
Helped by the night, new graces find,
Which by the splendour of her view,
Dazzled before, we never knew.

 While we converse with her we mark
No want of day, nor think it dark:
Her shining image is a light
Fixed in our hearts and conquers night.

 Like jewels to advantage set
Her beauty by the shades does get:
There blushes, frowns, and cold disdain,
All that our passion might restrain,
Is his, and our indulgent mind
Presents the fair idea kind.

 Yet friended by the night we dare
Only in whispers tell our care:
He that on her his bold hand lays
With Cupid's pointed arrows plays:
They with a touch (they are so keen)
Wound us unshot, and she unseen.

 All near approaches threaten death;
We may be shipwrecked by her breath:
Love, favoured once with that sweet gale,
Doubles his haste and fills his sail,
Till he arrive where she must prove
The haven or the rock of love.

 So we the Arabian coast do know
At distance when the spices blow,
By the rich odour taught to steer,
Though neither day nor stars appear.

COMMENDATORY POEMS

TO MR HENRY LAWES

Verse makes heroic virtue live,
But you can life to verses give.
As when in open air we blow
The breath, though strained, sounds flat and low,
5   But if a trumpet take the blast
It lifts it high and makes it last,
So in your airs our numbers dressed,
Make a shrill sally from the breast
Of nymphs, who, singing what we penned,
10   Our passions to themselves commend,
While love, victorious with thy art,
Governs at once their voice and heart.
    You by the help of tune and time
Can make that song that was but rhyme.
15   Noye pleading no man doubts the cause,
Or questions verses set by Lawes.
    For as a window, thick with paint,
Lets in a light but dim and faint,
So others with division hide
20   The light of sense, the poet's pride.
But you alone may truly boast
That not a syllable is lost:
The writer's and the setter's skill
At once the ravished ears do fill.
25   Let those which only warble long
And gargle in their throats a song,
Content themselves with ut, re, mi:
Let words and sense be set by thee.

TO VANDYCK

Rare artisan, whose pencil moves
Not our delights alone, but loves:
From thy shop of beauty we
Slaves return that entered free.
5   The headless lover does not know
Whose eyes they are that wound him so,

But, confounded with thy art,
Enquires her name that has his heart;
Another, who did long refrain,
10   Feels his old wound bleed fresh again,
With dear remembrance of that face
Where now he reads new hopes of grace:
Nor scorn nor cruelty does find,
But gladly suffers a false wind
15   To blow the ashes of despair
From the reviving brand of care:
Fool that forget'st her stubborn look,
This softness from thy finger took:
Strange that thy hand should not inspire
20   The beauty only but the fire;
Not the form alone and grace,
But act and power of a face.
Mayst thou yet thyself as well
As all the world beside excel;
25   So thou th' unfeigned truth rehearse
(That I may make it live in verse)
Why thou couldst not at one assay
That face to aftertimes convey,
Which this admires; was it thy wit
30   To make her oft before thee sit?
Confess and we'll forgive thee this,
For who would not repeat that bliss,
And frequent sight of such a dame
Buy with the hazard of his fame?
35   Yet who can tax thy blameless skill
Though thy good hand had failèd still,
When nature's self so often errs?
She for this many thousand years
Seems to have practised with much care
40   To frame the race of women fair,
Yet never could a perfect birth
Produce before to grace the earth,
Which waxèd old ere it could see
Her that amazed thy art and thee.
45   But now 'tis done, O let me know
Where those immortal colours grow
That could this deathless piece compose
In lilies or the fading rose:
No, for this theft thou hast climbed higher
50   Than did Prometheus for his fire.

TO MY LORD OF LEICESTER

Not that thy trees at Penshurst groan
Oppressèd with their timely load,
And seem to make their silent moan
That their great lord is now abroad:
5   They to delight his taste or eye
      Would spend themselves in fruit and die.

Not that thy harmless deer repine
And think themselves unjustly slain
By any other hand than thine,
10   Whose arrows they would gladly stain:
      No, nor thy friends which hold too dear
      That peace with France which keeps thee there.

All these are less than that great cause,
Which now exacts your presence here,
15   Wherein there meet the diverse laws
Of public and domestic care:
      For one bright nymph our youth contends
      And on your prudent choice depends.

Not the bright shield of Thetis' son
20   For which such stern debate did rise
That the great Ajax Telamon
Refused to live without the prize:
      Those Achave peers did more engage
      Than she the gallants of our age.

25   That beam of beauty which begun
To warm us when that thou wert here,
Now scorches like the raging sun
When Syrius does first appear:
      O fix this flame and let despair
30   Redeem the rest from endless care!

TO MY YOUNG LADY LUCY SIDNEY

Why came I so untimely forth
Into a world which, wanting thee,
Could entertain us with no worth
Or shadow of felicity?
5   That time should me so far remove
      From that which I was born to love?

Yet, fairest blossom, do not slight
That age which you must know so soon:
The rosy morn resigns her light
10   And milder glory to the moon:
    And then what wonders shall you do
    Whose dawning beauty warms us so?

Hope waits upon the flow'ry prime,
And summer, though it be less gay,
15   Yet is not looked on as a time
Of declination or decay:
    For with a full hand that doth bring
    All that was promised by the spring.

TO MY LORD NORTHUMBERLAND UPON THE DEATH OF HIS LADY

To this great loss a sea of tears is due,
But the whole debt not to be paid by you:
Charge not yourself with all, nor render vain
Those showers the eyes of us your servants rain.
5   Shall grief contract the largeness of that heart
In which nor fear nor anger has a part?
Virtue would blush if time should boast (which dries,
Her sole child dead, their tender mother's eyes)
Your mind's relief where reason triumphs so
10   Over all passions, that they ne'er could grow
Beyond their limits in your noble breast,
To harm another or impeach your rest.
This we observed, delighting to obey
One who did never from his great self stray;
15   Whose mild example seemèd to engage
The obsequious seas and teach them not to rage.
The brave Emilius his great charge laid down,
(The force of Rome and fate of Macedon)
In his lost sons did feel the cruel stroke
20   Of changing fortune, and thus highly spoke
Before Rome's people: 'We did oft implore
That if the heavens had any ill in store
For your Emilius they would pour it still
On his own house, and let you flourish still.'
25   You on the barren sea, my lord, have spent
Whole springs and summers to the public lent;
Suspended all the pleasures of your life
And shortened the short joy of such a wife;

For which your country's more obligèd then
30 For many lives of old, less happy men.
You that have sacrificed so great a part
Of youth and private bliss, ought to impart
Your sorrow too, and give your friends a right
As well in your affliction as delight.
35 Then with Emilian courage bear this cross,
Since public persons only public loss
Ought to affect, and though her form and youth,
Her application to your will and truth,
That noble sweetness and that humble state,
40 All snatched away by such a hasty fate,
Might give excuse to any common breast
With the huge weight of so much grief oppressed,
Yet let no portion of your life be stained
With passion, but your character maintained
45 To the last act: it is enough her stone
May honoured be with superscription
Of the sole lady who had power to move
The great Northumberland to grieve and love.

ON MY LADY ISABELLA PLAYING ON THE LUTE

Such moving sounds, from such a careless touch,
So unconcerned herself and we so much:
What art is this that with so little pains
Transports us thus and o'er the spirit reigns?
5 The trembling strings above her fingers proud,
And tell their joy for every kiss aloud:
Small force there needs to make thee tremble so—
Touched by that hand who would not tremble too?
Here love takes stand, and while she charms the ear
10 Empties his quiver on the listening deer:
Music so softens and disarms the mind
That not an arrow does resistance find.
Thus the fair tyrant celebrates the prize
And acts herself the triumph of her eyes.
15 So Nero once with harp in hand surveyed
His flaming Rome, and as it burned he played.

UPON BEN JONSON

Mirror of poets, mirror of our age,
Which, her whole face beholding on thy stage,

Pleased and displeased with her own faults, endures
A remedy like those whom music cures.
5   Thou hast alone those various inclinations
Which nature gives to ages, sexes, nations;
Hast trackèd with thy all-resembling pen
Whatever custom has imposed on men,
Or ill-got habit which deserts them so
10 That scarce one brother can the brother know,
Is representing to the wond'ring eyes
Of all that see or read thy comedies.
Whoever in those glasses look may find
The spots returned or graces of the mind;
15 And by the help of so divine an art
At leisure view and dress his nobler part.
Narcissus, cozened by that flattering well,
And nothing could but of his beauty tell,
Had here discovering that the deformed estate
20 Of his fond mind preserved himself with hate.
But virtue too, as well as vice, is clad
In flesh and blood so well that Plato had
Beheld what his high fancy once embraced,
Virtue with colours, speech and motion graced.
25 The sundry postures of thy copious muse
Who would express a thousand tongues must use;
Whose fate's no less peculiar than thy art,
For as thou couldst all characters impart,
So none could render thine, who still escapes
30 Like Proteus in variety of shapes:
Who was nor this nor that, but all we find
And all we can imagine in mankind.

TO MY LADY MORTON, ON
NEW YEAR'S DAY, 1650

Madam, new years may well expect to find
Welcome from you, to whom they are so kind;
Still as they pass they court and smile on you,
And make your beauty, as themselves, seem new.
5   To the fair Villiers we Dalkeith prefer,
And fairest Morton now as much to her:
So like the sun's advance your titles show,
Which as he rises does the warmer grow.
But thus to style you fair, your sex's praise,
10 Gives you but myrtle who may challenge bays.

From armèd foes to bring a royal prize
Shows your brave heart victorious as your eyes.
If Judith, marching with the general's head,
Can give us passion when her story's read,
15 What may the living do which brought away
Though a less bloody, yet a nobler prey;
Who from our flaming Troy, with a bold hand
Snatched her fair charge, the princess, like a brand?
A brand, preserved to warm some prince's heart
20 And make whole kingdoms take her brother's part:
So Venus from prevailing Greeks did shroud
The hope of Rome and save him in a cloud.
   This gallant act may cancel all our rage,
Begin a better and absolve this age.
25 Dark shades become the portrait of our time:
Here weeps misfortune, and there triumphs crime.
Let him that draws it hide the rest in night:
This portion only may endure the light,
Where the kind nymph, changing her faultless shape,
30 Becomes unhandsome handsomely to 'scape,
When through the guards, the river, and the sea,
Faith, beauty, wit, and courage made their way.
As the brave eagle does with sorrow see
The forest wasted and that lofty tree
35 Which holds her nest about to be o'erthrown,
Before the feathers of her young are grown,
She will not leave them, nor she cannot stay,
But bears them boldly on her wings away;
So fled the dame and o'er the ocean bore
40 Her princely burden to the Gallic shore.
Born in the storms of war this royal fair
Produced like lightning in tempestuous air,
Though now she flies her native isle (less kind,
Less safe for her than either sea or wind)
45 Shall, when the blossom of her beauty's blown,
See her great brother on the British throne:
Where peace shall smile and no dispute arise
But which rules most, his sceptre or her eyes.

A PANEGYRIC TO MY LORD PROTECTOR

While with a strong and yet a gentle hand
You bridle faction and our hearts command,
Protect us from ourselves and from the foe,
Make us unite and make us conquer too—

5   Let partial spirits still aloud complain,
Think themselves injured that they cannot reign,
And own no liberty but where they may
Without control upon their fellows prey.

Above the waves as Neptune showed his face,
10   To chide the winds and save the Trojan race,
So has your highness, raised above the rest,
Storms of ambition tossing us repressed.

Your drooping country, torn with civil hate,
Restored by you is made a glorious state,
15   The seat of empire where the Irish come,
And the unwilling Scotch, to fetch their doom.

The sea's our own, and now all nations greet
With bending sails each vessel of our fleet;
Your power extends as far as winds can blow,
20   Or swelling sails upon the globe may go.

Heaven (that has placed this island to give law,
To balance Europe and her states to awe)
In this conjunction does on Britain smile:
The greatest leader and the greatest isle!

25   Whether this portion of the world were rent,
By the rude ocean, from the continent,
Or thus created, it was sure designed
To be the sacred refuge of mankind.

Hither the oppressèd shall henceforth resort,
30   Justice to crave, and succour, at your court,
And then your highness not for ours alone
But for the world's protector shall be known.

Fame, swifter than your wingèd navy, flies
Through every land that near the ocean lies,
35   Sounding your name and telling dreadful news
To all that piracy and rapine use.

With such a chief the meanest nation blessed
Might hope to lift her head above the rest:
What may be thought impossible to do
40   By us, embracèd by the sea and you?

Lords of the world's great waste, the ocean, we
Whole forests send to reign upon the sea,
And every coast may trouble or relieve,
But none can visit us without your leave.

45   Angels and we have this prerogative
      That none can at our happy seat arrive,
      While we descend at pleasure to invade
      The bad with vengeance and the good to aid.

      Our little world, the image of the great,
50   Like that, amidst the boundless ocean set,
      Of her own growth has all that nature craves,
      And all that's rare as tribute from the waves.

      As Egypt does not on the clouds rely,
      But to the Nile owes more than to the sky,
55   So what our earth and what our heaven denies
      Our ever-constant friend, the sea, supplies.

      The taste of hot Arabia's spice we know,
      Free from the scorching sun that makes it grow;
      Without the worm in Persian silks we shine;
60   And without planting drink of every vine.

      To dig for wealth we weary not our limbs:
      Gold, though the heaviest metal, hither swims.
      Ours is the harvest where the Indians mow:
      We plough the deep and reap what others sow.

65   Things of the noblest kind our own soil breeds,
      Stout are our men and warlike are our steeds:
      Rome, though her eagle through the world had flown,
      Could never make this island all her own.

      Here the third Edward, and the Black Prince too,
70   France-conquering Henry, flourished, and now you,
      For whom we stayed as did the Grecian state
      Till Alexander came to urge their fate.

      When for more worlds the Macedonian cried,
      He wist not Thetis in her lap did hide
75   Another yet—a world reserved for you.
      To make more great than that he did subdue.

      He safely might old troops to battle lead,
      Against the unwarlike Persians and the Mede,
      Whose hasty flight did, from a bloodless field,
80   More spoil than honour to the victor yield.

      A race unconquered, by their clime made bold,
      The Caledonians, armed with want and cold,
      Have by a fate indulgent to your name
      Been from all ages kept for you to tame.

85   Whom the old Roman wall so ill confined
With a new chain of garrisons you bind:
Here foreign gold no more shall make them come—
Our English iron holds them fast at home.

They that henceforth must be content to know
90   No warmer region than their hills of snow,
May blame the sun, but must extol your grace,
Which in our senate has allowed them place.

Preferred by conquest, happily o'erthrown,
Falling they rise to be with us made one;
95   So kind dictators made, when they came home,
Their vanquished foes free citizens of Rome.

Like favour find the Irish with like fate,
Advanced to be a portion of our state,
While by your valour and your courteous mind
100   Nations divided by the sea are joined.

Holland, to gain your friendship, is content
To be our outguard on the continent;
She from her fellow-provinces would go
Rather than hazard to have you her foe.

105   In our late fight, when cannons did diffuse,
Preventing posts, the terror and the news,
Our neighbouring princes trembled at their roar,
But our conjunction makes them tremble more.

Your never-failing sword made war to cease,
110   And now you heal us with the acts of peace;
Our minds with bounty and with awe engage,
Invite affection and restrain our rage.

Less pleasure take brave minds in battles won
Than in restoring such as are undone:
115   Tigers have courage and the rugged bear,
But man alone can whom he conquers spare.

To pardon willing, and to punish loath,
You strike with one hand but you heal with both;
Lifting up all that prostrate lie you grieve
120   You cannot make the dead again to live.

When fate or error had our age misled,
And o'er these nations such confusion spread,
The only cure which could from heaven come down
Was so much power and piety in one!

125   One whose extraction from an ancient line
     Gives hope again that well-born men may shine;
     The meanest in your nature mild and good,
     The noblest rest secur'd in your blood.

     Oft have we wondered how you hid in peace
130   A mind proportioned to such things as these:
     How such a ruling spirit you could restrain,
     And practise first over yourself to reign.

     Your private life did a just pattern give
     How fathers, husbands, pious sons should live;
135   Born to command, your princely virtues slept
     Like humble David's, while the flock he kept.

     But when your troubled country called you forth,
     Your flaming courage and your matchless worth,
     Dazzling the eyes of all that did pretend,
140   To fierce contention gave a prosperous end.

     Still as you rise the state, exalted too,
     Finds no distemper while 'tis changed by you;
     Changed by the world's great scene, when, without noise
     The rising sun night's vulgar light destroys.

145   Had you, some ages past, this race of glory
     Run, with amazement we should read your story,
     But living virtue, all achievements past,
     Meets envy still to grapple with at last.

     This Caesar found, and that ungrateful age
150   With losing him fell back to blood and rage:
     Mistaken Brutus thought to break their yoke,
     But cut the bond of union with that stroke.

     That sun once set a thousand meaner stars
     Gave a dim light to violence and wars,
155   To such a tempest as now threatens all,
     Did not your mighty arm prevent the fall.

     If Rome's great senate could not wield that sword
     Which of the conquered world had made them lord,
     What hope had ours, while yet their power was new,
160   To rule victorious armies but by you?

     You, that had taught them to subdue their foes,
     Could order teach and their high spirits compose,
     To every duty could their minds engage,
     Provoke their courage and command their rage.

165 So when a lion shakes his dreadful mane
And angry grows, if he that first took pain
To tame his youth approach the haughty beast,
He bends to him but frights away the rest.

As the vexed world, to find repose, at last
170 Itself into Augustus' arms did cast,
So England now does, with like toil oppressed,
Her weary head upon your bosom rest.

Then let the muses with such notes as these
Instruct us what belongs unto our peace:
175 Your battles they hereafter shall indite
And draw the image of our Mars in fight;

Tell of towns stormed, of armies overcome,
Of mighty kingdoms by your conduct won;
How, while you thundered, clouds of dust did choke
180 Contending troops and seas lay hid in smoke.

Illustrious acts high raptures do infuse
And every conqueror creates a muse:
Here in low strains your milder deeds we sing,
But there, my lord, we'll bays and olive bring

185 To crown your head, while you in triumph ride
O'er vanquished nations, and the sea beside,
While all your neighbour princes unto you,
Like Joseph's sheaves, pay reverence and bow.

OCCASIONAL AND MISCELLANEOUS POEMS

OF THE DANGER HIS MAJESTY (BEING PRINCE) ESCAPED ON THE ROAD AT SANTANDER

Nor had his highness bid farewell to Spain
And reached the sphere of his own power, the main,
With British bounty in his ship he feasts
Th'Hesperian princes, his amazèd guests,
5 To find that wat'ry wilderness exceed
The entertainment of their great Madrid.
Healths to both kings attended with the roar
Of cannon echoed from th'affrighted shore;
With loud resemblance of his thunder prove
10 Bacchus the seed of cloud-compelling Jove,

While to his harp divine Arion sings
The loves and conquests of our Albion kings.
  Of the fourth Edward was his noble song,
Fierce, goodly, valiant, beautiful and young.
15 He rent the crown from vanquished Henry's head,
Raised the white rose and trampled on the red;
Till love triumphing o'er the victor's pride
Brought Mars and Warwick to the conquered side:
Neglected Warwick (whose bold hand, like fate,
20 Gives and resumes the sceptre of our state)
Woos for his master, and with double shame
Himself deluded, mocks the princely dame,
The Lady Bona whom just anger burns
And foreign war with civil rage returns.
25 Ah, spare your words where beauty is to blame:
Love gave th'affront and must repair the same,
When France shall boast of her whose conquering eyes
Have made the best of English hearts their prize;
Have power to alter the decree of fate
30 And change again the councils of our state.
  What the prophetic muse intends alone
To him that feels the secret wound is known;
With the sweet sound of this harmonious lay
About the keel delighted dolphins play,
35 Too sure a sign of seas' ensuing rage
Which must anon this royal troop engage,
To whom soft sleep seems more secure and sweet
Within the town commanded by our fleet.
These mighty peers placed in the gilded barge
40 Proud with the burden of so brave a charge:
With painted oars the youth begin to sweep
Neptune's smooth face and cleave the yielding deep,
Which soon becomes the seat of sudden war
Between the wind and tide that fiercely jar:
45 As when a sort of lusty shepherds try
Their force at football, care of victory
Makes them salute so rudely breast to breast
That their encounters seem too rough for jest.
They ply their feet and still the restless ball
50 Tossed to and fro is urgèd by them all:
So fares the doubtful barge 'twixt tide and winds,
And like effect of their contention finds.
Yet the bold Britons still securely rowed:
Charles and his virtue was their sacred load,
55 Than which a greater pledge heaven could not give
That the good boat this tempest should outlive.
But storms increase and now no hope of grace
Among them shines save in the prince's face.

The rest resign their courage, skill and sight
60   To danger, horror and unwelcome night.
        The gentle vessel wont with state and pride
On the smooth back of silver Thames to ride,
Wanders astonished in the angry main
As Titan's car did while the golden rain
65   Filled the young hand of his adventrous son
When the whole world an equal hazard run
To this of ours; the light of whose desire
Waves threaten now, as that was scared by fire.
        The impatient sea grows impotent and raves
70   That (night assisting) his impetuous waves
Should find resistance from so light a thing:
These surges ruin, those our safety bring.
Th'oppressed vessel doth the charge abide
Only because assailed on every side.
75   So men with rage and passion set on fire
Trembling for haste impeach their own desire.
        The pale Iberians had expired with fear,
But that their wonder did divert their care,
To see the prince with danger moved no more
80   Than with the pleasures of their court before.
Godlike his courage seemed, whom nor delight
Could soften, nor the face of death affright.
Next to the power of making tempests cease
Was in that storm to have so calm a peace.
85   Great Maro could no greater tempest feign
When the loud winds usurping on the main,
For any Juno laboured to destroy
The hated relics of confounded Troy:
His bold Aeneas, on like billows tossed
90   In a tall ship, and all his countries lost,
Dissolves with fear, and both his hands upheld,
Proclaims them happy whom the Greeks had quelled.
        In honourable fight our hero set
In a small, shallow fortune in his debt,
95   So near a hope of crowns and sceptres more
Than ever Priam when he flourished wore:
His loins yet full of ungot princes, all
His glory in the bud, lets nothing fall
That argues fear: if any thought annoys
100 The gallant youth, 'tis love's untasted joys,
And dear remembrance of that fatal glance
For which he lately pawned his heart in France,
Where he had lately seen a brighter nymph than she
That sprung out of his present foe, the sea.
105 That noble ardour, more than mortal fire,
The conquered ocean could not make expire,

Nor angry Thetis raise her waves above
The heroic prince, his courage, or his love.
'Twas indignation and not fear he felt
110   The shrine should perish where that image dwelt.
    Ah, love forbid the noblest of thy strain
Should not survive to let her know his pain,
Who nor his peril minding, nor his flame,
Is entertained with some less serious game
115   Among the bright nymphs of the Gallic court,
All highly born, obsequious to her sport.
They roses seem within their early pride,
But half reveal and half their beauties hide.
She the glad morning which her beams doth throw
120   Upon their smiling leaves and gild them so,
Like bright Aurora, whose refulgent ray
Foretells the fervour of ensuing day,
And warns the shepherd with his flocks retreat
To leafy shadows from the threatened heat.
125   From Cupid's string of many shafts that fled
Winged with those plumes which noble fame had shed,
As through the wondering world she flew and told
Of his adventures haughty, brave and bold:
Some had already touched the royal maid
130   But love's first summons seldom are obeyed.
Light was the wound, the prince's care unknown,
She might not, would not, yet reveal her own.
    His glorious name had so possessed her ears
That with delights those antique tales she hears
135   Of Jason, Theseus, and such worthies old,
As with his story best resemblance hold.
    And now she views, as on the wall it hung,
What old Musaeus so divinely sung:
Which art with life and love did so inspire
140   That she discerns and favours that desire,
Which there provokes th'adventurous youth to swim,
And in Leander's dangers pities him,
Whose not new love alone but fortune seeks
To frame his story like that amorous Greek's.
145   For from the stern of some good ship appears
A friendly light which moderates their fears:
New courage from reviving hope they take
And climbing o'er the waves that taper make,
On which the hope of all their lives depends,
150   As his on that fair hero's hand extends.
    The ship at anchor like a fixèd rock
Breaks the proud billows which her large sides knock,
Whose rage, restrainèd, foaming higher swells,
And from her port the weary barge repels,

155   Threat'ning to make her, forcèd out again,
        Repeat the dangers of the troubled main.
           Twice was the cable hurled in vain; the fates
        Would not be movèd for our sister states:
        For England is the third, successful throw,
160   And then the genius of that land they know,
        Whose prince must be (as their own books devise)
        Lord of the scene where now the danger lies.
           Well sung the Roman bard, all human things
        Of dearest value hang on slender strings.
165   O, see the then sole hope, and in design
        Of heaven our joy, supported by a line,
        Which for that instant was heaven's care above
        The chain that's fixèd to the throne of Jove;
        On which the fabric of our world depends,
170   One link dissolved, the whole creation ends.

AT PENSHURST

        While in this park I sing, the listening deer
        Attend my passion and forget to fear.
        When to the beeches I report my flame
        They bow their heads as if they felt the same.
5   To gods appealing when I reach their bowers
        With loud complaints, they answer me in showers.
        To thee a wild and cruel soul is given,
        More deaf than trees and prouder than the heaven.
        Love's foe professed, why dost thou falsely feign
10   Thyself a Sidney? From which noble strain
        He sprung that could so far exalt the name
        Of love and warm our nation with his flame,
        That all we can of love or high desire
        Seems but the smoke of amorous Sidney's fire.
15   Nor call her mother, who so well do prove
        One breast may hold both chastity and love.
        Never can she that so exceeds the spring
        In joy and bounty be supposed to bring
        One so destructive: to no human stock
20   We owe this fierce unkindness, but the rock,
        The cloven rock, produced thee, by whose side
        Nature, to recompence the fatal pride
        Of such stern beauty, placed those healing springs
        Which not more help than that destruction brings.
25   Thy heart no ruder than the rugged stone
        I might like Orpheus, with my numerous moan

Melt to compassion: now my traitorous song
With thee conspires to do the singer wrong:
While thus I suffer not myself to lose
30   The memory of what augments my woes,
But with my own breath still foment the fire
Which flames as high as fancy can aspire.
     This last complaint th'indulgent ears did pierce
Of just Apollo, president of verse,
35   Highly concernèd that the muse should bring
Damage to one whom he had taught to sing.
Thus he advised me on yon agèd tree,
'Hang up thy lute and hie thee to the sea
That there with wonders thy diverted mind
40   Some truce at least may with affection find.'
     Ah, cruel nymph, from whom her humble swain
Flies for relief unto the raging main,
And from the winds and tempests doth expect
A milder fate than from her cold neglect.
45   Yet there he'll pray that the unkind may prove
Blessed in her choice, and vows this endless love
Springs from no hope of what she can confer,
But from those gifts which heaven has heaped on her.

AT PENSHURST

Had Dorothea lived when mortals made
Choice of their deities, this sacred shade
Had held an altar to her power, that gave
The peace and glory which these always have
5   Embroidered so with flowers where she stood
That it became a garden of the wood.
Her presence has such more than human grace
That it can civilize the rudest place,
And beauty too, and order, can impart
10   Where nature ne'er intended it, nor art.
The plants acknowledge this, and her admire
No less than those of old did Orpheus' lyre.
If she sit down with tops all toward her bowed
They round about her into arbors crowd;
15   Or if she walk in even ranks they stand
Like some well-marshalled and obsequious band.
Amphion so made stones and timber leap
Into fair figures from a confused heap—
And in the symmetry of her parts is found
20   A power like that of harmony in sound.

Ye lofty beeches tell this matchless dame
That if together ye feed all on one flame,
It could not equalize the hundred part
Of what her eyes have kindled in my heart.
25   Go, boy, and carve this passion on the bark
Of yonder tree, which stands the sacred mark
Of noble Sidney's birth, when such benign,
Such more than mortal-making stars did shine,
That there they cannot but forever prove
30   The monument and pledge of humble love:
His humble love whose hope shall ne'er rise higher
Than for a pardon that he dares admire.

OF SALLE

Of Jason, Theseus and such worthies old,
Light seem the tales antiquity has told:
Such beasts and monsters as their force oppressed,
Some places only, and some times infest.
5   Salle, that scorned all power and laws of men,
Goods with their owners hurrying to their den,
And future ages threatening with a rude
And savage race successively renewed;
Their king despising with rebellious pride
10   And foes professed to all the world beside:
This pest of mankind gives our hero fame
And through th'obligèd world dilates his name.
    The prophet once to cruel Agag said
'As thy fierce sword has mothers childless made
15   So shall the sword make thine': and with that word
He hewed the man in pieces with his sword.
Just Charles like measure has returned to these,
Whose pagan hands had stained the troubled seas;
With ships they made the spoilèd merchant mourn,
20   With ships their city and themselves are torn.
One squadron of our wingèd castles sent
O'er-threw their fort and all their navy rent:
For not content the dangers to increase
And act the part of tempest in the seas,
25   Like hungry wolves these pirates from our shore
Whole flocks of sheep and ravished cattle bore.
Safely they did on other nations prey:
Fools to provoke the sovereign of the sea.
Mad Cacus so whom like ill fate persuades
30   The herd of fair Alcmena's seed invades;

Who for revenge and mortals' glad relief
Sacked the dark cave and crushed that horrid thief.
   Morocco's monarch, wond'ring at this fact,
Save that his presence his affairs exact,
35   Had come in person to have seen and known
The injured world's revenger and his own.
Hither he sends the chief among his peers,
Who in his dark well-chosen presents bears
To the renowned for piety and force,
40   Poor captives manumized and matchless horse.

OF A WAR WITH SPAIN AND A FIGHT AT SEA

Now for some ages had the pride of Spain
Made the sun shine on half the world in vain,
While she bid war to all that durst supply
The place of those her cruelty made die.
5   Of nature's bounty men forbore to taste
And the best portion of the earth lay waste:
From the new world her silver and her gold
Came like a tempest to confound the old;
Feeding with these the bribed Electors' hopes
10   Alone she gave us emperors and popes,
With these accomplishing her vast designs;
Europe was shaken with her Indian mines.
   When Britain, looking with a just disdain
Upon this gilded majesty of Spain,
15   And knowing well that empire must decline
Whose chief support and sinews are of coin,
Our nation's solid virtue did oppose
To the rich troublers of the world's repose.
   And now some months, encamping on the main,
20   Our naval army had besiegèd Spain:
They that the whole world's monarchy designed
Are to their ports by our bold fleet confined,
From whence our Red Cross they triumphant see
Riding without a rival on the sea.
25   Others may use the ocean as their road:
Only the English make it their abode,
Whose ready sails with every wind can fly
And make a covenant with the inconstant sky;
Our oaks secure, as if they there took root,
30   We tread on billows with a steady foot.
   Meanwhile the Spaniards in America
Near to the line the sun approaching saw,

And hoped their European coasts to find
Cleared from our ships by the autumnal wind.
35   Their huge capacious galleons stuffed with plate
The labouring winds drive slowly towards their fate.
Before St Lucar they their guns discharge,
To tell their joy or to call forth a barge.
This heard some ships of ours, though out of view,
40   And, swift as eagles, to the quarry flew:
So heedless lambs, which for their mothers bleat,
Wake hungry lions and become their meat.
   Arrived, they soon began that tragic play,
And with their smoky cannons banish day:
45   Night, horror, slaughter, with confusion meets
And in their sable arms embrace their fleets.
Through yielding planks the angry bullets fly
And of one wound hundreds together die:
Born under different stars one fate they have—
50   The ship their coffin and the sea their grave.
Bold were the men who on the ocean first
Spread their new sails, when shipwreck was the worst;
More danger now from man alone we find
Than from the rocks, the billows, or the wind.
55   They that had sailed from near the Antarctic pole,
Their treasure safe, and all their vessels whole,
In sight of their dear country ruined be,
Without the guilt of either rock or sea.
What they would spare our fiercer art destroys,
60   Surpassing storms in terror and in noise.
Once Jove from Ida did both hosts survey
And, when he pleased to thunder, part the fray:
Here heaven in vain that kind retreat should sound,
The louder cannon had the thunder drowned.
65   Some we made prize, while others, burned and rent,
With their rich lading to the bottom went:
Down sinks at once (so Fortune with us sports!)
The pay of armies and the pride of courts.
Vain man, whose rage buries as low that store
70   As avarice had digged for it before;
What earth in her dark bowels could not keep
From greedy hands, lies safer in the deep,
Where Thetis kindly does from mortals hide
Those seeds of luxury, debate and pride.
75   And now into her lap the richest prize
Fell, with the noblest of our enemies.
The marquis (glad to see the fire destroy
Wealth that prevailing foes were to enjoy)
Out from his flaming ship his children sent
80   To perish in a milder element,

Then laid him by his burning lady's side
And, since he could not save her, with her died.
Spices and gums about them melting fry,
And, phoenix-like, in that rich nest they die:
85   Alive in flames of equal love they burned,
And now together are to ashes turned—
Ashes more worth than all their funeral cost,
Than the huge treasure which was with them lost.
These dying lovers and their floating sons
90   Suspend the fight and silence all our guns.
Beauty and youth about to perish finds
Such noble pity in brave English minds
That (the rich spoil forgot, their valour's prize)
All labour now to save their enemies.
95   How frail our passions! How soon changèd are
Our wrath and fury to a friendly care!
They that but now for honour and for plate
Made the sea blush for blood, resign their hate,
And, their young foes endeavouring to retrieve,
100   With greater hazard than they fought they dive.
With these returns victorious Montague,
With laurels in his hand, and half Peru.
Let the brave generals divide that bough,
Our great Protector hath such wreaths enow:
105   His conquering head has no more room for bays;
Then let it be as the glad nation prays;
Let the rich ore forthwith be melted down,
And the state fixed by making him a crown:
With ermine clad and purple let him hold
110   A royal sceptre made of Spanish gold.

INSTRUCTIONS TO A PAINTER

(For the drawing of the posture and progress of his majesty's forces at
sea, under the command of his Royal Highness; together with the
battle and victory obtained over the Dutch, June 3, 1665)

First draw the sea, that portion which between
The greater world and this of ours is seen.
Here place the British, there the Holland fleet,
Vast floating armies, both prepared to meet.
5   Draw this whole world, expecting who shall reign
After this combat o'er the conquered main.
Make heaven concerned, and an unusual star
Declare the importance of the approaching war;
Make the sea shine with gallantry and all
10   The English youth flock to their admiral,

The valiant duke whose early deeds abroad
Such rage in fight and art in conduct showed.
His bright sword now a dearer interest draws,
His brother's glory and his country's cause.
15   Let thy bold pencil hope and courage spread
Through the whole navy by that hero led;
Make all appear, where such a prince is by,
Resolved to conquer, or resolved to die.
With his extraction and his glorious mind
20   Make the proud sails swell more than with the wind;
Preventing cannon, make his louder fame
Check the Batavians and their fury tame.
So hungry wolves, though greedy of their prey,
Stop when they find a lion in their way;
25   Make him bestride the ocean, and mankind
Ask his consent to use the sea and wind.
While his tall ships in the barred channel stand
He grasps the Indies in his armèd hand.
    Paint an east wind and make it blow away
30   The excuse of Holland for their navy's stay;
Make them look pale and, the bold prince to shun,
Through the cold north and rocky regions run.
To find the coast where morning first appears
By the dark pole the wary Belgian steers,
35   Confessing now he dreads the English more
Than all the dangers of a frozen shore,
While from our arms, security to find,
They fly so far they leave the day behind.
Describe their fleet abandoning the sea,
40   And all their merchants left a wealthy prey;
Our first success in war make Bacchus crown
And half the vintage of the year our own.
The Dutch their wine and all their brandy lose,
Disarmed of that from which their courage grows,
45   While the glad English to relieve their toils
In healths to their great leader drink the spoils.
    His high command to Afric's coast extend
And make the Moors before the English bend.
Those barbarous pirates willingly receive
50   Conditions such as we are pleased to give.
Deserted by the Dutch, let nations know
We can our own and their great business do,
False friends chastise and common foes restrain,
Which, worse than tempests, did infest the main.
55   Within those straits make Holland's Smyrna fleet
With a small squadron of the English meet:
Like falcons these, those like a numerous flock
Of fowl which scatter to avoid the shock.

There paint confusion in a various shape:
60   Some sink, some yield, and—flying—some escape.
Europe and Africa from either shore
Spectators are and hear our cannon roar,
While the divided world in this agree,
Men that fight so deserve to rule the sea.
65   But nearer home thy pencil use once more,
And place our navy by the Holland shore:
The world they compassed while they fought with Spain,
But here already they resign the main.
Those greedy mariners, out of whose way
70   Diffusive Nature could no region lay,
At home preserved from rocks and tempests lie,
Compelled like others in their beds to die.
Their single towns th'Iberian armies pressed:
We all their provinces at once invest,
75   And in a month ruin their traffic more
Than that long war could in an age before.
        But who can always on the billows lie?
The wat'ry wilderness yields no supply.
Spreading our sails to Harwich we resort
80   And meet the beauties of the British court.
Th'illustrious duchess and her glorious train
(Like Thetis with her nymphs) adorn the main.
The gazing sea-gods, since the Paphian queen
Sprung from among them, no such sight had seen.
85   Charmed with the graces of a troop so fair
Those deathless powers for us themselves declare,
Resolved the aid of Neptune's court to bring
And help the nation where such beauties spring.
The soldier here his wasted store supplies
90   And takes new valour from the ladies' eyes.
        Meanwhile, like bees when stormy winter's gone,
The Dutch, as if the sea were all their own,
Desert their ports and, falling in their way,
Our Hamburg merchants are become their prey.
95   Thus flourish they before th'approaching fight,
As dying tapers give a blazing light.
        To check their pride our fleet half-victualled goes,
Enough to serve us till we reach our foes,
Who now appear so numerous and bold
100   The action worthy of our arms we hold.
A greater force than that which here we find
Ne'er pressed the ocean nor employed the wind.
Restrained a while by the unwelcome night
Th'impatient English scarce attend the light.
105   But now the morning, heaven severely clear,
To the fierce work indulgent does appear,

And Phoebus lifts above the waves his light
That he might see and thus record the fight.
　　As when loud winds from different quarters rush,
110　Vast clouds encountering one another crush,
With swelling sails so, from their several coasts,
Join the Batavian and the British hosts.
For a less prize, with less concern and rage,
The Roman fleets at Actium did engage;
115　They for the empire of the world they knew,
These for the old contend and for the new.
At the first shock, with blood and powder stained,
Nor heaven nor sea their former face retained;
Fury and art produce effects so strange
120　They trouble nature and her visage change.
Where burning ships the banished sun supply
And no light shines but that by which men die,
There York appears, so prodigal is he
Of royal blood as ancient as the sea!
125　Which down to him, so many ages told,
Has through the veins of mighty monarchs rolled.
The great Achilles marched not to the field
Till Vulcan that impenetrable shield
And arms had wrought, yet there no bullets flew,
130　But shafts and darts which the weak Phrygians threw:
Our bolder hero on the deck does stand
Exposed, the bulwark of his native land;
Defensive arms laid by as useless here
Where massy balls the neighbouring rocks do tear.
135　Some power unseen those princes does protect
Who for their country thus themselves neglect.
　　Against him first Opdam his squadron leads,
Proud of his late success against the Swedes,
Made by that action and his high command
140　Worthy to perish by a prince's hand.
The tall Batavian in a vast ship rides,
Bearing an army in her hollow sides;
Yet, not inclined the English ship to board,
More on his guns relies than on his sword,
145　From whence a fatal volley we received:
It missed the Duke but his great heart it grieved.
Three worthy persons from his side it tore
And died his garment with their scattered gore.
Happy to whom this glorious death arrives,
150　More to be valued than a thousand lives!
On such a theatre as this to die,
For such a cause and such a witness by,
Who would not thus a sacrifice be made
To have his blood on such an altar laid?

155 The rest about him struck with horror stood
    To see their leader covered o'er with blood.
    So trembled Jacob when he thought the stains
    Of his son's coat had issued from his veins.
    He feels no wound but in his troubled thought:
160 Before for honour, now revenge he fought.
    His friends in pieces torn (the bitter news
    Not brought by Fame) with his own eyes he views:
    His mind at once reflecting on their youth,
    Their worth, their love, their valour, and their truth,
165 The joys of court, their mothers and their wives,
    To follow him, abandoned, and their lives!
    He storms and shoots, but flying bullets now
    To execute his rage appear too slow:
    They miss or sweep but common souls away—
170 For such a loss Opdam his life must pay.
    Encouraging his men he gives the word,
    With fierce intent that hated ship to board,
    And make the guilty Dutch with his own arm
    Wait on his friends while yet their blood is warm.
175 His wingèd vessel like an eagle shows,
    When through the clouds to truss a swan she goes:
    The Belgian ship unmoved, like some huge rock
    Inhabiting the sea, expects the shock.
    From both the fleets men's eyes are bent this way,
180 Neglecting all the business of the day.
    Bullets their flight and guns their noise suspend:
    The silent ocean does th'event attend,
    Which leader shall the doubtful victory bless
    And give an earnest of the war's success,
185 When Heaven itself, for England to declare,
    Turns ships and men and tackle into air.
        Their new commander from his charge is tossed
    Which that young prince had so unjustly lost,
    Whose great progenitors, with better fate
190 And better conduct, swayed their infant state.
    His flight towards heaven th'aspiring Belgian took,
    But fell, like Phaeton, with thunder struck—
    From vaster hopes than his he seemed to fall
    That durst attempt the British admiral.
195 From her broadsides a ruder flame is thrown
    Than from the fiery chariot of the sun:
    That bears the radiant ensign of the day,
    And she the flag that governs in the sea.
        The Duke, ill pleased that fire should thus prevent
200 The work which for his brighter sword he meant,
    Anger still burning in his valiant breast
    Goes to complete revenge upon the rest:

So on the guardless herd, their keeper slain,
Rushes a tiger in the Lybian plain.
205 The Dutch, accustomed to the raging sea,
And in black storms the frowns of heaven to see,
Never met tempest which more urged their fears
Than that which in the prince's look appears.
Fierce, goodly, young—Mars he resembles when
210 Jove sends him down to scourge perfidious men:
Such as with foul ingratitude have paid
Both those that led and those that gave them aid.
Where he gives on, disposing of their fates,
Terror and death on his loud cannon waits,
215 With which he pleads his brother's cause so well
He shakes the throne to which he does appeal.
The sea with spoils his angry bullets strow,
Widows and orphans making as they go;
Before his ship fragments of vessels torn,
220 Flags, arms, and Belgian carcasses are borne,
And his despairing foes, to flight inclined,
Spread all their canvas to invite the wind.
So the rude Boreas, where he lists to blow,
Makes clouds above and billows fly below,
225 Beating the shore, and with a boisterous rage,
Does heaven at once, and earth and sea engage.
　　The Dutch, elsewhere, did through the wat'ry field
Perform enough to have made others yield,
But English courage, growing as they fight,
230 In danger, noise, and slaughter takes delight:
Their bloody task unwearied still they ply,
Only restrained by death or victory.
Iron and lead, from earth's dark entrails torn,
Like showers of hail from either side are borne:
235 So high the rage of wretched mortals goes,
Hurling their mother's bowels at their foes!
Ingenious to their ruin every age
Improves the arts and instruments of rage.
Death-hastening ills Nature enough has sent
240 And yet men still a thousand more invent!
　　But Bacchus now, which led the Belgians on,
So fierce at first, to favour us begun:
Brandy and wine, their wonted friends, at length
Render them useless and betray their strength.
245 So corn in fields, and in the garden, flowers,
Revive and raise themselves with moderate showers;
But overcharged with never-ceasing rain
Become too moist and bend their heads again.
Their reeling ships on one another fall,
250 Without a foe enough to ruin all.

Of this disorder and the favouring wind
The watchful English such advantage find
Ships fraught with fire among the heap they throw,
And up the so-entangled Belgians blow.
255 The flame invades the powder-rooms and then
Their guns shoot bullets and their vessels men.
The scorched Batavians on the billows float,
Sent from their own to pass in Charon's boat.
    And now our royal admiral success
260 (With all the marks of victory) does bless:
The burning ships, the taken and the slain,
Proclaim his triumph o'er the conquered main.
Nearer to Holland, as their hasty flight
Carries the noise and tumult of the fight,
265 His cannons' roar, forerunners of his fame,
Makes their Hague tremble and their Amsterdam:
The British thunder does their houses rock,
And the Duke seems at every door to knock.
His dreadful streamer (like a comet's hair
270 Threatening destruction) hastens their despair;
Makes them deplore their scattered fleet as lost
And fear our present landing on their coast.
    The trembling Dutch the approaching Prince behold,
As sheep a lion leaping towards their fold:
275 Those piles which serve them to repel the main
They think too weak his fury to restrain.
'What wonders may not English valour work
Led by the example of victorious York,
Or what defence against him can they make
280 Who, at such distance, does their country shake?
His fatal hand their bulwarks will o'erthrow
And let in both the ocean and the foe'—
Thus cry the people, and, their land to keep,
Allow our title to command the deep;
285 Blaming their States' ill conduct, to provoke
Those arms which freed them from the Spanish yoke.
    Painter, excuse me if I have awhile
Forgot thy art and used another style;
For though you draw armed heroes as they sit,
290 The task in battle does the muses fit:
They in the dark confusion of a fight
Discover all, instruct us how to write;
And light and honour to brave actions yield,
Hid in the smoke and tumult of the field:
295 Ages to come shall know that leader's toil,
And his great name, on whom the muses smile.
Their dictates here let thy famed pencil trace
And this relation with thy colours grace.

  Then draw the parliament, the nobles met,

300   And our great monarch high above them set:
Like young Augustus let his image be,
Triumphing for that victory at sea,
Where Egypt's queen and eastern kings o'erthrown,
Made the possession of the world his own.
305   Last draw the Commons at his royal feet,
Pouring out treasure to supply his fleet.
They vow with lives and fortunes to maintain
Their kind's eternal title to the main,
And with a present to the Duke, approve
310   His valour, conduct, and his country's love.

ON THE STATUE OF KING CHARLES I

That the first Charles does here in triumph ride,
See his son reign where he a martyr died,
And people pay that reverence as they pass
(Which then he wanted) to the sacred brass,
5   Is not the effect of gratitude alone,
To which we owe the statue and the stone:
But heaven this lasting monument has wrought
That mortals may eternally be taught
Rebellion, though successful, is but vain,
10   And kings so killed rise conquerors again.
This truth the royal image does proclaim
Loud as the trumpet of surviving fame.

TO ONE MARRIED TO AN OLD MAN

Since thou wouldst need, bewitched with some ill charms,
Be buried in those monumental arms,
All we can wish is 'May that earth lie light
Upon thy tender limbs—and so good night!'

AN EPIGRAM ON A PAINTED LADY WITH ILL TEETH

Were men so dull they could not see
That Lycè painted, should they flee
Like simple birds into a net
So grossly woven and ill set,

5 Her own teeth would undo the knot
And let all go that she had got.
Those teeth fair Lycè must not show
If she would bite: her lovers, though
Like birds they stoop at seeming grapes,
10 Are disabused when first she gapes:
The rotten bones discovered there
Show 'tis a painted sepulchre.

OF ENGLISH VERSE

Poets may boast, as safely vain,
Their works shall with the world remain:
Both, bound together, live or die,
The verses and the prophecy.

5 But who can hope his lines should long
Last in a daily changing tongue?
When they are new envy prevails,
And as that dies our language fails.

When architects have done their part
10 The matter may betray their art:
Time, if we use ill-chosen stone,
Soon brings a well-built palace down.

Poets that lasting marble seek
Must carve in Latin or in Greek:
15 We write in sand, our language grows
And like the tide our work o'erflows.

Chaucer his sense can only boast,
The glory of his numbers lost:
Years have defaced his matchless strain,
20 And yet he did not sing in vain.

The beauties which adorned that age,
The shining subjects of his rage,
Hoping they should immortal prove
Rewarded with success his love.

25 This was the generous poet's scope,
And all an English pen can hope:
To make the fair approve his flame
That can so far extend their fame.

Verse thus designed has no ill fate
If it arrive but at the date
Of fading beauty; if it prove
But as long-lived as present love.

OF TEA, COMMENDED BY HER MAJESTY

Venus her myrtle, Phoebus has his bays:
Tea both excels, which she vouchsaves to praise.
The best of queens and best of herbs we owe
To that bold nation which the way did show
To the fair region where the sun does rise,
Whose rich productions we so justly prize.
The muse's friend, tea does our fancy aid,
Repress those vapours which the head invade,
And keeps that palace of the soul serene
Fit on her birthday to salute the queen.

EPITAPH ON SIR GEORGE SPEKE

Upon this stone lies virtue, youth,
Unblemished probity and truth;
Just unto all relations known,
A worthy patriot, pious son;
Whom neighbouring towns so often sent
To give their sense in parliament;
With lives and fortunes trusting one
Who so discreetly used his own.
Sober he was, wise, temperate,
Contented with an old estate,
Which no foul avarice did increase
Nor wanton luxury make less.
While yet but young his father died
And left him to a happy guide:
Not Lemuel's mother with more care
Did counsel or instruct her heir,
Or teach with more success her son
The vices of the time to shun.
An heiress she: while yet alive
All that was hers to him did give,
And he just gratitude did show
To one that had obliged him so.

Nothing too much for her he thought
By whom he was so bred and taught.
25   So—early made that path to tread
Which did his youth to honour lead—
His short life did a pattern give
How neighbours, husbands, friends should live.
    The virtues of a private life
30   Exceed the glorious noise and strife
Of battle won: in those we find
The solid interest of mankind.
    Approved by all and loved so well,
Though young, like fruit that's ripe, he fell.

LONG AND SHORT LIFE

Circles are praised not that abound
In largeness, but the exactly round:
So life we praise that does excel
Not in much time, but acting well.

OF THE LAST VERSES IN THE BOOK

When we for age could neither read nor write
The subject made us able to indite:
The soul with nobler resolutions decked,
The body stooping, does herself erect,
5   No mortal parts are requisite to raise
Her that unbodied can her Maker praise.
    The seas are quiet when the winds give o'er:
So, calm are we when passions are no more,
For then we know how vain it was to boast
10   Of fleeting things, so certain to be lost.
Clouds of affection from our younger eyes
Conceal that emptiness which age descries.
    The soul's dark cottage, battered and decayed,
Lets in new light through chinks that time has made:
15   Stronger by weakness wiser men become
As they draw near to their eternal home.
Leaving the old, both worlds at once they view
That stand upon the threshold of the new.

Henry Vaughan (1622–95)

SECULAR POEMS

TO MY INGENUOUS FRIEND R.W.

When we are dead and now no more
Our harmless mirth, our wit and score
Distracts the town; when all is spent
That the base niggard world hath lent
Thy purse or mine; when the loathed noise
Of drawers, prentices and boys
Hath left us, and the clamorous bar
Items no pints i' the Moon or Star;
When no calm whisperers wait the doors
To fright us with forgotten scores,
And such agèd long bills carry
As might start an antiquary;
When the sad tumults of the maze,
Arrests, suits, and the dreadful face
Of sergeants are not seen, and we
No lawyers, ruffs, or gowns must fee:
When all these mulcts are paid, and I
From thee, dear wit, must part and die,
We'll beg the world would be so kind
To give's one grave as we'd one mind:
There (as the wiser few suspect
That souls after death affect)
Our souls shall meet, and thence will they,
Freed from the tyranny of clay,
With equal wings and ancient love
Into the Elysian fields remove,
Where in those blessèd walks they'll find
More of thy genius and my mind.
    First, in the shade of his own bays
Great Ben they'll see, whose sacred lays
The learnèd ghosts admire, and throng
To catch the subject of his song.
Then Randolph in those holy meads,
His *Lovers* and *Amyntas* reads,
Whilst his nightingale close by
Sings his and her own elegy.

[45]

From thence dismissed by subtle roads
Through airy paths and sad abodes,
They'll come into the drowsy fields
40   Of Lethe, which such virtue yields
That, if what poets sing be true,
The streams all sorrow can subdue.
Here on a silent, shady green,
The souls of lovers oft are seen,
45   Who in their lives' unhappy space
Were murdered by some perjured face.
All these the enchanted streams frequent
To drown their cares and discontent,
That the inconstant, cruel sex
50   Might not in death their spirits vex.
    And here our souls, big with delight
Of their new state, will cease their flight;
And now the last thoughts will appear
They'll have of us or any here;
55   But on those flowery banks will stay
And drink all sense and cares away.
    So they that did of these discuss
    Shall find their fables true in us.

TO AMORET GONE FROM HIM

Fancy and I last evening walked,
And, Amoret, of thee we talked.
The west just then had stol'n the sun
And his last blushes were begun:
5   We sat and marked how everything
Did mourn his absence—how the spring
That smiled and curled about his beams
Whilst he was here, now checked her streams:
The wanton eddies of her face
10   Were taught less noise and smoother grace,
And in a slow, sad channel went,
Whispering the banks their discontent.
The careless ranks of flowers that spread
Their perfumed bosoms to his head,
15   And with an open, free embrace
Did entertain his beamy face:
Like absent friends point to the west
And on that weak reflection feast.
If creatures, then, that have no sense
20   But the loose tie of influence

(Though fate and time each day remove
Those things that element their love)
At such vast distance can agree,
   Why, Amoret, why should not we?

A RHAPSODY

Darkness and stars i' the mid-day! They invite
Our active fancies to believe it night:
For taverns need no sun, but for a sign,
Where rich tobacco and quick tapers shine,
5   And royal, witty sack, the poet's soul,
With brighter suns than he doth gild the bowl,
As though the pot and poet did agree
Sack should to both illuminator be.
That artificial cloud with its curled brow
10   Tells us 'tis late, and that blue space below
Is fired with many stars: mark how they break
In silent glances o'er the hills, and speak
The evening to the plains, where—shot from far—
They meet in dumb salutes as one great star.
15   The room methinks grows darker, and the air
Contracts a sadder colour and less fair.
Or is't the drawer's skill? Hath he no arts
To blind us so we can't know pints from quarts?
No, no, 'tis night: look where the jolly clown
20   Musters his bleating herd and quits the down.
Hark how his rude pipe frets the quiet air
Whilst every hill proclaims Lycoris fair.
Rich, happy man that canst thus watch and sleep
Free from all cares but thy wench, pipe and sheep.
25   But, see, the moon is up, view where she stands
Sentinel o'er the door, drawn by the hands
Of some base painter that for gain hath made
Her face the landmark to the tippling trade.
This cup to her, that to Endymion give:
30   'Twas wit at first, and wine, that made them live.
Choke may the painter, and his box disclose
No other colours than his fiery nose!
And may we no more of his pencil see
Than two churchwardens and mortality.
35   Should we go now a-wandering we should meet
With catchpoles, whores and carts in every street.
Now when each narrow lane, each nook and cave,
Signposts and shop-doors pimp for every knave,

When riotous, sinful plush and telltale spurs
40 Walk Fleet Street and the Strand; when the soft stirs
Of bawdy, ruffled silks turn night to day,
And the loud whip and coach scolds all the way;
When lust of all sorts and each itchy blood
From the Tower Wharf to Cymbeline and Lud
45 Hunts for a mate, and the tired footman reels
'Twixt chairmen, torches, and the hackney wheels.
     Come, take the other dish. It is to him
That made his horse a senator. Each brim
Look big as mine: the gallant, jolly beast
50 Of all the herd, you'll say, was not the least.
     Now crown the second bowl, rich as his worth
I'll drink it to: he that like fire broke forth
Into the senate's faces, crossed Rubicon
And the state's pillars with their laws thereon,
55 And made the dull greybeards and furred gowns fly
Into Brundisium to consult and lie.
     This to brave Sylla: why should it be said
We drink more to the living than the dead?
Flatterers and fools do use it: let us laugh
60 At our own honest mirth, for they that quaff
To honour others do like those that sent
Their gold and plate to strangers to be spent.
     Drink deep; this cup be pregnant and the wine
Spirit of wit to make us all divine,
65 That big with sack and mirth we may retire
Possessors of more souls and nobler fire,
And by the influx of this painted sky
And laboured forms to higher matters fly:
So if a nap shall take us we shall all
70 After full cups have dreams poetical.

Let's laugh now and the pressed grape drink,
Till the drowsy day star wink;
And in our merry, mad mirth run
Faster and faster than the sun;
75 And let none his cup forsake
Till that star again doth wake;
So we men below shall move
Equally with the gods above.

TO HIS FRIEND ———

I wonder, James, through the whole history
Of ages such entails of poverty

Are laid on poets. Lawyers, they say, have found
A trick to cut them, would they were but bound
5   To practise on us, though for this thing we
Should pay, if possible, their bribes and fee.
Search, as thou canst, the old and modern store
Of Rome and hours, in all the witty score
Thou shalt not find a rich one. Take each clime
10 And run o'er all the pilgrimage of time,
Thou'lt meet them poor and everywhere descry
A threadbare, goldless genealogy.
Nature, it seems, when she meant us for earth
Spent so much of her treasure in the birth
15 As ever after niggards her, and she—
Thus stored within—beggars us outwardly.
Woeful profusion, at how dear a rate
Are we made up? All hope of thrift and state
Lost for a verse. When I by thoughts look back
20 Into the womb of time, and see the rack
Stand useless there until we are produced
Unto the torture and our souls infused
To learn afflictions, I begin to doubt
That as some tyrants use from their chained rout
25 Of slaves to pick out one whom for their sport
They keep afflicted by some lingering art,
So we are merely thrown upon the stage,
The mirth of fools and legend of the age.
When I see in the ruins of a suit
30 Some nobler breast, and his tongue sadly mute,
Feed on the vocal silence of his eye,
And knowing cannot reach the remedy;
When souls of baser stamp shine in their store
And he of all the throng is only poor;
35 When French apes for foreign fashions pay
And English legs are dressed the outlandish way,
So fine too that they their own shadows woo,
While he walks in the sad and pilgrim-shoe,
I'm mad at fate and angry even to sin
40 To see deserts and learning clad so thin.
To think how the earthly usurer can brood
Upon his bags and weigh the precious food
With palsied hands as if his soul did fear
The scales could rob him of what he laid there:
45 Like devils that on hid treasures sit, or those
Whose jealous eyes trust not beyond their nose,
They guard the dirt, and the bright idol hold
Close and commit adultery with gold.
A curse upon their dross! How have we sued
50 For a few scattered chips? How oft pursued

Petitions with a blush in hope to squeeze
For their souls' health, more than our wants, a piece?
Their steel-ribbed chests and purse (rust eat them both!)
Have cost us with much paper many an oath,
55   And protestations of such solemn sense
As if our souls were sureties for the pence.
Should we a full night's learnèd cares present
They'll scarce return us one short hour's content.
'Las, they're but quibbles, things we poets feign,
60   The short-lived squibs and crackers of the brain.
    But we'll be wiser, knowing 'tis not they
That must redeem the hardship of our way.
Whether a higher power or that star
Which, nearest heaven, is from earth most far,
65   Oppress us thus, or angeled from that sphere
By our strict guardians are kept luckless here,
It matters not, we shall one day obtain
Our native and celestial scope again.

UPON A CLOAK LENT HIM BY MR J. RIDSLEY

Here, take again thy sackcloth and thank heaven
Thy courtship hath not killed me! Is't not even
Whether we die by piecemeal or at once—
Since both but ruin, why then for the nonce
5   Didst husband my afflictions and cast o'er
Me this forced hurdle to inflame the score?
Had I near London in this rug been seen
Without doubt I had executed been
For some bold Irish spy, and 'cross a sledge
10   Had lain messed up for their four gates and bridge.
When first I bore it my oppressèd feet
Would needs persuade me 'twas some leaden sheet:
Such deep impressions and such dangerous holes
Were made that I began to doubt my soles,
15   And every step (so near necessity)
Devoutly wished some honest cobbler by.
Besides it was so short the Jewish rag
Seemed circumcised, but had a Gentile shag.
Hadst thou been with me on that day when we
20   Left craggy Biston and the fatal Dee,
When, beaten with fresh storms and late mishap,
It shared the office of a cloak and cap,
To see how 'bout my clouded head it stood
Like a thick turban or some lawyer's hood,

25 While the stiff, hollow pleats on every side
   Like conduit-pipes rained from the bearded hide,
   I know thou wouldst in spite of that day's fate
   Let loose thy mirth at my new shape and state,
   And with a shallow smile or two profess
30 Some Saracen had lost the clouted dress.
   Didst ever see the good-wife, as they say,
   March in her short cloak on the Christening day,
   With what soft motions she salutes the church
   And leaves the bedrid mother in the lurch?
35 Just so jogged I while my dull horse did trudge
   Like a circuit beast plagued with a gouty judge.
       But this was civil. I have since known more
   And worser pranks: one night (as heretofore
   Th'hast known) for want of change (a thing which I
40 And Bias used before me) I did lie
   Pure Adamite, and simply for that end
   Resolved and made this for my bosom friend.
   O that thou hadst been there next morn that I
   Might teach thee new microcosmography!
45 Thou wouldst have ta'en me, as I naked stood,
   For one of the seven pillars before the flood:
   Such characters and hieroglyphics were
   In one night worn, that thou mightst justly swear
   I'd slept in cerecloth or at Bedlam where
50 The madmen lodge in straw. I'll not forbear
   To tell thee all—his wild impress and tricks
   Like Speed's old Britons made me look, or Picts.
   His villanous, biting wire-embraces
   Had sealed in me more strange forms and faces
55 Than children see in dreams, or thou hast read
   In Arras, puppet plays, or gingerbread,
   With angled schemes and crosses that bred fear
   Of being handled by some conjurer,
   And nearer thou wouldst think (such strokes were drawn)
60 I'd been some rough statue of Fetter Lane,
   Nay I believe had I that instant been
   By surgeons or apothecaries seen,
   They had condemned my razèd skin to be
   Some walking herbal or anatomy.
65   But (thanks to the day!) 'tis off. I'd now advise
   Thee friend to put this piece to merchandise:
   The pedlars of our age have business yet
   And gladly would against the fair day fit
   Themselves with such a roof, that can secure
70 Their wares from dogs and cats rained in shower.
   It shall perform; or if this will not do
   'Twill make the ale wives sure—'twill make them two

Fine rooms of one and, spread upon a stick,
Is a partition without lime or brick.
75 Horned obstinacy! How my heart doth fret
To think what mouths and elbows it would set
In a wet day! Have you for two pence e'er
Seen King Harry's chapel at Westminster,
Where in their dusty gowns of brass and stone
80 The judges lie? And marked you how each one
In sturdy marble pleats about the knee
Bears up to show his legs and symmetry?
Just so would this, that I think't weaved upon
Some stiff-necked Brownist's exercising loom.
85 O, that thou hadst it when this juggling fate
Of soldiery first seized me! At what rate
Would I have bought it then, what was there but
I would have given for the compendious hut?
I do not doubt but—if the weight could please—
90 'Twould guard me better than a Lapland lease,
Or a German shirt with enchanted lint
Stuffed through, and the devil's beard and face weaved in't.
    But I have done. And think not friend that I
This freedom took to jeer thy courtesy:
95 I thank thee for it, and I believe my muse
So known to thee thou'lt not suspect abuse:
She did this 'cause, perhaps, thy love paid thus
Might with my thanks outlive thy cloak and us.

TO AMORET. THE SIGH

Nimble sigh on thy warm wings
    Take this message and depart,
Tell Amoret that smiles and sings
At what thy airy voyage brings
5   That thou cam'st lately from my heart.

Tell my lovely foe that I
    Have no more such spies to send
    But one or two that I intend,
Some few minutes ere I die,
10   To her white bosom to commend.

Then whisper by that holy spring
    Where for her sake I would have died,
Whilst those water nymphs did bring
    Flowers to cure what she had tried,
15   And of my faith and love did sing,

That if my Amoret, if she
   In aftertimes would have it read
How her beauty murdered me,
   With all my heart I will agree,
20   If she'll but love me being dead.

TO AMORET, WALKING IN A STARRY EVENING

If Amoret that glorious eye,
   In the first birth of light
     And death of night,
Had with those elder fires you spy
5   Scattered so high
   Receivèd form and sight,

We might suspect in the vast ring,
   Amidst these golden glories
     And fiery stories,
10 Whether the sun had been the king
     And guide of day,
Or your brighter eye should sway.

But, Amoret, such is my fate
   That if thy face a star
     Had shined from far,
15 I am persuaded in that state
     'Twixt thee and me
   Of some predestined sympathy.

For sure such two conspiring minds,
   Which no accident or sight
     Did thus unite,
20 Whom no distance can confine,
     Start or decline,
   One for another were designed.

A SONG TO AMORET

If I were dead and in my place
   Some fresher youth designed,
To warm thee with new fires, and grace
   Those arms I left behind;

5   Were he as faithful as the sun
          That's wedded to the sphere,
       His blood as chaste and temperate run
          As April's mildest tear;

       Or were he rich and with his heap
10   And spacious share of earth
       Could make divine affection cheap,
          And court his golden birth:

       For all these arts I'd not believe
          (No, though he should be thine)
15   The mighty amorist could give
          So rich a heart as mine.

       Fortune and beauty thou might'st find
          And greater men than I:
       But my true resolvèd mind
20   They never shall come nigh.

       For I not for an hour did love,
          Or for a day desire,
       But with my soul had from above
          This endless holy fire.

POEMS FROM SILEX SCINTILLANS

REGENERATION

       A ward and still in bonds, one day
          I stole abroad:
       It was high spring and all the way
          Primrosed and hung with shade;
5   Yet was it frost within
             And surly winds
       Blasted my infant buds, and sin
          Like clouds eclipsed my mind.

       Stormed thus I straight perceived my spring
10   Mere stage and show,
       My walk a monstrous, mountained thing
          Rough-cast with rocks and snow;

And as a pilgrim's eye
  Far from relief
15 Measures the melancholy sky
  Then drops and rains for grief,

So sighed I upwards still: at last,
  'Twixt steps and falls,
I reached the pinnacle, where placed
20 I found a pair of scales.
  I took them up and laid
    In the one late pains;
The other smoke and pleasures weighed
  But proved the heavier grains.

25 With that some cried 'Away': straight I
    Obeyed, and led
Full east, a fair, fresh field could spy;
  Some called it Jacob's bed,
  A virgin soil which no
30   Rude feet e'er trod,
Where, since he stepped there, only go
  Prophets and friends of God.

Here I reposed; but, scarce well set,
  A grove descried
35 Of stately height, whose branches met
  And mixed on every side.
  I entered, and once in
    (Amazed to see't)
Found all was changed, and a new spring
40 Did all my senses greet.

The unthrift sun shot vital gold
  A thousand pieces,
And heaven its azure did unfold
  Chequered with snowy fleeces:
45 The air was all in spice
    And every bush
A garland wore. Thus fed my eyes
  But all the ear lay hush.

Only a little fountain lent
50 Some use for ears,
And on the dumb shades' language spent
  The music of her tears.
  I drew her near and found
    The cistern full
55 Of diverse stones, some bright and round,
  Others ill-shaped and dull.

The first—pray mark—as quick as light
    Danced through the flood,
But the last, more heavy than the night,
60   Nailed to the centre stood.
    I wondered much, but tired
      At last with thought,
My restless eye that still desired
    As strange an object brought:

65 It was a bank of flowers, where I descried
    (Though 'twas midday)
Some fast asleep, others broad-eyed
    And taking in the ray.
    Here musing long I heard
70   A rushing wind
Which still increased, but whence it stirred
    Nowhere I could not find.

I turned me round and to each shade
    Dispatched an eye,
75 To see if any leaf had made
    Least motion or reply:
    But while I listening sought
      My mind to ease
By knowing where 'twas or where not,
80   It whispered 'Where I please'.

    'Lord,' then said I, 'On me one breath,
    And let me die before my death.'

Cant. Cap. 5. ver. 17
Arise, O north, and come thou south wind, and blow upon my garden,
that the spices thereof may flow out.

RESURRECTION AND IMMORTALITY

Heb. Cap. 10. ver. 20
By that new, and living way, which he hath prepared for us, through
the veil, which is his flesh.

Body
Oft have I seen, when that renewing breath
    That binds and loosens death
Inspired a quickening power through the dead
    Creatures abed,

5　　　　　Some drowsy silk-worm creep
　　　　　　　From that long sleep
　　And in weak, infant hummings chime and knell
　　　　About her silent cell,
　　Until at last full with the vital ray
10　　　　　She winged away,
　　　　　And proud with life and sense,
　　　　　　Heaven's rich expense,
　　Esteemed (vain things!) of two whole elements
　　　　As mean and span-extents.
15　Shall I then think such providence will be
　　　　　　Less friend to me?
　　　Or that he can endure to be unjust
　　　Who keeps his covenant even with our dust?

Soul

　　Poor, querulous handful! Was't for this
20　　　　I taught thee all that is?
　　Unbowelled nature, showed thee her recruits
　　　　　And change of suits,
　　　And how of death we make
　　　　　A mere mistake,
25　For no thing can to nothing fall, but still
　　　　Incorporates by skill,
　　And then returns and from the womb of things
　　　　　Such treasure brings
　　　　As phoenix-like renew'th
30　　　　Both life and youth;
　　For a preserving spirit doth still pass
　　　　Untainted through this mass,
　　Which doth resolve, produce and ripen all
　　　　　That to it fall;
35　　　Nor are those births which we
　　　　　Thus suffering see
　　Destroyed at all: but when time's restless wave
　　　　　Their substance doth deprave
　　And the more noble essence finds his house
40　　　　Sickly and loose,
　　　　He, ever young, doth wing
　　　　　Unto that spring
　　And source of spirits, where he takes his lot
　　　Till time no more shall rot
45　His passive cottage; which, though laid aside,
　　　　Like some spruce bride
　　Shall one day rise, and clothed with shining light
　　　　All pure and bright,
　　　Remarry to the soul, for 'tis most plain
50　　Thou only fall'st to be refined again.

Then I that here saw darkly in a glass
    But mists and shadows pass,
And by their own weak shine did search the springs
    And course of things
55   Shall with enlightened rays
      Pierce all their ways;
And as thou saw'st I in a thought could go
    To Heaven or earth below
To read some star, or mineral, and in state
60   There often sat,
      So shalt thou then with me
      (Being winged and free)
Rove in that mighty and eternal light
    Where no rude shade or night
65 Shall dare approach us: we shall there no more
      Watch stars or pore
    Through melancholy clouds and say
      'Would it were day!'
    One everlasting sabbath there shall run
70   Without succession and without a sun.

Dan: Cap. 12. ver. 13

But go thou thy way until the end be, for thou shalt rest and stand up
in thy lot, at the end of the days.

THE SEARCH

'Tis now clear day: I see a rose
Bud in the bright east and disclose
The pilgrim sun. All night have I
Spent in a roving ecstasy
5   To find my saviour. I have been
As far as Bethle'm and have seen
His inn and cradle. Being there
I met the wise men, asked them where
He might be found, or what star can
10 Now point him out, grown up a man.
To Egypt hence I fled, ran o'er
All her parched bosom to Nile's shore,
Her yearly nurse; came back, enquired
Amongst the doctors and desired
15 To see the temple, but was shown
A little dust and for the town
A heap of ashes, where some said
A small, bright sparkle was abed,

Which would one day (beneath the pole)
20 Awake and then refine the whole.
    Tired, here I come to Sychar; thence
To Jacob's Well, bequeathèd since
Unto his sons, where often they
In those calm, golden evenings lay
25 Wat'ring their flocks and, having spent
Those white days, drove home to the tent
Their well-fleeced train. And here, O fate,
I sit where once my Saviour sat:
The angry spring in bubbles swelled
30 Which broke in sighs still as they filled,
And whispered 'Jesus had been there
But Jacob's children would not hear'.
Loath hence to part at last I rise
But with the fountain in my eyes,
35 And here a fresh search is decreed:
He must be found where he did bleed.
I walk the garden and there see
Ideas of his agony,
And moving anguishments that set
40 His blessed face in a bloody sweat.
I climbed the hill, perused the cross
Hung with my gain and his great loss.
Never did tree bear fruit like this,
Balsam of souls, the body's bliss.
45 But O his grave, where I saw lent
(For he had none) a monument:
An undefiled and new-hewed one,
But there was not the cornerstone.
'Sure,' then said I, 'my quest is vain,
50 He'll not be found where he was slain,
So mild a lamb can never be
'Midst so much blood and cruelty.
I'll to the wilderness and can
Find beasts more merciful than man:
55 He lived there safe; 'twas his retreat
From the fierce Jew and Herod's heat,
And forty days withstood the fell
And high temptations of hell.
With seraphims there talkèd he
60 His father's flaming ministry,
He heavened their walks, and with his eyes
Made those wild shades a paradise:
Thus was the desert sanctified
To be the refuge of his bride.
65 I'll thither then: see, it is day,
The sun's broke through to guide my way.'

Henry Vaughan

But as I urged thus and writ down
What pleasures should my journey crown,
What silent paths, what shades and cells,
70   Fair, virgin flowers and hallowed wells
I should rove in and rest my head
Where my dear Lord did often tread,
Sug'ring all dangers with success,
Methought I heard one singing thus:

75   Leave, leave thy gadding thoughts:
      Who pores
      and spies
     Still out of doors
      descries
80   Within them naught.

The skin and shell of things
      Though fair
      are not
     Thy wish nor prayer,
85   but got
     By mere despair
      of wings.

To rack old elements
     Or dust,
90   and say
     Sure here he must
      needs stay
     Is not the way
      nor just.

95   Search well another world: who studies this
     Travels in clouds; seeks manna where none is.

Acts Cap. 17. ver. 27, 28.
That they should seek the Lord, if haply they might feel after him,
and find him, though he be not far off from every one of us, for in him
we live, and move, and have our being.

THE LAMP

'Tis dead night round about: horror doth creep
And move on with the shades; stars nod and sleep,
And through the dark air spin a fiery thread
Such as doth gild the lazy glow-worm's bed.

5   Yet burn'st thou here a full day, while I spend
      My rest in cares and to the dark world lend
      These flames, as thou dost thine to me. I watch
      That hour which must thy life and mine dispatch:
      But still thou dost outgo me—I can see
10   Met in thy flames all acts of piety.
      Thy light is charity, thy heat is zeal,
      And thy aspiring, active fires reveal
      Devotion still on wing. Then thou dost weep
      Still as thou burn'st, and the warm droppings creep
15   To measure out thy length as if thou'ldst know
      What stock and how much time were left thee now;
      Nor dost thou spend one tear in vain, for still
      As thou dissolv'st to them and they distill
      They're stored up in the socket, where they lie
20   When all is spent, thy last and sure supply,
      And such is true repentance: every breath
      We spend in sighs is treasure after death.
      Only one point escapes thee—that thy oil
      Is still out with thy flame, and so both fail.
25   But whensoe'er I'm out, both shall be in,
      And where thou mad'st an end there I'll begin.

Mark Cap. 13. ver. 35

Watch you therefore, for you know not when the master of the house cometh, at even, or at midnight, or at the cock crowing, or in the morning.

MOUNT OF OLIVES

      Sweet, sacred hill on whose fair brow
      My saviour sat, shall I allow
        Language to love
      And idolize some shade or grove,
5   Neglecting thee? Such ill-placed wit,
      Conceit or call it what you please,
        Is the brain's fit
        And mere disease.

      Cotswold and Cooper's both have met
10   With learnèd swains and echo yet
        Their pipes and wit:
      But thou sleep'st in a deep neglect
      Untouched by any, and what need
      The sheep bleat thee a silly lay
15   That heard'st both reed
        And sheep-ward play?

Yet if poets mind thee well
They shall find thou art their hill
   And fountain too:
20   Their lord with thee had most to do—
He wept once, walked whole nights on thee,
And from thence, his sufferings ended,
     Unto glory
     Was attended.

25   Being there this spacious ball
Is but his narrow footstool all,
   And what we think
Unsearchable, now with one wink
He doth comprise: but in this air
30   When he did stay to bear our ill
     And sin, this hill
     Was then his chair.

ʃ

Thou that know'st for whom I mourn
   And why these tears appear,
That keep'st account till he return
   Of all his dust left here,
5   As easily thou might'st prevent
   As now produce these tears,
And add unto that day he went
   A fair supply of years.
But 'twas my sin that forced thy hand
10   To cull this primrose out,
That, by thy early choice forewarned,
   My soul might look about.
O what a vanity is man!
   How like the eye's quick wink
15   His cottage fails, whose narrow span
   Begins even at the brink!
Nine months thy hands are fashioning us,
   And many years (alas!)
Ere we can lisp or aught discuss
20   Concerning thee must pass.
Yet I have known thy slightest things—
   A feather or a shell,
A stick or rod which some chance brings—
   The best of us excel;
25   Yea I have known these shreds outlast
   A fair-compacted frame,

And for one twenty we have passed
   Almost outlive our name.
Thus hast thou placed in man's outside
30   Death to the common eye
That heaven within him might abide
   And close eternity.
Hence youth and folly, man's first shame,
   Are put unto the slaughter,
35   And serious thoughts begin to tame
   The wise man's madness, laughter.
Dull, wretched worms, that would not keep
   Within our first fair bed,
But out of Paradise must creep
40   For every foot to tread:
Yet had our pilgrimage been free
   And smooth without a thorn,
Pleasures had foiled eternity
   And tares had choaked the corn.
45   Thus by the cross salvation runs,
   Affliction is a mother
Whose painful throes yield many sons
   Each fairer than the other.
A silent tear can pierce thy throne
50   When loud joys want a wing,
And sweeter airs stream from a groan
   Than any arted string.
Thus, Lord, I see my gain is great,
   My loss but little to it,
55   Yet something more I must entreat
   And only thou canst do it.
O let me (like him) know my end,
   And be as glad to find it,
And whatsoe'er thou shalt commend
60   Still let thy servant mind it.
Then make my soul white as his own,
   My faith as pure and steady,
And deck me, Lord, with the same crown
   Thou hast crowned him already!

THE RETREAT

Happy those early days when I
Shined in my angel-infancy;
Before I understood this place
Appointed for my second race,

5   Or taught my soul to fancy aught
       But a white, celestial thought;
       When yet I had not walked above
       A mile or two from my first love,
       And looking back, at that short space,
10   Could see a glimpse of his bright face;
       When on some gilded cloud or flower
       My gazing soul would dwell an hour,
       And in those weaker glories spy
       Some shadows of eternity;
15   Before I taught my tongue to wound
       My conscience with a sinful sound,
       Or had the black art to dispense
       A several sin to every sense,
       But felt through all this fleshy dress
20   Bright shoots of everlastingness.
         O how I long to travel back
       And tread again that ancient track,
       That I might once more reach that plain
       Where first I left my glorious train,
25   From whence the enlightened spirit sees
       That shady city of palm trees;
       But (ah!) my soul with too much stay
       Is drunk and staggers in the way.
       Some men a forward motion love
30   But I by backward steps would move,
       And when this dust falls to the urn
       In that state I came return.

∫

       Come, come, what do I here?
           Since he is gone
       Each day is grown a dozen year,
           And each hour one.
5   Come, come!
           Cut off the sum
           By these soiled tears!
           (Which only thou
           Know'st to be true)
10   Days are my fears.

       There's not a wind can stir,
           Or beam pass by,
       But straight I think, though far,
           Thy hand is nigh;

15   Come, come!
        Strike these lips dumb:
        This restless breath
        That soils thy name
        Will ne'er be tame
20   Until in death.

        Perhaps some think a tomb
            No house of store,
        But a dark and sealed-up womb
            Which ne'er breeds more.
25   Come, come!
        Such thoughts benumb:
        But I would be
        With him I weep
        Abed, and sleep
30   To wake in thee.

THE MORNING WATCH

        O joys! Infinite sweetness! With what flowers
        And shoots of glory my soul breaks and buds!
            All the long hours
            Of night, and rest
5   Through the still shrouds
            Of sleep and clouds,
        This dew fell on my breast.
            O how it bloods
        And spirits all my earth! Hark in what rings
10   And hymning circulations the quick world
            Awakes and sings;
            The rising winds
            And falling springs,
            Birds, beasts, all things
15   Adore him in their kinds!
            Thus all is hurled
        In sacred hymns and order: the great chime
        And symphony of nature. Prayer is
            The world in tune,
20   A spirit voice,
            And vocal joys
        Whose echo is heaven's bliss.
            O let me climb
        When I lie down! The pious soul by night
25   Is like a clouded star, whose beams though said

To shed their light
Under some cloud,
Yet are above
And shine and move
30   Beyond that misty shroud.
So in my bed,
That curtained grave, though sleep like ashes hide
My lamp and life, both shall in thee abide.

THE EVENING WATCH: A DIALOGUE

Body
Farewell, I go to sleep, but when
The day-star springs I'll wake again.
Soul
Go, sleep in peace, and when thou liest
Unnumbered in thy dust, when all this frame
5   Is but one dram, and what thou now descriest
In several parts shall want a name,
Then may his peace be with thee, and each dust
Writ in his book, who ne'er betrayed man's trust.
Body
Amen! But, hark, ere we two stray,
10 How many hours dost think till day?
Soul
Ah, go: th'art weak and sleepy. Heaven
Is a plain watch and without figures winds
All ages up: who drew this circle even
He fills it—days and hours are blinds.
15 Yet this take with thee: the last gasp of time
Is thy first breath and man's eternal prime.

∫

Silence and stealth of days! 'Tis now
Since thou art gone
Twelve hundred hours, and not a brow
But clouds hang on.
5   As he that in some cave's thick damp
Locked from the light,
Fixeth a solitary lamp
To brave the night,
And, walking from his sun, when past
10   That glimmering ray

Cuts through the heavy mists in haste
  Back to his day,
So o'er fled minutes I retreat
  Unto that hour
15 Which showed thee last but did defeat
  Thy light and power.
I search and rack my soul to see
  Those beams again,
But nothing but the snuff to me
20 Appeareth plain;
That, dark and dead, sleeps in its known
  And common urn,
But those fled to their Maker's throne
  There shine and burn.
25 O could I track them! But souls must
  Track one the other,
And now the spirit, not the dust
  Must be thy brother.
Yet I have one pearl by whose light
30 All things I see,
And in the heart of earth and night
  Find Heaven and thee.

∫

Sure, there's a tie of bodies, and as they
  Dissolve with it to clay
Love languisheth and memory doth rust,
  O'ercast with that cold dust.
5 For things thus centered, without beams or action
  Nor give nor take contaction,
And man is such a marigold, these fled,
  That shuts and hangs the head.

Absents within the line conspire, and sense
10 Things distant doth unite;
Herbs sleep unto the east, and some fowls thence
  Watch the returns of light.
But hearts are not so kind: false, short delights
  Tell us the world is brave,
15 And wraps us in imaginary flights
  Wide of a faithful grave:
Thus Lazarus was carried out of town,
  For 'tis our foes' chief art
By distance all good objects first to drown
20 And then besiege the heart.

But I will be my own death's-head; and though
   The flatterer say I live,
Because incertainties we cannot know
   Be sure not to believe.

PEACE

My soul, there is a country
   Far beyond the stars,
Where stands a wingèd sentry
   All skilful in the wars.
5   There above noise and danger
   Sweet peace sits crowned with smiles,
And one born in a manger
   Commands the beauteous files.
He is thy gracious friend
10   And (O my soul, awake!)
Did in pure love descend
   To die here for thy sake.
If thou canst get but thither,
   There grows the flower of peace,
15   The rose that cannot wither,
   Thy fortress and thy ease.
Leave then thy foolish ranges,
   For none can thee secure,
But one who never changes,
20   Thy God, thy life, thy cure.

Rom. Cap. 8. ver. 19

Etenim res creatae exerto capite observantes expectant revelationem
filiorum dei.

And do they so? Have they a sense
   Of aught but influence?
Can they their heads lift, and expect,
   And groan too? Why the elect
5   Can do no more: my volumes said
   They were all dull and dead;
They judged them senseless and their state
   Wholly inanimate.
   Go, go seal up thy looks
10   And burn thy books.

I would I were a stone or tree
   Or flower by pedigree,
Or some poor highway herb, or spring
   To flow, or bird to sing!
15   Then should I (tied to one sure state)
   All day expect my date;
But I am sadly loose, and stray
   A giddy blast each way:
   O let me not thus range!
20   Thou canst not change.

Sometimes I sit with thee and tarry
   An hour or so, then vary.
Thy other creatures in this scene
   Thee only aim and mean:
25   Some rise to seek thee, and with heads
   Erect peep from their beds;
Others whose birth is in the tomb
   And cannot quit the womb,
   Sigh there and groan for thee,
30   Their liberty.

O let not me do less! Shall they
   Watch while I sleep or play?
Shall I thy mercies still abuse
   With fancies, friends or news?
35   O brook it not! Thy blood is mine
   And my soul should be thine;
O brook it not! Why wilt thou stop
   After whole showers one drop?
   Sure thou wilt joy to see
40   Thy sheep with thee.

THE RELAPSE

My God, how gracious art thou! I had slipped
   Almost to hell,
And on the verge of that dark, dreadful pit
   Did hear them yell:
5   But O thy love! Thy rich, almighty love
   That saved my soul,
And checked their fury, when I saw them move
   And heard them howl.
O my sole comfort, take no more these ways,
10   This hideous path,

And I will mend my own without delays:
    Cease thou thy wrath!
I have deserved a thick Egyptian damp,
    Dark as my deeds,
15 Should mist within me and put out that lamp
    Thy spirit feeds:
A darting conscience full of stabs and fears,
    No shade but yew,
Sullen and sad eclipses, cloudy spheres,
20   Those are my due.
But he that with his blood (a price too dear)
    My scores did pay,
Bid me, by virtue from him, challenge here
    The brightest day:
25 Sweet, downy thoughts, soft lily shades, calm streams,
    Joys full and true,
Fresh, spicy mornings, and eternal beams—
    These are his due.

THE RESOLVE

I have considered it, and find
    A longer stay
Is but excused neglect: to mind
    One path and stray
5 Into another, or to none,
    Cannot be love.
When shall that traveller come home
    That will not move?
If thou wouldst thither, linger not,
10   Catch at the place,
Tell youth and beauty they must rot,
    They're but a case.
Loose, parcelled hearts will freeze: the sun
    With scattered locks
15 Scarce warms, but by contraction
    Can heat rocks.
Call in thy powers, run and reach
    Home with the light;
Be there before the shadows stretch
20   And span up night.
Follow the cry no more: there is
    An ancient way
All strewed with flowers and happiness,
    And fresh as May;

25   There turn, and turn no more: let wits
         Smile at fair eyes
     Or lips, but who there weeping sits
         Hath got the prize.

CORRUPTION

Sure it was so: man in those early days
    Was not all stone and earth;
He shined a little, and by those weak rays
    Had some glimpse of his birth.
5   He saw Heaven o'er his head, and knew from whence
    He came, condemnèd, hither,
And, as first love draws strongest, so from hence
    His mind sure progressed thither.
Things here were strange unto him: sweat and till,
10   All was a thorn or weed.
Nor did those last but, like himself, died still
    As soon as they did seed:
They seemed to quarrel with him, for that act
    That 'fell him, foiled them all—
15 He drew the curse upon the world and cracked
    The whole frame with his fall.
This made him long for home, as loth to stay
    With murmurers and foes:
He sighed for Eden and would often say
20   'Ah what bright lights were those?'
Nor was Heaven cold unto him, for each day
    The valley or the mountain
Afforded visits, and still Paradise lay
    In some green shade or fountain.
25 Angels lay lieger here: each bush and cell,
    Each oak and highway knew them.
Walk but the fields or sit down at some well,
    And he was sure to view them.
Almighty love! Where art thou now? Mad man
30   Sits down and freezeth on:
He raves and swears to stir nor fire nor fan
    But bids the thread be spun.
I see thy curtains are close-drawn; thy bow
    Looks dim too in the cloud;
35 Sin triumphs still and man is sunk below
    The centre and his shroud;
All's in deep sleep and night; thick darkness lies
    And hatcheth o'er thy people:
But hark! What trumpet's that? What angel cries
40   'Arise! Thrust in thy sickle'?

UNPROFITABLENESS

How rich, O Lord, how fresh thy visits are!
'Twas but just now my bleak leaves hopeless hung,
   Sullied with dust and mud:
Each snarling blast shot through me and did share
5   Their youth and beauty; cold showers nipped and wrung
   Their spiciness and blood.
But since thou didst in one sweet glance survey
Their sad decays I flourish, and once more
   Breathe all perfumes and spice;
10 I smell a dew like myrrh and all the day
Wear in my bosom a full sun: such store
   Hath one beam from thy eyes.
But, ah! my God, what fruit hast thou of this?
What one poor leaf did ever I yet fall
15   To wait upon thy wreath?
Thus thou all day a thankless weed dost dress,
And when th'hast done a stench or fog is all
   The odour I bequeath.

IDLE VERSE

Go, go, quaint follies, sug'red sin,
   Shadow no more my door,
I will no longer cobwebs spin—
   I'm too much on the score.

5   For since amidst my youth and night
   My great preserver smiles,
We'll make a match, my only light,
   And join against their wiles;

Blind, desperate fits that study how
10   To dress and trim our shame,
That gild rank poison and allow
   Vice in a fairer name.

The purls of youthful blood and bowels
   Lust in the robes of love,
15   The idle talk of feverish souls
   Sick with a scarf or glove.

Let it suffice my warmer days
   Simpered and shined on you;
Twist not my cypress with your bays,
20   Or roses with my yew:

Go, go seek out some greener thing,
   It snows and freezeth here:
Let nightingales attend the spring,
    Winter is all my year.

THE DAWNING

Ah, what time wilt thou come, when shall that cry
  'The bridegroom's coming' fill the sky?
Shall it in the evening run
When our words and works are done,
5 Or will thy all-surprising light
   Break at midnight?
When either sleep or some dark pleasure
Possesseth mad man without measure;
Or shall these early, fragrant hours
10   Unlock thy bowers?
And with their blush of light descry
Thy locks crowned with eternity;
Indeed it is the only time
That with thy glory doth best chime:
15 All now are stirring, every field
   Full hymns doth yield;
The whole creation shakes off night
And for thy shadow looks the light;
Stars now vanish without number,
20 Sleepy planets set and slumber,
The pursy clouds disband and scatter,
All expect some sudden matter,
Not one beam triumphs, but from far
   That morning star.

25 O at what time soever thou
(Unknown to us) the heavens wilt bow,
And with thy angels in the van
Descend to judge poor, careless man,
Grant I may not like puddle lie
30 In a corrupt security,
Where if a traveller water crave
He finds it dead and in a grave;

But as this restless, vocal spring
All day and night doth run and sing,
35   And though here born yet is acquainted
Elsewhere, and flowing keeps untainted;
So let me all my busy age
In thy free services engage,
And though, while here, of force I must
40   Have commerce sometimes with poor dust,
And in my flesh, though vile and low,
As this doth in her channel flow,
Yet let my course, my aid, my love,
And chief acquaintance be above;
45   So when that day and hour shall come
In which thyself will be the sun,
Thou'lt find me dressed and on my way,
Watching the break of thy great day.

AFFLICTION

Peace, peace, it is not so. Thou dost miscall
    Thy physic; pills that change
    Thy sick accessions into settled health,
This is the great elixir that turns gall
5   To wine and sweetness, poverty to wealth,
        And brings man home when he doth range.
        Did not he who ordained the day
            Ordain night too,
        And in the greater world display
10   What in the lesser he would do?
All flesh is clay thou knowest, and but that God
            Doth use his rod,
And by a fruitful change of frosts and showers
        Cherish and bind thy powers,
15   Thou wouldst to weeds and thistles quite disperse
        And be more wild than is thy verse.
Sickness is wholesome and crosses are but curbs
        To check the mule, unruly man:
They are Heaven's husbandry, the famous fan
20   Purging the floor which chaff disturbs.
Were all the year one constant sunshine we
        Should have no flowers—
All would be drought and leanness: not a tree
        Would make us bowers.

25 Beauty consists in colours, and that's best
　　Which is not fixed, but flies and flows:
The settled red is dull, and whites that rest
　　Something of sickness would disclose.
　　　　Vicissitude plays all the game;
30 　　　　Nothing that stirs
　　　　Or hath a name
　　But waits upon this wheel.
Kingdoms too have their physic and for steel
　　Exchange their peace and furs.
35 Thus doth God key disordered man
　　(Which none else can)
Tuning his breast to rise or fall;
And by a sacred, needful art
Like strings stretch every part
40 Making the whole most musical.

LOVE AND DISCIPLINE

Since in a land not barren still
(Because thou dost thy grace distil)
My lot is fallen, blessed be thy will!

And since these biting frosts but kill
5 Some tares in me which choke or spill
That seed thou sow'st, blessed be thy skill!

Blessed be thy dew and blessed thy frost,
And happy I to be so crossed
And cured by crosses at thy cost.

10 The dew doth cheer what is distressed,
The frost's ill weeds nip and molest,
In both thou work'st unto the best.

Thus while thy several mercies plot
And work on me now cold, now hot,
15 The work goes on and slacketh not,

For as thy hand the weather steers,
So thrive I best 'twixt joys and tears,
And all the year have some green ears.

Henry Vaughan

THE WORLD

I saw eternity the other night
   Like a great ring of pure and endless light,
   All calm as it was bright;
And round beneath it Time in hours, days, years,
5   Driven by the spheres
Like a vast shadow moved, in which the world
   And all her train were hurled:
The doting lover in his quaintest strain
   Did there complain;
10 Near him his lute, his fancy and his flights,
   Wits so our delights,
With gloves and knots, the silly snares of pleasure—
   Yet his dear treasure
All scattered lay, while he his eyes did pour
15   Upon a flower.

The darksome statesman, hung with weights and woe,
Like a thick midnight fog moved there so slow
   He did nor stay nor go:
Condemning thoughts, like sad eclipses, scowl
20   Upon his soul,
And clouds of crying witnesses without
   Pursued him with one shout.
Yet digged the mole and lest his ways be found
   Worked underground,
25 Where he did clutch his prey, but one did see
    That policy;
Churches and altars fed him; perjuries
   Were gnats and flies;
It rained about him blood and tears but he
30   Drank them as free.

The fearful miser on a heap of rust
Sat pining all his life there, did scarce trust
   His own hands with the dust,
Yet would not place one piece above, but lives
35   In fear of thieves.
Thousands there were as frantic as himself
   And hugged each one his pelf.
The downright epicure placed heaven in sense
   And scorned pretence,
40 While others, slipped into a wide excess,
    Said little less.

The weaker sort slight, trivial wares enslave
    Who think them brave,
And poor, despisèd truth sat counting by
45   Their victory.

Yet some, who all this while did weep and sing,
And sing and weep, soared up into the king,
    But most would use no wing.
'O fools,' said I, 'thus to prefer dark night
50   Before true light;
To live in grots and caves and hate the day
    Because it shows the way;
The way which from this dead and dark abode
    Leads up to God;
55 A way where you might tread the sun and be
        More bright than he.'
But as I did their madness so discuss,
    One whispered thus:
'The ring the bridegroom did for none provide
60   But for his bride.'

John Cap. 2. Ver. 16, 17
All that is in the world, the lust of the flesh, the lust of the eyes, and
the pride of life, is not of the father, but is of the world.
And the world passeth away, and the lusts thereof, but he that doth
the will of God abideth for ever.

THE MUTINY

Weary of this same clay and straw I laid
Me down to breathe, and casting in my heart
The after-burthens and griefs yet to come,
    The heavy sum
5 So shook my breast that, sick and sore dismayed,
My thoughts, like water which some stone doth start,
Did quit their troubled channel and retire
Unto the banks, where storming at those bounds
They murmured sore: but I, who felt them boil
10   And knew their coil,
Turning to him who made poor sand to tire
And tame proud waves, 'If yet these barren grounds
  And thirsty brick must be,' said I,
    'My task and destiny,

15 Let me so strive and struggle with thy foes,
    Not thine alone, but mine too, that when all
    Their arts and force are built unto the height,
        That Babel-weight
    May prove thy glory and their shame: so close
20 And knit me to thee, that though in this vale
    Of sin and death I sojourn, yet one eye
    May look to thee, to thee the finisher
    And author of my faith; to show me home
        That all this foam
25 And frothy noise which up and down doth fly
    May find no lodging in mine eye or ear:
        O seal them up, that these may fly
            Like other tempests by.

    Not but I know thou hast a shorter cut
30 To bring me home than through a wilderness,
    A sea or sands and serpents; yet since thou,
        As thy words show,
    Though in this desert I were wholly shut,
    Canst light and lead me there with such redress
35 That no decay shall touch me, O be pleased
    To fix my steps, and whatsoever path
    Thy sacred and eternal will decreed
        For thy bruised reed
    O give it full obedience, that so seized
40 Of all I have, I may nor move thy wrath
        Nor grieve thy dove, but soft and mild
            Both live and die thy child.'

Revel. Cap. 2. ver. 17
To him that overcometh will I give to eat of the hidden manna, and
I will give him a white stone, and in the stone a new name written,
which no man knoweth, saving he that receiveth it.

MAN

    Weighing the steadfastness and state
    Of some mean things which here below reside,
    Where birds like watchful clocks the noiseless date
        And intercourse of times divide;
5   Where bees at night get home and hive, and flowers
            Early as well as late
    Rise with the sun and set in the same bowers;

I would, said I, my God would give
The staidness of these things to man, for these
10 To his divine appointments ever cleave,
And no new business breaks their peace:
The birds nor sow nor reap, yet sup and dine,
The flowers without clothes live,
Yet Solomon was never dressed so fine.

15 Man hath still ever toys or care,
He hath no root nor to one place is tied,
But ever restless and irregular
About this earth doth run and ride:
He knows he hath a home, but scarce knows where—
20 He says it is so far
That he hath quite forgot how to go there.

He knocks at all doors, strays and roams,
Nay hath not so much wit as some stones have,
Which in the darkest nights point to their homes
25 By some hid sense their maker gave:
Man is the shuttle, to whose winding quest
And passage through these looms
God ordered motion, but ordained no rest.

∫

I walked the other day (to spend my hour)
Into a field
Where I sometimes had seen the soil to yield
A gallant flower,
5 But winter now had ruffled all the bower
And curious store
I knew there heretofore.

Yet I whose search loved not to peep and peer
I' the face of things
10 Thought with myself there might be other springs
Besides this here
Which, like cold friends, sees us but once a year,
And so the flower
Might have some other bower.

15 Then taking up what I could nearest spy
I digged about
That place where I had seen him to grow out,

      And by and by
I saw the warm recluse alone to lie
      Where, fresh and green,
20   He lived of us unseen.

Many a question intricate and rare
      Did I there strow,
But all I could extort was that he now
25   Did there repair
Such losses as befell him in this air,
      And would ere long
      Come forth most fair and young.

This past, I threw the clothes quite o'er his head,
30   And stung with fear
Of my own frailty, dropped down many a tear
      Upon his bed;
Then sighing whispered 'Happy are the dead!'
      What peace doth now
35   Rock him asleep below?

And yet how few believe such doctrine springs
      From a poor root,
Which all the winter sleeps here under foot
      And hath no wings
40   To raise it to the truth and light of things,
      But is still trod
      By every wandering clod.

O thou, whose spirit did at first inflame
      And warm the dead,
45   And by a sacred incubation fed
      With life this frame,
Which once had neither being, form, nor name,
      Grant I may so
      Thy steps track here below

50   That in these masques and shadows I may see
      Thy sacred way,
And by those hid ascents climb to that day
      Which breaks from thee
Who art in all things, though invisibly;
55   Show me thy peace,
      Thy mercy, love and ease,

And from this care, where dreams and sorrows reign,
      Lead me above
Where light, joy, leisure, and true comforts move

60 Without all pain:
There, hid in thee, show me his life again
    At whose dumb urn
    Thus all the year I mourn.

BEGGING

King of mercy, king of love,
In whom I live, in whom I move,
Perfect what thou hast begun,
Let no night put out this sun,
5 Grant I may—my chief desire—
Long for thee, to thee aspire,
Let my youth, my bloom of days
Be my comfort and thy praise,
That hereafter, when I look
10 O'er the sullied, sinful book,
I may find thy hand therein
Wiping out my shame and sin.
O it is thy only art
To reduce a stubborn heart,
15 And since thine is victory
Strongholds should belong to thee—
Lord then take it, leave it not
Unto my dispose or lot,
But since I would not have it mine,
20 O my God, let it be thine!

ʃ

They are all gone into the world of light!
    And I alone sit lingering here:
Their very memory is fair and bright,
    And my sad thoughts doth clear.

5 It glows and glitters in my cloudy breast
    Like stars upon some gloomy grove,
Or those faint beams in which this hill is dressed
    After the sun's remove.

I see them walking in an air of glory,
10   Whose light doth trample on my days;
My days which are at best but dull and hoary,
    Mere glimmering and decays.

O holy hope and high humility,
　　High as the heavens above!
15　These are your walks, and you have showed them me
　　To kindle my cold love.

Dear, beauteous death! The jewel of the just,
　　Shining nowhere but in the dark:
What mysteries do lie beyond thy dust,
20　　Could man outlook that mark!

He that hath found some fledged bird's nest may know
　　At first sight if the bird be flown;
But what fair well or grove he sings in now,
　　That is to him unknown.

25　And yet, as angels in some brighter dreams
　　Call to the soul when man doth sleep,
So some strange thoughts transcend our wonted themes
　　And into glory peep.

If a star were confined into a tomb
30　　Her captive flames must needs burn there,
But when the hand that locked her up gives room
　　She'll shine through all the sphere.

O father of eternal life, and all
　　Created glories under thee,
35　Resume thy spirit from this world of thrall
　　Into true liberty.

Either disperse these mists, which blot and fill
　　My perspective, still, as they pass,
Or else remove me hence unto that hill
40　　Where I shall need no glass.

COCK-CROWING

Father of lights! What sunny seed,
What glance of day hast thou confined
Into this bird? To all the breed
This busy ray thou hast assigned:
5　　Their magnetism works all night,
　　And dreams of paradise and light.

Their eyes watch for the morning hue,
Their little grain, expelling night,
  So shines and sings as if it knew
10   The path unto the house of light.
      It seems their candle, how'ever done,
      Was tinned and lighted at the sun.

If such a tincture, such a touch,
So firm a longing can impower,
15 Shall thy own image think it much
    To watch for thy appearing hour?
      If a mere blast so fill the sail
      Shall not the breath of God prevail?

O thou immortal light and heat!
20 Whose hand so shines through all this frame,
  That by the beauty of the seat
    We plainly see who made the same.
      Seeing thy seed abides in me,
      Dwell thou in it and I in thee.

25 To sleep without thee is to die;
Yea 'tis a death partakes of hell:
  For where thou dost not close the eye
    It never opens, I can tell.
      In such a dark, Egyptian border,
30   The shades of death dwell and disorder.

If joys and hopes and earnest throes
And hearts, whose pulse still beats for light,
Are given to birds, who but thee knows
A love-sick soul's exalted flight?
35   Can souls be tracked by any eye
      But his who gave them wings to fly?

Only this veil which thou hast broke,
And must be broken yet in me,
This veil, I say, is all the cloak
40 And cloud which shadows thee from me.
    This veil thy full-eyed love denies,
    And only gleams and fractions spies.

O take it off! Make no delay,
But brush me with thy light, that I
45 May shine unto a perfect day
And warm me at thy glorious eye!
    O take it off, or 'till it flee,
    Though with no lily, stay with me!

THE GARLAND

Thou who dost flow and flourish here below,
To whom a falling star and nine days' glory,
Or some frail beauty makes the bravest show,
Hark, and make use of this ensuing story.

5   When first my youthful, sinful age
    Grew master of my ways,
   Appointing error for my page
    And darkness for my days;
   I flung away, and with full cry
10   Of wild affections rid
   In post for pleasures, bent to try
    All gamesters that would bid.
   I played with fire, did counsel spurn,
    Made life my common stake,
15   But never thought that fire would burn
    Or that a soul could ache.
   Glorious deceptions, gilded mists,
    False joys, fantastic flights,
   Pieces of sackcloth with silk lists—
20   These were my prime delights.
   I sought choice bowers, haunted the spring,
    Culled flowers and made me posies;
   Gave my fond humours their full wing,
    And crowned my head with roses.
25   But at the height of this career
    I met with a dead man,
   Who noting well my vain abear,
    Thus to me began:
   'Desist, fond fool, be not undone,
30   What thou hast cut today
   Will fade at night and with this sun
    Quite vanish and decay'.
Flowers gathered in this world die here; if thou
Wouldst have a wreath that fades not, let them grow,
35 And grow for thee; who spares them here shall find
A garland where comes neither rain, nor wind.

THE BIRD

Hither thou com'st: the busy wind all night
Blew through thy lodging, where thy own warm wing
Thy pillow was: many a sullen storm
(For which course man seems much the fitter born)

5   Rained on thy bed
      And harmless head.
And now as fresh and cheerful as the light
Thy little heart in early hymns doth sing
Unto that providence whose unseen arm
10   Curbed them and clothed thee well and warm.
      All things that be praise him, and had
      Their lesson taught them when first made.

So hills and valleys into singing break,
And though poor stones have neither speech nor tongue,
15   While active winds and streams both run and speak,
Yet stones are deep in admiration.
Thus praise and prayer here beneath the sun
Make lesser mornings when the great are done.

For each enclosèd spirit is a star
      Enlightening his own little sphere,
20   Whose light, though fetched and borrowèd from far,
      Both morning makes and evening there.
But as these birds of light make a land glad,
Chirping their solemn matins on each tree,
25   So in the shades of night some dark fowls be
Whose heavy notes make all that hear them sad.

      The turtle then in palm trees mourns,
        While owls and satyrs howl;
      The pleasant land to brimstone turns
30   And all her streams grow foul.

Brightness and mirth and love and faith all fly,
Till the day-spring breaks forth again from high.

BEGGING

Ay, do not go: thou know'st I'll die!
My spring and fall are in thy book;
Or if thou go'st do not deny
To lend me, though from far, one look!

5   My sins long since have made thee strange,
A very stranger unto me;
No morning meetings since this change,
Nor evening walks have I with thee.

Why is my God thus slow and cold,
10　　When I am most, most sick and sad?
Well fare those blessèd days of old
When thou didst hear the weeping lad!

O do not thou do as I did,
Do not despise a lovesick heart!
15　　What though some clouds defiance bid?
Thy sun must shine in every part.

Though I have spoiled, O spoil not thou!
Hate not thine own dear gift and token!
Poor birds sing best and prettiest show
20　　When their nest is fall'n and broken.

Dear Lord, restore thy ancient peace,
Thy quick'ning friendship, man's bright wealth!
And if thou wilt not give me ease
From sickness, give my spirit health!

THE KNOT

Bright queen of Heaven, God's virgin spouse
　　The glad word's blessèd maid!
Whose beauty tied life to thy house
　　And brought us saving aid.

5　　Thou art the true love's-knot; by thee
　　　　God is made our ally,
And man's inferior essence he
　　With his did dignify.

For coalescent by that band
10　　　　We are his body grown,
Nourished with favours from his hand
　　Whom for our head we own.

And such a knot what arm dares loose,
　　What life, what death can sever?
15　　Which us in him and him in us
　　United keeps forever.

THE SEED GROWING SECRETLY
St Mark 4. 26

If this world's friends might see but once
What some poor man may often feel,
Glory and gold and crowns and thrones
They would soon quit and learn to kneel.

5   My dew, my dew! My early love,
My soul's bright food, thy absence kills!
Hover not long, eternal dove!
Life without thee is loose and spills.

Something I had which long ago
10   Did learn to suck and sip and taste,
But now grown sickly, sad and slow,
Doth fret and wrangle, pine and waste.

O spread thy sacred wings and shake
One living drop: one drop life keeps!
15   If pious griefs Heaven's joys awake,
O fill his bottle, thy child weeps!

Slowly and sadly doth he grow,
And soon as left shrinks back to ill;
O feed that life, which makes him blow
20   And spread and open to thy will.

For thy eternal, living wells
None stained or withered shall come near;
A fresh, immortal green there dwells
And spotless white is all the wear.

25   Dear secret greenness! Nursed below,
Tempests and winds and winter nights
Vex not, that but one sees thee grow,
That one made all these lesser lights.

If those bright joys he singly sheds
30   On thee, were all met in one crown,
Both sun and stars would hide their heads,
And moons, though full, would get them down.

Let glory be their bait, whose minds
Are all too high for a low cell:
35   Though hawks can prey through storms and winds
The poor bee in her hive must dwell.

Glory, the crowd's cheap tinsel still
To what most takes them, is a drudge,
And they too oft take good for ill,
40   And thriving vice for virtue judge.

What needs a conscience calm and bright
Within itself an outward test?
Who breaks his glass to take more light
Makes way for storms into his rest.

45   Then bless thy secret growth, nor catch
At noise, but thrive unseen and dumb:
Keep clean, bear fruit, earn life and watch
Till the white-winged reapers come!

THE ASS
St Matt. 21

Thou who didst place me in this busy street
Of flesh and blood, where two ways meet:
The one of goodness, peace and life,
The other of death, sin and strife;
5   Where frail visibles rule the mind
And present things find men most kind;
Where obscure cares the mean defeat
And splendid vice destroys the great;
As thou didst set no law for me
10   But that of perfect liberty,
Which neither tires nor doth corrode,
But is a pillow, not a load,
So give me grace ever to rest
And build on it because the best.
15   Teach both mine eyes and feet to move
Within those bounds set by thy love;
Grant I may soft and lowly be,
And mind those things I cannot see;
Tie me to faith, though above reason,
20   Who question power, they speak treason:
Let me, thy ass, be only wise
To carry, not search mysteries.
Who carries thee is by thee led,
Who argues follows his own head.
25   To check bad motions keep me still
Amongst the dead, where thriving ill
Without his brags and conquests lies,
And truth (oppressed here) gets the prize.

At all times, whatsoe'er I do
30 Let me not fail to question who
Shares in the act and puts me to't,
And if not thou let me not do't.
Above all make me love the poor,
Those burthens to the rich man's door,
35 Let me admire those and be kind
To low estates and a low mind.
If the world offers to me aught
That by thy book must not be sought,
Or though it should be lawful may
40 Prove not expedient for thy way;
To shun that peril let thy grace
Prevail with me to shun the place.
Let me be wise to please thee still
And let men call me what they will.
45 While thus thy mild, instructing hand
Finds thy poor foal at thy command,
When he from wild is become wise,
And slights that most which men most prize;
When all things here to thistles turn
50 Pricking his lips till he doth mourn
And hang his head, sighing for those
Pastures of life where the Lamb goes.
O then, just then, break or untie
These bonds, this sad captivity,
55 This leaden state, which men miscall
Being and life but is dead thrall.
And when, O God, the ass is free,
In a state known to none but thee,
O let him by his Lord be led
60 To living springs and there be fed,
Where light, joy, health and perfect peace
Shut out all pain and each disease;
Where death and frailty are forgotten
And bones rejoice which once were broken!

CHILDHOOD

I cannot reach it, and my striving eye
Dazzles at it as at eternity.
Were now that chronicle alive,
Those white designs which children drive,
5 And the thoughts of each harmless hour,
With their content too in my power,

Quickly would I make my path even
And by mere playing go to Heaven.
   Why should men love
10   A wolf more than a lamb, or dove?
Or choose hell fire and brimstone streams
Before bright stars and God's own beams?
Who kisseth thorns will hurt his face,
But flowers do both refresh and grace,
15   And sweetly living (fie on men!)
Are when dead medicinal then.
If seeing much should make staid eyes
And long experience should make wise,
Since all that age doth teach is ill
20   Why should I not love childhood still?
Why, if I see a rock or shelf
Shall I from thence cast down myself,
Or by complying with the world
From the same precipice be hurled?
25   Those observations are but foul
Which make me wise to lose my soul.
And yet the practice worldlings call
Business and weighty action all,
Checking the poor child for his play,
30   But gravely cast themselves away.
   Dear, harmless age! The short, swift span
Where weeping virtue parts with man,
Where love without lust dwells and bends
What way we please, without self-ends.
35   An age of mysteries, which he
Must live twice, that would God's face see;
Which angels guard and with it play,
Angels, which foul men drive away.
How I do study now and scan
40   Thee, more than ere I studied man,
And only see through a long night
Thy edges and thy bordering light!
O for thy centre and midday—
For sure that is the narrow way.

ABEL'S BLOOD

Sad, purple well, whose bubbling eye
Did first against a murderer cry,
Whose streams still vocal still complain
   Of bloody Cain,
5   And now at evening are as red
As in the morning when first shed.

If single thou
(Though single voices are but low)
Couldst such a shrill and long cry rear
10   As speaks still in thy maker's ear,
What thunders shall those men arraign
Who cannot count those they have slain,
Who bathe not in a shallow flood
But in a deep, wide sea of blood?
15   A sea whose loud waves cannot sleep,
But deep still calleth upon deep;
Whose urgent sound like unto that
Of many waters beateth at
The everlasting doors above,
20   Where souls behind the altar move,
And with one strong, incessant cry
Enquire 'How long?' Of the most high.
    Almighty judge!
At whose just laws no just men grudge;
25   Whose blessèd, sweet commands do pour
Comforts and joy and hopes each hour
On those that keep them: O accept
Of his vowed heart, whom thou hast kept
From bloody men, and grant I may
30   That sworn memorial duly pay
To thy bright arm which was my light
And leader through thick death and night!
    Ay, may that flood,
That proudly spilt and despised blood,
35   Speechless and calm as infants sleep,
Or if it watch, forgive and weep
For those that spilt it! May no cries
From the low earth to high Heaven rise,
But what (like his whose blood peace brings)
40   Shall, when they rise, speak better things
Than Abel's doth! May Abel be
Still single heard while these agree
With his mild blood in voice and will,
Who prayed for those that did him kill.

ANGUISH

My God and king, to thee
    I bow my knee,
I bow my troubled soul and greet
With my foul heart thy holy feet.
5   Cast it or tread it! It shall do
Even what thou wilt and praise thee too.

My God, could I weep blood,
   Gladly I would;
Or if thou wilt give me that art
10   Which through the eyes pours out the heart,
I will exhaust it all and make
Myself all tears, a weeping lake.

O 'tis an easy thing
   To write and sing,
15   But to write true, unfeignèd verse
Is very hard! O God disperse
These weights and give my spirits leave
To act as well as to conceive!

O my God hear my cry,
20   Or let me die! . . .

THE AGREEMENT

I wrote it down. But one that saw
And envied that record did since
Such a mist over my mind draw
It quite forgot that purposed glimpse.
5   I read it sadly oft but still
    Simply believed 'twas not my quill.

At length my life's kind angel came,
And with his bright and busy wing
Scattering that cloud showed me the flame
10   Which straight like morning stars did sing,
    And shine and point me to a place
    Which all the year sees the sun's face.

O beamy book, O my midday
Exterminating fears and night!
15   The mount whose white ascendants may
Be in conjunction with true light!
    My thoughts, when towards thee they move,
    Glitter and kindle with thy love.

Thou art the oil and the wine house:
20   Thine are the present healing leaves,
Blown from the tree of life to us
By his breath whom my dead heart heaves.
    Each page of thine hath true life in't,
    And God's bright mind expressed in print.

25 Most modern books are blots on thee,
Their doctrine chaff and windy fit;
Darkened along as their scribes be
With those foul storms when they were writ,
  While the man's zeal lays out and blends
30   Only self-worship and self-ends.

Thou art the faithful, pearly rock,
The hive of beamy, living lights,
Ever the same, whose diffused stock
Entire still wears out blackest nights.
35   Thy lines are rays the true sun sheds:
  Thy leaves are healing wings he spreads.

For until thou didst comfort me
I had not one poor word to say:
Thick, busy clouds did multiply
40 And said I was no child of day;
  They said my own hands did remove
  That candle given me from above.

O God, I know and do confess
My sins are great and still prevail,
45 Most heinous sins and numberless,
But thy compassions cannot fail!
  If thy sure mercies can be broken
  Then all is true my foes have spoken.

But while time runs, and after it
50 Eternity, which never ends;
Quite through them both, still infinite
Thy covenant by Christ extends:
  No sins of frailty, nor of youth
  Can foil his merits and thy truth.

55 And this I hourly find, for thou
Dost still renew and purge and heal:
Thy care and love which jointly flow
New cordials, new cathartics deal.
  But were I once cast off by thee
60   I know, my God, this would not be.

Wherefore with tears (tears by thee sent)
I beg my faith may never fail,
And when in death my speech is spent,
O let that silence then prevail!
65   O chase in that cold calm my foes
  And hear my heart's last private throes!

So thou who didst the work begin,
For I till drawn came not to thee,
Wilt finish it, and by no sin
70 Will thy free mercies hindered be:
         For which, O God, I only can
         Bless thee and blame unthankful man.

THE DAY OF JUDGEMENT

O day of life, of light, of love,
The only day dealt from above!
A day so fresh, so bright, so brave
'Twill show us each forgotten grave,
5   And make the dead like flowers arise
Youthful and fair to see new skies.
All other days, compared to thee,
Are but light's weak minority;
They are but veils and ciphers drawn
10 Like clouds before thy glorious dawn,
O come, arise, shine, do not stay
         Dearly loved day!
The fields are long since white and I
With earnest groans for freedom cry;
15 My fellow creatures too say 'Come!'
And stones, though speechless, are not dumb.
When shall we hear that glorious voice
         Of life and joys?
That voice which to each secret bed
20   Of my Lord's dead
Shall bring true day and make dust see
The way to immortality.
When shall those first white pilgrims rise,
Whose holy, happy histories
25 (Because they sleep so long) some men
Count but the blots of a vain pen?
         Dear Lord make haste,
Sin every day commits more waste,
And thy old enemy, which knows
30 His time is short, more raging grows.
Nor moan I only, though profuse,
Thy creature's bondage and abuse,
But what is highest sin and shame,
The vile despite done to thy name;
35 The forgeries which impious wit
And power force on Holy Writ,

With all detestable designs
That may dishonour those pure lines.
O God! Though mercy be in thee
40   The greatest attribute we see,
And the most needful for our sins,
Yet when thy mercy nothing wins
But mere disdain, let not man say
'Thy arm doth sleep', but write this day
45   Thy judging one: descend, descend,
Make all things new and without end!

DEATH

Though since thy first sad entrance by
    Just Abel's blood
'Tis now six thousand years well nigh,
And still thy sovereignty holds good,
5   Yet by none art thou understood.

We talk and name thee with much ease
    As a tried thing,
And everyone can slight his lease
As if it ended in a spring
10   Which shades and bowers doth rent-free bring.

To thy dark land these heedless go:
    But there was one
Who searched it quite through to and fro,
And then returning, like the sun,
15   Discovered all that there is done.

And since his death we th'roughly see
    All thy dark way:
Thy shades but thin and narrow be,
Which his first looks will quickly fray:
20   Mists make but triumphs for the day.

As harmless violets, which give
    Their virtues here
For salves and syrops, while they live,
Do after calmly disappear
25   And neither grieve, repine nor fear,

So die his servants, and as sure
    Shall they revive.
Then let not dust your eyes obscure,
But lift them up, where still alive,
30   Though fled from you their spirits hive.

THE WATERFALL

With what deep murmurs through time's silent stealth
Doth thy transparent, cool and watery wealth
    Here flowing fall
    And chide and call,
5   As if his liquid, loose retinue stayed
Ling'ring, and were of this steep place afraid;
    The common pass
    Where, clear as glass,
    All must descend
10   Not to an end,
But quickened by this deep and rocky grave
Rise to a longer course more bright and brave.

Dear stream, dear bank, where often I
Have sat and pleased my pensive eye,
15   Why, since each drop of thy quick store
Runs thither whence it flowed before,
Should poor souls fear a shade or night
Who came, sure, from a sea of light?
Or since those drops are all sent back
20   So sure to thee that none doth lack,
Why should frail flesh doubt any more
That what God takes he'll not restore?
O useful element and clear,
My sacred wash and cleanser here,
25   My first consigner unto those
Fountains of life where the Lamb goes!
What sublime truths and wholesome themes
Lodge in thy mystical, deep streams!
Such as dull man can never find
30   Unless that spirit lead his mind,
Which first upon thy face did move
And hatched all with his quickening love.
As this loud brook's incessant fall
In streaming rings restagnates all,
35   Which reach by course the bank and then
Are no more seen, just so pass men.

O my invisible estate,
My glorious liberty, still late!
Thou art the channel my soul seeks,
40 Not this with cataracts and creeks.

THE BOOK

Eternal God, maker of all
That have lived here since the man's fall;
The rock of ages, in whose shade
They live unseen when here they fade!

5 Thou knew'st this papyr when it was
Mere seed, and after that but grass;
Before 'twas dressed or spun, and when
Made linen who did wear it then;
What were their lives, their thoughts and deeds,
10 Whether good corn or fruitless weeds.

Thou knew'st this tree when a green shade
Covered it, since a cover made,
And where it flourished, grew and spread
As if it never should be dead.

15 Thou knew'st this harmless beast, when he
Did live and feed by thy decree
On each green thing, then slept (well fed)
Clothed with this skin, which now lies spread
A covering o'er this agèd book,
20 Which makes me wisely weep and look
On my own dust—mere dust it is,
But not so dry and clean as this.
Thou knew'st and saw'st them all, and though
Now scattered thus, dost know them so.

25 O knowing, glorious spirit! When
Thou shalt restore trees, beasts and men;
When thou shalt make all new again,
Destroying only death and pain,
Give him amongst thy works a place
30 Who in them loved and sought thy face!

Sir John Denham (1615–69)

COOPER'S HILL

Sure there are poets which did never dream
Upon Parnassus, nor did taste the stream
Of Helicon: we therefore may suppose
Those made not poets, but the poets those.
5   And as courts make not kings but kings the court,
So where the muses and their train resort
Parnassus stands: if I can be to thee
A poet, thou Parnassus art to me.
Nor wonder if, advantaged in my flight
10   By taking wing from thy auspicious height,
Through untraced ways and airy paths I fly,
More boundless in my fancy than my eye—
My eye, which swift as thought contracts the space
That lies between, and first salutes the place
15   Crowned with that sacred pile, so vast, so high,
That whether 'tis a part of earth or sky
Uncertain seems, and may be thought a proud,
Aspiring mountain or descending cloud:
Paul's, the late theme of such a muse, whose flight
20   Has bravely reached and soared above thy height,
Now shalt thou stand though sword, or time, or fire,
Or zeal more fierce than they thy fall conspire:
Secure whilst thee the best of poets sings,
Preserved from ruin by the best of kings.
25   Under his proud survey the city lies
And like a mist beneath a hill doth rise;
Whose state and wealth the business and the crowd
Seems at this distance but a darker cloud,
And is to him who rightly things esteems,
30   No other in effect than what it seems;
Where with like haste, though several ways, they run
Some to undo and some to be undone;
While luxury and wealth, like war and peace,
Are each the other's ruin and increase,
35   As rivers lost in seas some secret vein
Thence reconveys, there to be lost again.

O happiness of sweet, retired content,
To be at once secure and innocent.
Windsor the next (where Mars with Venus dwells:
40   Beauty with strength) above the valley swells
Into my eye and doth itself present
With such an easy and unforced ascent
That no stupendious precipice denies
Access, no horror turns away our eyes;
45   But such a rise as doth at once invite
A pleasure and a reverence from the sight.
Thy mighty master's emblem, in whose face
Sat meekness heightened with majestic grace—
Such seems thy gentle height, made only proud
50   To be the basis of that pompous load,
Than which a nobler weight no mountain bears
But Atlas only, that supports the spheres.
When Nature's hand this ground did thus advance
'Twas guided by a wiser power than chance:
55   Marked out for such a use as if 'twere meant
T'invite the builder and his choice prevent.
Nor can we call it choice when what we choose
Folly or blindness only could refuse.
A crown of such majestic towers doth grace
60   The gods' great mother when her heavenly race
Do homage to her, yet she cannot boast,
Amongst that numerous and celestial host,
More heroes than can Windsor, nor doth Fame's
Immortal book record more noble names.
65   Not to look back so far, to whom this isle
Owes the first glory of so brave a pile,
Whether to Caesar, Albanact, or Brute,
The British Arthur or the Danish Cnut,
(Though this of old no less contest did move
70   Than when for Homer's birth seven cities strove—
Like him in birth thou shouldst be like in fame,
As thine his fate if mine had been his flame),
But whosoe'er it was, Nature designed
First a brave place, and then as brave a mind—
75   Not to recount those several kings to whom
It gave a cradle, or to whom a tomb,
But thee, great Edward, and thy greater son
(The lilies which his father wore he won)
And thy Bellona, who the consort came
80   Not only to thy bed but to thy fame:
She to thy triumph led one captive king
And brought that son which did the second bring.
Then didst thou found that order (whether love
Or victory thy royal thoughts did move)

85   Each was a noble cause and nothing less
     Than the design has been the great success;
     Which foreign kings and emperors esteem
     The second honour to their diadem.
     Had thy great destiny but given thee skill
90   To know as well, as power to act her will,
     That from those kings who then thy captives were
     In aftertimes should spring a royal pair
     Who should possess all that thy mighty power,
     Or thy designs more mighty, did devour;
95   To whom their better fate reserves whate'er
     The victor hopes for or the vanquished fear,
     That blood which thou and thy great grandsire shed,
     And all that since these sister nations bled,
     Had been unspilt had happy Edward known
100 That all the blood he spilt had been his own.
     When he that patron chose in whom are joined
     Soldier and martyr, and his arms confined
     Within the azure circle, he did seem
     But to foretell and prophesy of him,
105 Who to his realms that azure round hath joined
     Which nature for their bound at first designed.
     That bound which to the world's extremest ends,
     Endless itself, its liquid arms extends.
     Nor doth he need these emblems which we paint,
110 But is himself the soldier and the saint.
     Here should my wonder dwell and here my praise,
     But my fixed thoughts my wandering eye betrays,
     Viewing a neighbouring hill whose top of late
     A chapel crowned, till in the common fate
115 The adjoining abbey fell (may no such storm
     Fall on our times where ruin must reform).
     Tell me, my muse, what monstrous, dire offence
     What crime could any Christian king incense
     To such a rage? Was't luxury or lust?
120 Was he so temperate, so chaste, so just?
     Were these their crimes? They were his own much more:
     But wealth is crime enough to him that's poor;
     Who having spent the treasures of his crown
     Condemns their luxury to feed his own:
125 And yet this act, to varnish o'er the shame
     Of sacrilege, must bear devotion's name.
     No crime so bold but would be understood
     A real, or at least a seeming good.
     Who fears not to do ill, yet fears the name,
130 And free from conscience is a slave to fame.
     Thus he the church at once protects and spoils:
     But princes' swords are sharper than their stiles:

And thus to th'ages past he makes amends;
Their charity destroys, their faith defends.
135   Then did religion in a lazy cell
In empty, airy contemplations dwell,
And like the block unmovèd lay: but ours,
As much too active, like the stork, devours.
Is there no temperate region can be known
140   Betwixt their frigid and our torrid zone?
Could we not wake from that lethargic dream
But to be restless in a worse extreme?
And for that lethargy was there no cure
But to be cast into a calenture?
145   Can knowledge have no bound, but must advance
So far to make us wish for ignorance,
And rather in the dark to grope our way
Than led by a false guide to err by day?
Who sees these dismal heaps, but would demand
150   What barbarous invader sacked the land?
But when he hears no Goth or Turk did bring
This desolation, but a Christian king;
When nothing but the name of zeal appears
'Twixt our best actions and the worst of theirs,
155   What does he think our sacrilege would spare
When such th'effects of our devotions are?
Parting from thence 'twixt anger, shame and fear:
Those for what's past and this for what's too near,
My eye descending from the hill surveys
160   Whence Thames amongst the wanton valleys strays:
Thames, the most loved of all the ocean's sons,
By his old sire to his embraces runs,
Hasting to pay his tribute to the sea,
Like mortal life to meet eternity.
165   Though with those streams he no resemblance hold
Whose foam is amber and their gravel gold;
His genuine and less guilty wealth t'explore
Search not his bottom but survey his shore,
O'er which he kindly spreads his spacious wing
170   And hatches plenty for th'ensuing spring.
Nor then destroys it with too fond a stay
Like mothers which their infants overlay.
Nor with a sudden and impetuous wave
Like profuse kings resumes the wealth he gave.
175   No unexpected inundations spoil
The mower's hopes nor mock the ploughman's toil,
But godlike his unwearied bounty flows:
First loves to do then loves the good he does.
Nor are his blessings to his banks confined,
180   But free and common as the sea or wind,

When he to boast or to disperse his stores
Full of the tributes of his grateful shores,
Visits the world and in his flying towers
Brings home to us and makes both Indies ours;
185   Finds wealth where 'tis, bestows it where it wants,
Cities in deserts, woods in cities plants.
So that to us no thing, no place is strange
While his fair bosom is the world's exchange.
O could I flow like thee and make thy stream
190   My great example, as it is my theme:
Though deep yet clear, though gentle yet not dull,
Strong without rage, without o'erflowing full.
Heaven her Eridanus no more shall boast
Whose fame in thine, like lesser currents lost;
195   Thy nobler streams shall visit Jove's abodes
To shine amongst the stars and bathe the gods.
Here Nature, whether more intent to please
Us or herself with strange varieties,
(For things of wonder give no less delight
200   To the wise maker's than beholder's sight.
Though these delights from several causes move,
For so our children, thus our friends we love)
Wisely she knew the harmony of things
As well as that of sounds, from discords springs.
205   Such was the discord which did first disperse
Form, order, beauty through the universe:
While dryness moisture, coldness heat resists
All that we have and that we are subsists.
While the steep, horrid roughness of the wood
210   Strives with the gentle calmness of the flood.
Such huge extremes when nature doth unite
Wonder from thence results, from thence delight.
The stream is so transparent, pure and clear
That had the self-enamoured youth gazed here
215   So fatally deceived he had not been,
While he the bottom not his face had seen.
But his proud head the airy mountain hides
Among the clouds; his shoulders and his sides
A shady mantle clothes; his curlèd brows
220   Frown on the gentle stream, which calmly flows
While winds and storms his lofty forehead beat:
The common fate of all that's high or great.
Low at his foot a spacious plain is placed
Between the mountain and the stream embraced,
225   Which shade and shelter from the hill derives,
While the kind river wealth and beauty gives:
And in the mixture of all these appears
Variety, which all the rest endears.

This scene had some bold Greek or British bard
230   Beheld of old, what stories had we heard
Of fairies, satyrs, and the nymphs, their dames,
Their feasts, their revels and their amorous flames:
'Tis still the same, although their airy shape
All but a quick poetic sight escape:
235   There Faunus and Sylvanus keep their courts
And thither all the hornèd host resorts
To graze the ranker mead, that noble herd
On whose sublime and shady fronts is reared
Nature's great masterpiece, to show how soon
240   Great things are made, but sooner are undone.
Here have I seen the king, when great affairs
Give leave to slacken and unbend his cares,
Attended to the chase by all the flower
Of youth, whose hopes a nobler prey devour.
245   Pleasure with praise and danger they would buy
And wish a foe that would not only fly.
The stag now conscious of his fatal growth,
At once indulgent to his fear and sloth,
To some dark covert his retreat had made
250   Where nor man's eye nor heaven's should invade
His soft repose; when the unexpected sound
Of dogs and men his wakeful ear doth wound.
Roused with the noise he scarce believes his ear,
Willing to think th'illusions of his fear
255   Had given this false alarm: but straight his view
Confirms that more than all he fears is true.
Betrayed in all his strengths, the wood beset,
All instruments, all arts of ruin met,
He calls to mind his strength and then his speed,
260   His wingèd heels and then his armèd head:
With these t'avoid, with that his fate to meet:
But fear prevails and bids him trust his feet.
So fast he flies that his reviewing eye
Has lost the chasers and his ear the cry;
265   Exulting till he finds their nobler sense
Their disproportioned speed does recompense.
Then curses his conspiring feet, whose scent
Betrays that safety which their swiftness lent.
Then tries his friends among the baser herd
270   Where he so lately was obeyed and feared.
His safety seeks: the herd, unkindly wise,
Or chases him from thence or from him flies.
Like a declining statesman, left forlorn
To his friends' pity and pursuers' scorn,
275   With shame remembers while himself was one
Of the same herd himself the same had done.

Thence to the coverts and the conscious groves,
The scenes of his past triumphs and his loves;
Sadly surveying where he ranged alone,
280   Prince of the soil and all the herd his own;
And like a bold knight errant did proclaim
Combat to all and bore away the dame,
And taught the woods to echo to the stream
His dreadful challenge and his clashing beam.
285   Yet faintly now declines the fatal strife:
So much his love was dearer than his life.
Now every leaf and every moving breath
Presents a foe, and every foe a death.
Wearied, forsaken and pursued, at last
290   All safety in despair of safety placed,
Courage he thence resumes, resolved to bear
All their assaults since 'tis in vain to fear.
And now too late he wishes for the fight
That strength he wasted in ignoble flight.
295   But when he sees the eager chase renewed,
Himself by dogs, the dogs by men pursued,
He straight revokes his bold resolve, and more
Repents his courage than his fear before:
Finds that uncertain ways unsafest are
300   And doubt a greater mischief than despair.
Then to the stream, when neither friends, nor force,
Nor speed, nor art avail, he shapes his course:
Thinks not their rage so desperate t'assay
An element more merciless than they,
305   But fearless they pursue, nor can the flood
Quench their dire thirst: alas, they thirst for blood.
So towards a ship the oar-finned galleys ply,
Which wanting sea to ride or wind to fly,
Stands but to fall revenged on those that dare
310   Tempt the last fury of extreme despair.
So fares the stag among th'enragèd hounds,
Repels their force and wounds returns for wounds.
And as a hero, whom his baser foes
In troops surround, now these assails, now those,
315   Though prodigal of life disdains to die
By common hands; but if he can descry
Some nobler foe's approach, to him he calls,
And begs his fate and then contented falls.
So when the king a mortal shaft lets fly
320   From his unerring hand, then glad to die,
Proud of the wound, to it resigns his blood
And stains the crystal with a purple flood.
This a more innocent and happy chase
Than when of old, but in the self-same place,

325   Fair liberty pursued and, meant a prey
    To lawless power, here turned and stood at bay:
    When in that remedy all hope was placed
    Which was, or should have been at least, the last.
    Here was that charter sealed, wherein the crown
330   All marks of arbitrary power lays down.
    Tyrant and slave, those names of hate and fear,
    The happier style of king and subject bear:
    Happy when both to the same centre move,
    When kings give liberty and subjects love.
335   Therefore not long in force this charter stood:
    Wanting that seal it must be sealed in blood.
    The subjects armed, then more their princes gave,
    Th'advantage only took the more to crave.
    Till kings by giving give themselves away
340   And even that power that should deny betray.
    Who gives constrained but his own fear reviles,
    Not thanked but scorned, nor are they gifts but spoils:
    Thus kings by grasping more than they could hold
    First made their subjects by oppression bold:
345   And popular sway, by forcing kings to give
    More than was fit for subjects to receive,
    Ran to the same extremes; and one excess
    Made both, by striving to be greater, less.
    When a calm river raised with sudden rains,
350   Or snows dissolved, o'erflows the adjoining plains,
    The husbandmen with high-raised banks secure
    Their greedy hopes and this he can endure:
    But if with bays and dams they strive to force
    His channel to a new or narrow course,
355   No longer then within his banks he dwells,
    First to a torrent, then a deluge swells:
    Stronger and fiercer by restraint he roars,
    And knows no bound but makes his power his shores.

A SONG

    Morpheus the humble god that dwells
    In cottages and smoky cells,
    Hates gilded roofs and beds of down,
    And though he fears no prince's frown,
5   Flies from the circle of a crown.

Come I say, thou powerful god,
And thy leaden charming rod,
Dipped in the Lethean lake,
O'er his wakeful temples shake,
10   Lest he should sleep and never wake.

Nature, alas, why art thou so
Obligèd to thy greatest foe?
Sleep, that is thy best repast,
Yet of death it bears a taste—
15   And both are the same thing at last.

NEWS FROM COLCHESTER

All in the land of Essex,
Near Colchester the zealous,
    On the side of a bank
    Was played such a prank
5   As would make a stone-horse jealous.

Help Woodcock, Fox and Naylor,
For Brother Green's a stallion,
    Now alas what hope
    Of converting the pope
10   When a quaker turns Italian?

Even to our whole profession
A scandal 'twill be counted,
    When 'tis talked with disdain
    Amongst the profane
15   How Brother Green was mounted.

And in the good time of Christmas,
Which though our Saints have damned all,
    Yet when did they hear
    That a damned cavalier
20   E'er played such a Christmas gambol?

Had thy flesh, O Green, been pampered
With any cates unhallowed;
    Hadst thou sweetened thy gums
    With pottage of plums
25   Or profane minced pie have swallowed;

Rolled up in wanton swine's flesh
The fiend might have crept into thee:
   Then fulness of gut
   Might have caused thee to rut
30   And the devil so rid through thee.

But alas he had been feasted
With a spiritual collation,
   By our frugal mayor,
   Who can dine on a prayer
35   And sup on an exhortation.

'Twas mere impulse of spirit,
Though he used the weapon carnal:
   Filly foal, quoth he,
   My bride thou shalt be,
40   And how this is lawful learn all.

For if no respect of persons
Be due 'mongst sons of Adam,
   In a large extent
   Thereby may be meant
45   That a mare's as good as a madam.

Then without more ceremony,
Not bonnet vailed nor kissed her,
   But took her by force
   For better or worse,
50   And used her like a Sister.

Now when in such a saddle
A Saint will needs be riding,
   Though we dare not say
   'Tis a falling away,
55   May there not be some backsliding?

No surely, quoth John Naylor,
'Twas but an insurrection
   Of the carnal part,
   For a quaker in heart
60   Can never lose perfection.

For, as our masters teach us,
The intent being well directed,
   Though the devil trepan
   The Adamical man
65   The Saint stands uninfected.

But alas a pagan jury
Ne'er judges what's intended:
  Then say what we can
  Brother Green's outward man
70   I fear will be suspended.

And our adopted Sister
Will find no better quarter,
  But when him we enrol
  For a Saint filly foal
75   Shall pass herself for a martyr.

Rome that spiritual Sodom
No longer is thy debtor,
  O Colchester, now
  Who's Sodom but thou,
80   Even according to the letter?

THE PROLOGUE TO HIS MAJESTY

Greatest of monarchs, welcome to this place
Which majesty so oft was wont to grace
Before our exile, to divert the court
And balance weighty cares with harmless sport.
5   This truth we can to our advantage say:
They that would have no king would have no play.
The laurel and the crown together went,
Had the same foes and the same banishment.
The ghosts of your great ancestors they feared
10   Who, by the art of conjuring poets reared,
Our Harrys and our Edwards long since dead
Still on the stage a march of glory tread.
Those monuments of fame, they thought, would stain
And teach the people to despise their reign.
15   Nor durst they look into the muses' well
Lest the clear spring their ugliness should tell:
Affrighted with the shadow of their rage
They broke the mirror of the times, the stage.
The stage against them still maintained the war
20   When they debauched the pulpit and the bar.
Though to be hypocrites be our praise alone,
'Tis our peculiar boast that we were none.
Whate'er they taught we practised what was true
And something we had learned of honour too,
25   When by your danger and our duty pressed
We acted in the field and not in jest:

Then for the cause our tiring-house they sacked
And silenced us that they alone might act;
And to our shame most dexterously they do it—
30   Outact the players and outlie the poet;
But all the other arts appeared so scarce
Ours were the moral lectures, theirs the farce:
This spacious land their theatre became
And they grave councillors and lords in name,
35   Which these mechanics personate so ill
That even the oppressed with contempt they fill,
But when the lion's dreadful skin they took
They roared so loud that the whole forest shook:
The noise kept all the neighbourhood in awe,
40   Who thought 'twas the true lion by his paw.
If feignèd virtue could such wonders do,
What may we not expect from this that's true!
But this great theme must serve another age,
To fill our story and adorn our stage.

FRIENDSHIP AND SINGLE LIFE AGAINST
LOVE AND MARRIAGE

Love, in what poison is thy dart
Dipped when it makes a bleeding heart?
None know but they who feel the smart.

It is not thou but we are blind,
5   And our corporeal eyes, we find,
Dazzle the optics of our mind.

Love to our citadels resorts
Through those deceitful sally ports:
Our sentinels betray our forts.

10   What subtle witchcraft man constrains
To change his pleasures into pains
And all his freedom into chains?

May not a prison or a grave
Like wedlock honour's title have?
15   That word makes freeborn man a slave.

How happy he that loves not lives!
Him neither hope nor fear deceives
To fortune who no hostage gives.

How unconcerned in things to come!
20   If here uneasy, finds at Rome,
At Paris, or Madrid his home.

Secure from low and private ends,
His life, his zeal, his wealth attends
His prince, his country and his friends.

25   Danger and honour are his joy,
But a fond wife or wanton boy
May all those generous thoughts destroy.

Then he lays by the public care,
Thinks of providing for an heir,
30   Learns how to get and how to spare.

Nor fire, nor foe, nor fate, nor night
The Trojan hero did affright,
Who bravely twice renewed the fight:

Though still his foes in number grew,
35   Thicker their darts and arrows flew,
Yet left alone no fear he knew.

But death in all her forms appears,
From everything he sees and hears,
For whom he leads and whom he bears.

40   Love, making all things else his foes,
Like a fierce torrent overflows
Whatever doth his course oppose.

This was the cause the poets sung
Thy mother from the sea was sprung:
45   But they were mad to make thee young.

Her father not her son art thou:
From our desires our actions grow,
And from the cause the effect must flow.

Love is as old as place or time:
50   'Twas he the fatal tree did climb,
Grandsire of father Adam's crime.

Well mayst thou keep this world in awe:
Religion, wisdom, honour, law,
The tyrant in his triumph draw.

55 'Tis he commands the powers above:
Phoebus resigns his darts, and Jove
His thunder to the god of love.

To him doth his feigned mother yield,
Nor Mars her champion's flaming shield
60 Guards him when Cupid takes the field.

He clips hope's wings, whose airy bliss
Much higher than fruition is,
But less than nothing if it miss.

When matches Love alone projects,
65 The cause transcending the effects,
That wildfire's quenched in cold neglects;

Whilst those conjunctions prove the best
Where Love's of blindness dispossessed
By perspectives of interest.

70 Though Solomon with a thousand wives
To get a wise successor strives,
But one, and he a fool, survives.

Old Rome of children took no care:
They with their friends their beds did share,
75 Secure to adopt a hopeful heir.

Love, drowsy days and stormy nights
Makes, and breaks friendship whose delights
Feed but not glut our appetites.

Well chosen friendship, the most noble
80 Of virtues, all our joys makes double,
And into halves divides our trouble.

But when the unlucky knot we tie,
Care, avarice, fear and jealousy
Make friendship languish till it die.

85 The wolf, the lion and the bear
When they their prey in pieces tear
To quarrel with themselves forbear:

Yet timorous deer and harmless sheep,
When Love into their veins doth creep,
90 The law of nature cease to keep.

Who then can blame the amorous boy,
Who, the fair Helen to enjoy,
To quench his own set fire on Troy?

Such is the world's preposterous fate,
95   Amongst all creatures mortal hate
Love, though immortal, doth create.

But Love may beasts excuse for they
Their actions not by reason sway,
But their brute appetites obey.

100   But man's that savage beast whose mind,
From reason to self-love declined,
Delights to prey upon his kind.

NATURA NATURATA

Who gives us that fantastic fit,
That all our judgement and our wit
To vulgar custom we submit?

Treason, theft, murder, all the rest
5   Of that foul legion we detest,
Are in their proper names expressed.

Why is it then taught sin or shame
Those necessary parts to name
From whence we went and whence we came?

10   Nature, whate'er she wants, requires,
With love enflaming our desires
Finds engines fit to quench those fires.

Death she abhors, yet when men die
We are present: but no standerby
15   Looks on when we that loss supply.

Forbidden wares sell twice as dear—
Even sack prohibited last year,
A most abominable rate did bear.

'Tis plain our eyes and ears are nice
20   Only to raise by that device
Of those commodities the price.

> Thus reason's shadows us betray
> By tropes and figures led astray
> From nature, both her guide and way.

ON MY LORD CROFTS' AND MY JOURNEY INTO POLAND, FROM WHENCE WE BROUGHT £10,000 FOR HIS MAJESTY BY THE DECIMATION OF HIS SCOTTISH SUBJECTS THERE

Toll, toll
Gentle bell for the soul
Of the poor ones in Pole,
Which are damnèd in our scroll;

5   Who having felt a touch
Of Cockram's greedy clutch,
Which though it was not much,
Yet their stubbornness was such

That when we did arrive,
10   'Gainst the stream we did strive:
They would neither lead nor drive,

Nor lend
An ear to a friend,
Nor an answer would send
15   To our letter so well penned;

Nor assist our affairs
With their monies nor their wares,
As their answer now declares,
But only with their prayers.

20   Thus did they persist,
Did and said what they list,
Till the Diet was dismissed—
But then our breech they kissed:

For when
25   It was moved there and then
They should pay one in ten,
The Diet said amen.

And because they are loth
To discover the truth,
30   They must give word and oath,
Though they will forfeit both.

Thus the Constitution
Condemns them every one
From the father to the son.

35 But John
(Our friend) Molleson
Thought us to have outgone
With a quaint invention.

Like the prophets of yore
40 He complained long before
Of the mischiefs in store:
Ay, and thrice as much more.

And with that wicked lie
A letter they came by
45 From our king's majesty.

But fate
Brought the letter too late:
'Twas of too old a date
To relieve their damned state.

50 The letter's to be seen
With seal of wax so green,
At Danzig, where 'thas been
Turned into good Latin.

But he that gave the hint,
55 This letter for to print,
Must also pay his stint.

That trick,
Had it come in the nick
Had touched us to the quick,
60 But the messenger fell sick.

Had it later been wrought,
And sooner been brought,
They had got what they sought,
But now it serves for nought.

65 On Sandys they ran aground
And our return was crowned
With full ten thousand pound.

THE PROGRESS OF LEARNING

The Preface

My early mistress, now my ancient muse,
That strong Circaean liquor cease to infuse
Wherewith thou didst intoxicate my youth,
Now stoop with disenchanted wings to truth:
5   As the doves' flight did guide Aeneas, now
May thine conduct me to the golden bough:
Tell, like a tall oak tree, how learning shoots
To Heaven her branches and to Hell her roots.

When God from earth formed Adam in the east,
10   He his own image on the clay impressed:
As subjects then the whole creation came
And from their natures Adam them did name—
Not from experience (for the world was new)
He only from their cause their natures knew.
15   Had memory been lost with innocence
We had not known the sentence nor th'offence.
'Twas his chief punishment to keep in store
The sad remembrance what he was before;
And though th'offending part felt mortal pain
20   Th'immortal part its knowledge did retain.
After the flood arts to Chaldaea fell:
The father of the faithful there did dwell,
Who both their parent and instructor was.
From thence did learning into Egypt pass:
25   Moses in all the Egyptian arts was skilled
When heavenly power that chosen vessel filled,
And we to his high inspiration owe
That what was done before the flood we know.
From Egypt arts their progress made to Greece,
30   Wrapped in the fable of the golden fleece.
Musaeus first, then Orpheus civilize
Mankind and gave the world their deities:
To many gods they taught devotion
Which were the distinct faculties of one.
35   The eternal cause in their immortal lines
Was taught and poets were the first divines:
God Moses taught, then David did inspire
To compose anthems for his heavenly choir.
To the one the style of friend he did impart;
40   On the other stamped the likeness of his heart,
And Moses, in the old original,
Even God the poet of the world doth call.
Next those old Greeks Pythagoras did rise,
Then Socrates, whom the oracle called wise.

45 The divine Plato moral virtue shows,
  Then his disciple Aristotle rose
  Who nature's secrets to the world did teach,
  Yet that great soul our novelists impeach:
  Too much manuring filled that field with weeds,
50 Whilst sects, like locusts, did destroy the seeds.
  The tree of knowledge, blasted by disputes,
  Produces sapless leaves instead of fruits.
  Proud Greece all nations else barbarians held,
  Boasting her learning all the world excelled.
55 Flying from thence to Italy it came
  And to the realm of Naples gave the name;
  Till both their nation and their arts did come
  A welcome trophy to triumphant Rome;
  Then wheresoe'er her conquering eagles fled
60 Arts, learning and civility were spread;
  And as in this our microcosm, the heart,
  Heat, spirit, motion gives to every part,
  So Rome's victorious influence did disperse
  All her own virtues through the universe.
65 Here some digression I must make t'accuse
  Thee my forgetful and ingrateful muse:
  Couldst thou from Greece to Latium take thy flight
  And not to thy great ancestor do right?
  I can no more believe old Homer blind
70 Than those who say the sun hath never shined:
  The age wherein he lived was dark, but he
  Could not want sight who taught the world to see.
  They who Minerva from Jove's head derive
  Might make old Homer's skull the muses' hive,
75 And from his brain that Helicon distil
  Whose racy liquor did his offspring fill.
  Nor old Anacreon, Hesiod, Theocrite
  Must we forget, nor Pindar's lofty flight.
  Old Homer's soul, at last from Greece retired,
80 In Italy the Mantuan swan inspired.
  When great Augustus made war's tempests cease
  His halcyon days brought forth the arts of peace.
  He still in his triumphant chariot shines,
  By Horace drawn and Virgil's mighty lines.
85 'Twas certainly mysterious that the name
  Of prophets and of poets is the same.
  What the tragedian wrote, the late success
  Declares was inspiration and not guess:
  As dark a truth that author did unfold
90 As oracles or prophets e'er foretold:
  'At last the ocean shall unlock the bound
  Of things and a new world by Typhis found:

Then ages far remote shall understand
The isle of Thule is not the farthest land'.

95　Sure God by these discoveries did design
That his clear light through all the world should shine,
But the obstruction from that discord springs
The prince of darkness makes 'twixt Christian kings.
That peaceful age with happiness to crown,

100　From heaven the prince of peace himself came down.
Then the true sun of knowledge first appeared
And the old, dark, mysterious clouds were cleared;
The heavy cause of the old, accursèd flood
Sunk in the sacred deluge of his blood.

105　His passion man from his first fall redeemed;
Once more to paradise restored we seemed:
Satan himself was bound, till the iron chain
Our pride did break and let him loose again;
Still the old sting remained and man began

110　To tempt the serpent as he tempted man.
Then hell sends forth her furies—avarice, pride,
Fraud, discord, force, hypocrisy their guide.
Though the foundation on a rock were laid
The church was undermined and then betrayed;

115　Though the apostles these events foretold
Yet even the shepherd did devour the fold.
The fisher to convert the world began,
The pride convincing of vainglorious man:
But soon his follower grew a sovereign lord

120　And Peter's keys exchanged for Peter's sword,
Which still maintains for his adopted son
Vast patrimonies, though himself had none;
Wresting the text to the old giants' sense
That heaven once more must suffer violence.

125　Then subtle doctors scriptures made their prize,
Casuists, like cocks, struck out each other's eyes:
Then dark distinctions reason's light disguised
And into atoms truth anatomized.
Then Mahomet's crescent, by our feuds increased,

130　Blasted the learned remainders of the east.
That project, when from Greece to Rome it came,
Made mother Ignorance Devotion's dame:
Then he whom Lucifer's own pride did swell,
His faithful emissary, rose from hell

135　To possess Peter's chair, that Hildebrand
Whose foot on mitres, then on crowns did stand,
And before that exalted idol all
Whom we call gods on earth did prostrate fall.
Then darkness Europe's face did overspread

140　From lazy cells where superstition bred,

Which, linked with blind obedience, so increased
That the whole world some ages they oppressed;
Till through those clouds the sun of knowledge brake
And Europe from her lethargy did wake.
145 Then first our monarchs were acknowledged here
That they their churches' nursing fathers were.
When Lucifer no longer could advance
His works on the false ground of ignorance,
New arts he tries and new designs he lays:
150 Then his well-studied masterpiece he plays—
Loyola, Luther, Calvin he inspires
And kindles with infernal flames their fires;
Sends their forerunner (conscious of the event)
Printing, his most pernicious instrument.
155 Wild controversy then, which long had slept,
Into the press from ruined cloisters lept.
No longer by implicit faith we err
Whilst every man's his own interpreter;
No more conducted now by Aaron's rod
160 Lay elders from their ends create their God.
But seven wise men the ancient world did know:
We scarce know seven who think themselves not so.
When man learned undefiled religion
We were commanded to be all as one:
165 Fiery disputes that union have calcined,
Almost as many minds as men we find,
And when that flame finds combustible earth
Thence fatuous fires and meteors take their birth:
Legions of sects and insects come in throngs—
170 To name them all would tire a hundred tongues.
Such were the centaurs of Ixion's race
Who a bright cloud for Juno did embrace,
And such the monsters of chimera's kind,
Lions before and dragons were behind.
175 Then from the clashes between popes and kings,
Debate, like sparks from flint's collision, springs:
As Jove's loud thunderbolts were forged by heat,
The like our cyclops on their anvils beat.
All the rich mines of learning ransacked are
180 To furnish ammunition for this war.
Uncharitable zeal our reason whets
And double edges on our passion sets:
'Tis the most certain sign the world's accursed
That the best things, corrupted, are the worst.
185 'Twas the corrupted light of knowledge hurled
Sin, death and ignorance o'er all the world.
That sun, like this from which our sight we have,
Gazed on too long resumes the light he gave;

And when thick mists of doubts obscure his beams
190 Our guide is error and our visions dreams.
'Twas no false heraldry when madness drew
Her pedigree from those who too much knew.
Who in deep mines for hidden knowledge toils
Like guns o'ercharged breaks, misses or recoils:
195 When subtle wits have spread their thread too fine
'Tis weak and fragile, like Arachne's line:
True piety, without cessation tossed
By theories, the practic part is lost,
And like a ball bandied 'twixt pride and wit,
200 Rather than yield both sides the prize will quit:
Then whilst his foe each gladiator foils
The atheist, looking on, enjoys the spoils.
Through seas of knowledge we our course advance,
Discovering still new worlds of ignorance:
205 And these discoveries make us all confess
That sublunary science is but guess:
Matters of fact to man are only known,
And what seems more is mere opinion.
The standers by see clearly this event,
210 All parties say they're sure, yet all dissent:
With their new light our bold inspectors press
Like Cham to show their father's nakedness,
By whose example after ages may
Discover we more naked are than they:
215 All human wisdom to divine is folly—
This truth the wisest man made melancholy.
Hope or belief or guess gives some relief,
But to be sure we are deceived brings grief:
Who thinks his wife is virtuous, though not so,
220 Is pleased and patient till the truth he know.
Our God, when heaven and earth he did create,
Formed man, who should of both participate:
If our lives' motions theirs must imitate
Our knowledge, like our blood, must circulate.
225 When like a bridegroom from the east the sun
Sets forth, he thither whence he came doth run;
Into earth's spongy veins the ocean sinks
Those rivers to replenish which he drinks:
So learning which from reason's fountain springs
230 Back to the source some secret channel brings.
'Tis happy when our springs of knowledge flow
To fill their banks, but not to overflow.

Ut metit Autumnus fruges quas parturit Aestas,
Sic Ortum Natura, dedit Deus his quoque: Finem.

TO HIS MISTRESS

Go love-born accents of my dying heart,
Steal into hers and sweetly there impart
The boundless love with which my soul does swell,
And all my sighs there in soft echoes tell:
5   But if her heart does yet repugnant prove
To all the blessings that attend my love,
Tell her the flames that animate my soul
Are pure and bright as those Prometheus stole:
From heaven, though not like his by theft, they come,
10   But a free gift, by the eternal doom.
How partial, cruel fair one, are your laws,
To reward th'effect and yet condemn the cause?
Condemn my love and yet commend my lays:
That merits love more than these merit praise.
15   Yet I to you my love and verse submit:
Without your smile that hope and these want wit.
For as some hold no colours are in deed
But from reflection of the light proceed,
So as you shine my verse and I must live—
20   You can salvation and damnation give.

A SPEECH AGAINST PEACE AT THE CLOSE COMMITTEE

But will you now to peace incline
And languish in the main design,
    And leave us in the lurch?
I would not monarchy destroy
5   But as the only way to enjoy
    The ruin of the church.

Is not the Bishops' Bill denied
And we still threatened to be tried?
    You see the king's embraces.
10   Those councils he approved before:
Nor doth he promise, which is more,
    That we shall have their places.

Did I for this bring in the Scot?
For 'tis no secret now, the plot
   Was Saye's and mine together.
Did I for this return again
And spend a winter there in vain,
   Once more to invite them hither?

Though more our money than our cause
Their brotherly assistance draws,
   My labour was not lost:
At my return I brought you thence
Necessity, their strong pretence,
   And these shall quit the cost.

Did I for this my country bring
To help their knight against their king,
   And raise the first sedition?
Though I the business did decline,
Yet I contrived the whole design
   And sent them their petition.

So many nights spent in the city
In that invisible committee,
   The wheel that governs all.
From thence the change in church and state,
And all the mischiefs bear the date
   From Haberdashers' Hall.

Did we force Ireland to despair,
Upon the king to cast the war,
   To make the world abhor him,
Because the rebels used his name,
Though we ourselves can do the same,
   While both alike were for him?

Then the same fire we kindled here
With that was given to quench it there,
   And wisely lost that nation;
To do as crafty beggars use
To maim themselves thereby to abuse
   The simple man's compassion.

Have I so often passed between
Windsor and Westminster unseen,
   And did myself divide,
To keep his excellence in awe
And give the Parliament the law,
   For they knew none beside?

55 Did I for this take pains to teach
Our zealous ignorants to preach,
   And did their lungs inspire;
Gave them their text, set them their parts,
And taught them all their little arts
60   To fling abroad the fire?

Sometimes to beg, sometimes to threaten
And say the cavaliers are beaten,
   To stroke the people's ears:
Then straight when victory grows cheap,
65 And will no more advance the heap,
   To raise the price of fears?

And now the books and now the bells
And now our acts the preacher tells,
   To edify the people:
70 All our divinity is news
And we have made of equal use
   The pulpit and the steeple.

And shall we kindle all this flame
Only to put it out again,
75   And must we now give o'er,
And only end where we begun?
In vain this mischief we have done
   If we can do no more.

If men in peace can have their right,
80 Where's the necessity to fight,
   That breaks both law and oath?
They'll say they fight not for the cause,
Nor to defend the king and laws,
   But us against them both.

85 Either the cause at first was ill,
Or being good it is so still:
   And thence they will infer
That either now or at the first
They were deceived, or—which is worst—
90   That we ourselves may err.

But plague and famine will come in,
For they and we are near of kin
   And cannot go asunder:
But while the wicked starve, indeed
95 The Saints have ready at their need
   God's providence and plunder.

Princes we are if we prevail
And gallant villains if we fail,
   When to our fame 'tis told;
It will not be our least of praise,
Sin' a new state we could not raise,
   To have destroyed the old.

Then let us stay and fight and vote
Till London is not worth a groat:
   O 'tis a patient beast!
When we have galled and tired the mule
And can no longer have the rule,
   We'll have the spoil at least.

A WESTERN WONDER

Do you not know, not a fortnight ago,
   How they bragged of a Western wonder,
When a hundred and ten slew five thousand men
   With the help of lightning and thunder?

There Hopton was slain again and again,
   Or else my author did lie;
With a new thanksgiving for the dead who are living,
   To God and his servant Chudleigh.

But now on which side was this miracle tried
   I hope we at last are even,
For Sir Ralph and his knaves are risen from their graves
   To cudgel the clowns of Devon.

And there Stamford came for his honour was lame
   Of the gout three months together:
But it proved when they fought but a running gout,
   For his heels were lighter than ever:

For now he outruns his arms and his guns,
   And leaves all his money behind him,
But they follow after, unless he take water,
   At Plymouth again they will find him.

What Reading hath cost and Stamford hath lost
   Goes deep in the sequestrations:
These wounds will not heal with your new Great Seal
   Nor Jephson's declarations.

25   Now Peters and Case in your prayer and grace
        Remember the new thanksgiving:
    Isaac and his wife now dig for your life
        Or shortly you'll dig for your living.

A SECOND WESTERN WONDER

You heard of that wonder, of the lightning and thunder
    Which made the lie so much the louder,
Now list to another, that miracle's brother,
    Which was done with a firkin of powder.

5   O what a damp it struck through the camp!
        But as for honest Sir Ralph,
    It blew him to the Vies, without beard or eyes,
        But at least three heads and a half.

When out came the book which the news-monger took
10   From the preaching lady's letter,
Where in the first place stood the Conqueror's face,
    Which made it show much the better.

But now without lying you may paint him flying,
    At Bristol they say you may find him:
15   Great William the Con so fast he did run
        That he left half his name behind him.

And now came the post, saves all that was lost,
    But alas we are past deceiving
By a trick so stale, or else such a tale
20   Might amount to a new thanksgiving.

This made Mr Case with a pitiful face
    In the pulpit to fall a-weeping,
Though his mouth uttered lies, truth fell from his eyes,
    Which kept the Lord Mayor from sleeping.

25   Now shut up shops and spend your last drops,
        For the laws not your cause you that loathe 'um,
    Lest Essex should start and play the second part
        Of worshipful Sir John Hotham.

TO SIR RICHARD FANSHAW UPON HIS TRANSLATION OF *PASTOR FIDO*

Such is our pride, our folly, or our fate,
That few but such as cannot write translate.
But what in them is want of art or voice
In thee is either modesty or choice.
5   Whiles this great piece restored by thee doth stand
Free from the blemish of an artless hand.
Secure of fame thou justly dost esteem
Less honour to create than to redeem.
Nor ought a genius less than his that writ
10   Attempt translation, for transplanted wit
All the defects of air and soil doth share,
And colder brains like colder climates are:
In vain they toil since nothing can beget
A vital spirit but a vital heat.
15   That servile path thou nobly dost decline
Of tracing word by word and line by line.
Those are the laboured births of slavish brains—
Not the effects of poetry, but pains:
Cheap, vulgar arts whose narrowness affords
20   No flight for thoughts but poorly sticks at words.
A new and nobler way thou dost pursue
To make translations and translators too.
They but preserve the ashes, thou the flame:
True to his sense but truer to his fame.
25   Fording his current, where thou find'st it low
Let'st in thine own to make it rise and flow;
Wisely restoring whatsoever grace
It lost by change of times or tongues or place.
Nor fettered to his numbers and his times
30   Betray'st his music to unhappy rhymes;
Nor are the nerves of his compacted strength
Stretched and dissolved into unsinewed length:
Yet after all, lest we should think it thine,
Thy spirit to his circle dost confine.
35   New names, new dressings and the modern cast,
Some scenes, some persons altered had outfaced
The world it were thy work; for we have known
Some thanked and praised for what was less their own.
That master's hand which to the life can trace
40   The airs, the lines and features of a face,
May with a free and bolder stroke express
A varied posture or a flattering dress:
He could have made those like, who made the rest,
But that he knew his own design was best.

AN ELEGY UPON THE DEATH OF
THE LORD HASTINGS

Reader preserve thy peace: those busy eyes
Will weep at their own sad discoveries,
When every line they add improves thy loss,
Till having viewed the whole they sum a cross
5 Such as derides thy passion's best relief,
And scorns the succours of thy easy grief.
Yet lest thy ignorance betray thy name
Of man and pious, read and mourn: the shame
Of an exemption from just sense doth show
10 Irrational, beyond excessive, woe.
Since reason then can privilege a tear,
Manhood, uncensored, pay that tribute here
Upon this noble urn. Here, here remains
Dust far more precious than in India's veins;
15 Within these cold embraces ravished lies
That which completes the age's tyrannies,
Who weak to such another ill appear—
For what destroys our hope secures our fear.
What sin unexpiated in this land
20 Of groans hath guided so severe a hand?
The late, great victim that your altars knew,
You angry gods, might have excused this new
Oblation, and have spared one lofty light
Of virtue to inform our steps aright.
25 By whose example good, condemnèd we
Might have run on to kinder destiny.
But as the leader of the herd fell first,
A sacrifice to quench the raging thirst
Of inflamed vengeance for past crimes, so none
30 But this white, fatted youngling could atone,
By his untimely fate, that impious smoke
That sullied earth and did heaven's pity choke.
Let it suffice for us that we have lost
In him more than the widowed world can boast
35 In any lump of her remaining clay.
Fair as the grey-eyed morn he was: the day,
Youthful and climbing upwards still, imparts
No haste like that of his increasing parts:
Like the meridian beam his virtue's light
40 Was seen, as full of comfort and as bright.
Ah that that noon had been as fixed, as clear! But he
That only wanted immortality
To make him perfect, now submits to night.
In the black bosom of whose sable spite

45   He leaves a cloud of flesh behind and flies,
        Refined, all ray and glory, to the skies.
        Great saint, shine there in an eternal sphere,
        And tell those powers to whom thou now draw'st near,
        That, by our trembling sense, in Hastings dead,
50   Their anger and our ugly fates are read,
        The short lines of whose life did to our eyes
        Their love and majesty epitomize:
        Tell them whose stern decrees impose our laws
        The feasted grave may close her hollow jaws.
55   Though sin search nature to provide her here
        A second entertainment half so dear,
        She'll never meet a plenty like this hearse
        Till time present her with the universe.

A PANEGYRIC ON HIS EXCELLENCY, THE LORD GENERAL GEORGE MONK

        If England's bleeding story may transmit
        One renowned name to time yours must be it,
        Who with such art dost heal that we resound,
        Next to our cure, the glory of our wound.
5   Thou sav'st three shattered kingdoms' gasping life,
        Yet from our desperate gangrene keep'st thy knife.
        And though each searching weapon rallied stand
        And all fate's keen artillery wait at hand,
        Thou curb'st those terrors from inflicting harms:
10   Swords are thy instruments but not thy arms.
        Thou with thy pause and treaty rout'st thy foes,
        And thy tame conference a conquest grows.
        With the great Fabius, then, advance thy bays,
        Who sinking Rome restored by wise delays.
15   Let other victors count their dead and lay
        Sad wreaths of conscious laurel where they slay,
        Whilst thou alone dry trophies dost assume:
        They know to kill, but thou to overcome.
        Hence, though some foaming spleens and working hates
20   Make thee the Sampson to our city gates,
        At length thou introducest cooler votes
        To be the temper to impetuous throats.
        Choosing that safe sobriety of thy way,
        Not to eject their fury, but allay.
25   With like inspired prudence didst thou guide
        Thy doubtful answers when their fears applied

Their subtlest emissaries to disclose
Which struggling cause thy courage would oppose.
When though thy innocent breast resolvèd stood
30   The steady bulwark of the general good,
Thy then unripe affairs left them such scope
That who deserved no help might still have hope.
The superstitious thus returned of old
From their consulted oracles, that unfold
35   Two-handed fates, which when they false appear
Delphos spoke true, false the interpreter.
Apollo's awful tripos would not lie,
Yet the receiver's sense might misapply.
So thy consultors from their proud hopes fell:
40   They gave delusion; thou gav'st oracle.
Hence secret trains and snares thy steps pursue,
So dangerous 'mongst the false 'tis to be true.
Return, return, and shroud thy envied name
In those glad roofs thy sole arm screened from flame.
45   Thus threatened Troy no stronger fortress seeks
Than her palladium 'gainst the treacherous Greeks:
And that palladium ne'er was seen no more
When once by rapine from the temple tore.
What she to Troy, Troy did to her become,
50   And was the Pallas to palladium.
Thence did their mutual protections start:
Together both, neither were safe apart.
So thou without us safe canst hardly be
And we despise all safety without thee.
55   Return, return, enshrine thy glories here:
Thou whom both seas and shore do love and fear.
'Midst triumphs great like those thy valour stood
Whilst Holland's faithless gore did stain the flood:
When thy bold shot made their proud vessels creep
60   And cleanse their guilty navy in the deep.
Let land and water yet thy deeds proclaim
Till nature mints more elements for thy fame.

ON MR ABRAHAM COWLEY, HIS DEATH
AND BURIAL AMONGST THE ANCIENT
POETS

Old Chaucer, like the morning star,
To us discovers day from far,
His light those mists and clouds dissolved
Which our dark nation long involved:

5   But he descending to the shades,
    Darkness again the age invades.
    Next, like Aurora, Spenser rose,
    Whose purple blush the day foreshows.
    The other three, with his own fires,
10 Phoebus, the poet's god, inspires:
    By Shakespeare's, Jonson's, Fletcher's lines
    Our stage's lustre Rome's outshines:
    These poets near our princes sleep
    And in one grave their mansion keep;
15 They lived to see so many days,
    Till time had blasted all their bays:
    But cursèd be the fatal hour
    That plucked the fairest, sweetest flower
    That in the muses' garden grew
20 And amongst withered laurels threw.
    Time which made them their fame outlive
    To Cowley scarce did ripeness give.
    Old Mother Wit and nature gave
    Shakespeare and Fletcher all they have;
25 In Spenser and in Jonson art
    Of slower nature got the start:
    But both in him so equal are
    None knows which bears the happiest share.
    To him no author was unknown
30 Yet what he wrote was all his own:
    He melted not the ancient gold,
    Nor with Ben Jonson did make bold
    To plunder all the Roman stores
    Of poets and of orators.
35 Horace his wit and Virgil's state
    He did not steal but emulate,
    And when he would like them appear,
    Their garb but not their clothes did wear.
    He not from Rome alone, but Greece,
40 Like Jason, brought the golden fleece:
    To him that language, though to none
    Of th'others, as his own was known.
    On a stiff gale, as Flaccus sings,
    The Theban swan extends his wings;
45 When through the ethereal clouds he flies
    To the same pitch our swan doth rise:
    Old Pindar's flights by him are reached
    When on that gale his wings are stretched.
    His fancy and his judgement such,
50 Each to the other seemed too much;
    His severe judgement, giving law,
    His modest fancy kept in awe—

As rigid husbands jealous are
When they believe their wives too fair.
His English stream so pure did flow
As all that saw and tasted know.
But for his Latin vein, so clear,
Strong, full and high it doth appear,
That were immortal Virgil here
Him for his judge he would not fear;
Of that great portraiture, so true
A copy pencil never drew.
My muse her song had ended here
But both their genii straight appear:
Joy and amazement her did strike—
Two twins she never saw so like.
'Twas taught by wise Pythagoras
One soul might through more bodies pass:
Seeing such transmigration here
She thought it not a fable there.
Such a resemblance of all parts,
Life, death, age, fortune, nature, arts,
Then lights her torch at theirs, to tell
And show the world this parallel.
Fixed and contemplative their looks,
Still turning over nature's books:
Their works chaste, moral and divine,
Where profit and delight combine;
They gilding dirt, in noble verse
Rustic philosophy rehearse;
When heroes, gods or god-like kings
They praise, on their exalted wings
To the celestial orbs they climb,
And with the harmonious spheres keep time.
Nor did their actions fall behind
Their words, but with like candour shined.
Each drew fair characters, yet none
Of these they feigned excels their own.
Both by two generous princes loved
Who knew, and judged what they approved:
Yet, having each the same desire,
Both from the busy throng retire;
Their bodies to their minds resigned
Cared not to propagate their kind:
Yet though both fell before their hour
Time on their offspring hath no power,
Nor fire, nor fate their bays shall blast,
Nor death's dark veil their day o'ercast.

ON THE EARL OF STRAFFORD'S TRIAL AND DEATH

Great Strafford! Worthy of that name, though all
Of thee could be forgotten but thy fall,
Crushed by imaginary treasons' weight
Which too much merit did accumulate:
5   As chemists gold from brass by fire would draw,
Pretexts are into treason forged by law.
His wisdom such at once it did appear
Three kingdoms' wonder and three kingdoms' fear;
Whilst single he stood forth and seemed, although
10 Each had an army, as an equal foe.
Such was his force of eloquence to make
The hearers more concerned than he that spake:
Each seemed to act that part he came to see
And none was more a looker-on than he:
15 So did he move our passion some were known
To wish for the defence the crime their own.
Now private pity strove with public hate,
Reason with rage and eloquence with fate:
Now they could him if he could them forgive—
20 He's not too guilty but too wise to live.
Less seem those facts which treason's nickname bore
Than such a feared ability for more.
They after death their fears of him express:
His innocence and their own guilt confess.
25 Their legislative frenzy they repent,
Enacting it should make no precedent.
This fate he could have scaped but would not lose
Honour for life, but rather nobly chose
Death from their fears than safety from his own,
30 That his last action all the rest might crown.

TO THE FIVE MEMBERS OF THE HONOURABLE HOUSE OF COMMONS. THE HUMBLE PETITION OF THE POETS

After so many concurring petitions
From all ages and sexes and all conditions,
We come in the rear to present our follies
To Pym, Stroude, Haslerig, H. and H. . . .

 5 Though set form of prayer be an abomination,
    Set forms of petitions find great approbation:
    Therefore, as others from the bottom of their souls,
    So we from the depth and bottom of our bowls,
    According unto the blessed form you have taught us,
10 We thank you first for the ills you have brought us:
    For the good we receive we thank him that gave it
    And you for the confidence only to crave it.
    Next in course, we complain of the great violation
    Of privilege (like the rest of the nation)
15 But 'tis none of yours of which we have spoken
    Which never had being until they were broken:
    But ours is a privilege ancient and native,
    Hangs not on an ordinance or power legislative.
    And first, 'tis to speak whatever we please
20 Without fear of a prison or pursuivant's fees.
    Next, that we only may lie by authority,
    But in that also you have got the priority.
    Next, an old custom; our fathers did name it
    Poetical licence and always did claim it.
25 By this we have power to change age into youth,
    Turn nonsense to sense and falsehood to truth:
    In brief to make good whatsoever is faulty—
    This art some poet or the devil has taught ye:
    And this our property you have invaded
30 And a privilege of both houses have made it.
    But that trust above all in poets reposed
    That kings by them only are made and deposed—
    This, though you cannot do, yet you are willing:
    But when we undertake deposing or killing
35 They're tyrants and monsters, and yet then the poet
    Takes full revenge on the villains that do it;
    And when we resume a sceptre or a crown
    We are modest and seek not to make it our own.
    But is't not presumption to write verses to you
40 Who make the better poems of the two?
    For all those pretty knacks you compose,
    Alas, what are they but poems in prose?
    And between those and ours there's no difference
    But that yours want the rhyme, the wit and the sense:
45 But for lying (the most noble part of a poet)
    You have it abundantly and yourselves know it;
    And though you are modest and seem to abhor it
    'T has done you good service, and thank hell for it;
    Although the old maxim remains still in force
50 That a sanctified cause must have a sanctified course.
    If poverty be a part of our trade
    So far the whole kingdom poets you have made:

Nay even so far as undoing will do it
You have made King Charles himself a poet:
55   But provoke not his muse for all the world knows
Already you have had too much of his prose.

VERSES ON THE CAVALIERS IMPRISONED
IN 1655

Though the governing part cannot find in their heart
    To free the imprisoned throng,
Yet I dare affirm next Michaelmas term
    We'll set them all out in a song.

5   Then Marshall draw near, let the prisoners appear
    And read us their treasons at large,
For men think it hard to lie under a guard
    Without any probable charge.

Lord Petre we wonder what crime he falls under,
10   Unless it be *legem pone*;
He has ended the strife betwixt him and his wife
    But now the state wants alimony.

Since the whip's in the hand of another command
    Lord Maynard must have a smart jerk,
15   For the love that he bears to the new cavaliers,
    The presbet'ry and the kirk.

Lord Coventry's in, but for what loyal sin
    His fellows can hardly gather,
Yet he ought to disburse, for the seal and the purse
20   Which were so long kept by his father.

Lord Byron we know was accused of a bow,
    Or of some other dangerous plot,
But he's no such fool for then, by the rule,
    His bolt had been sooner shot.

25   Lord Lucas is fast and will be the last
    Because he's so learnèd a peer:
His law will not do't, nor his logic to boot
    Though he make the cause never so clear.

Lord St John, indeed, was presently freed,
30   For which he may thank his wife:
She did promise and vow he was innocent now
    And would be so all his life.

There's dainty Jack Russell that makes a great bustle
    And bled three times in a day:
35   But a Caulier swore that he was to bleed more
    Before he got clear away.

Sir Frederick Cornwallis, without any malice,
    Who carries more guts than crimes,
Has the fortune to hit and be counted a wit,
40   Which he could not in former times.

Ned Progers looks pale, but what does he ail?
    (For he diets with that fat droll)
He must dwindle at length that spends all his strength
    At the grill and the little hole.

45   We prisoners all pray that brave Shirley may
    Be gently assessed in your books,
'Cause under the line he has paid a good fine
    To the poor commonwealth of the rooks.

Dick Nichols, they say, and Lyttleton stay
50   For the governor's own delight:
One serves him with play at tennis by day,
    And the other with smoking at night.

Jack Paston was quit, by his hand underwrit,
    But his freedom he hardly enjoyed,
55   For as it is said he drunk himself dead
    On purpose to make his bond void.

Tom Panton, we think, is ready to sink
    If his friends do not lend their hands:
Still lower he goes, and all men suppose
60   Him swallowed up in the quicksands.

For the rest not here named I would not be blamed,
    As if they were scorned by our lyric,
For Waller intends to use them as ends
    To patch up his next panegyric.

65   And now to conclude I would not be rude,
    Nor press into reasons of state,
But surely some cause besides the known laws
    Has brought us unto this sad fate.

Must we pay the faults of our Argonauts,
70   And suffer for other men's sins?
'Cause like silly geese they have missed of the fleece
Poor prisoners are shorn to their skins.

Jamaica relations so tickle the nations,
And Venables looks so sullen,
75   That everyone cries the design was as wise
As those that are framed at Cullen.

Let them turn but our tax into paper and wax
(As some men have endeavoured)
And we shall not stand for notes of our hand:
80   They're sealed and we are delivered.

Yet the bonds they exact destroy their own act
Of pardon, which all men extol,
We thought we should be good subjects and free,
But now we are bondmen to Noll.

MARTIAL. EPIGRAM OUT OF AN EPIGRAM
OF MARTIAL

Prithee die and set me free
Or else be
Kind and brisk and gay like me:
I pretend not to the wise ones,
5   To the grave, to the grave,
Or the precise ones.

'Tis not cheeks, nor lips, nor eyes,
That I prize;
Quick conceits or sharp replies:
10   If wise thou wilt appear and knowing,
Repartee, repartee
To what I'm doing.

Prithee why the room so dark?
Not a spark
15   Left to light me to the mark;
I love daylight and a candle,
And to see, and to see
As well as handle.

20
Why so many bolts and locks,
　　Coats and smocks
And those drawers with a pox?
I could wish, could nature make it,
　　Nakedness, nakedness
Itself were naked.

25
But if a mistress I must have,
　　Wise and grave,
Let her so herself behave
All the day long Susan Civil,
　　Pap by night, pap by night,
30
Or such a devil.

SARPEDON'S SPEECH TO GLAUCUS IN
THE 12TH OF HOMER

　　Thus to Glaucus spake
Divine Sarpedon since he did not find
Others as great in place, as great in mind:
'Above the rest, why is our pomp, our power?
5
Our flocks, our herds, and our possessions more?
Why all the tributes land and sea affords
Heaped in great chargers, load our sumptuous boards?
Our cheerful guests carouse the sparkling tears
Of the rich grape whilst music charms their ears.
10
Why as we pass do those on Xanthus' shore
As gods behold us and as gods adore?
But that as well in danger as degree
We stand the first: that when our Lycians see
Our brave examples they admiring say
15
Behold our gallant leaders! These are they
Deserve the greatness, and unenvied stand:
Since what they act transcends what they command.
Could the declining of this fate, O friend,
Our date to immortality extend?
20
Or if death sought not them who seek not death
Would I advance? Or should my vainer breath
With such a glorious folly thee inspire?
But since with fortune nature doth conspire,
Since age, disease, or some less noble end,
25
Though not less certain, doth our days attend;
Since 'tis decreed and to this period led,
A thousand ways the noblest path we'll tread;
And bravely on till they or we or all
A common sacrifice to honour fall.

Richard Crashaw (? 1613–49)

MUSIC'S DUEL

Now westward Sol had spent the richest beams
Of noon's high glory when, hard by the streams
Of Tiber, on the scene of a green plat,
Under protection of an oak there sat
5   A sweet lutes-master, in whose gentle airs
He lost the day's heat and his own hot cares.
   Close in the covert of the leaves there stood
A nightingale, come from the neighbouring wood.
The sweet inhabitant of each glad tree,
10   Their muse, their siren (harmless siren she),
There stood she listening and did entertain
The music's soft report, and mould the same
In her own murmurs, that whatever mood
His curious fingers lent her voice made good.
15   The man perceived his rival and her art:
Disposed to give the light-foot lady sport
Awakes his lute, and 'gainst the fight to come
Informs it in a sweet praeludium
Of closer strains, and ere the war begin
20   He lightly skirmishes on every string
Charged with a flying touch; and straightway she
Carves out her dainty voice as readily
Into a thousand sweet, distinguished tones,
And reckons up in soft divisions
25   Quick volumes of wild notes, to let him know
By that shrill taste she could do something too.
   His nimble hands' instinct then taught each string
A cap'ring cheerfulness and made them sing
To their own dance: now negligently rash
30   He throws his arm and with a long-drawn dash
Blends all together; then distinctly trips
From this to that; then quick returning skips
And snatches this again and pauses there.
She measures every measure, everywhere
35   Meets art with art: sometimes, as if in doubt
Not perfect yet and fearing to be out,

[139]

Trails her plain ditty in one long-spun note
Through the sleek passage of her open throat—
A clear, unwrinkled song: then doth she point it
40 With tender accents and severely joint it
By short diminutives, that being reared
In controverting warbles evenly shared
With her sweet self she wrangles. He, amazed
That from so small a channel should be raised
45 The torrent of a voice whose melody
Could melt into such sweet variety,
Strains higher yet; that, tickled with rare art,
The tattling strings, each breathing in his part,
Most kindly do fall out: the grumbling bass
50 In surly groans disdains the treble's grace.
The high-perched treble chirps at this and chides,
Until his finger, moderator, hides
And closes the sweet quarrel, rousing all,
Hoarse, shrill, at once, as when the trumpets call
55 Hot Mars to the harvest of death's field and woo
Men's hearts into their hands: this lesson too
She gives him back. Her supple breast thrills out
Sharp airs, and staggers in a warbling doubt
Of dallying sweetness, hovers o'er her skill,
60 And folds in wavèd notes with a trembling bill
The pliant series of her slippery song.
Then starts she suddenly into a throng
Of short, thick sobs, whose thund'ring volleys float,
And roll themselves over her lubric throat
65 In panting murmurs, 'stilled out of her breast,
That ever-bubbling spring; the sug'red nest
Of her delicious soul that there does lie
Bathing in streams of liquid melody;
Music's best seed-plot, when in ripened airs
70 A golden-headed harvest fairly rears
IIis honey-dropping tops, ploughed by her breath,
Which there reciprocally laboureth
In that sweet soil. It seems a holy choir
Founded to the name of great Apollo's lyre,
75 Whose silver roof rings with the sprightly notes
Of sweet-lipped angel-imps that swill their throats
In cream of morning Helicon and then
Prefer soft anthems to the ears of men
To woo them from their beds, still murmuring
80 That men can sleep while they their matins sing—
Most divine service, whose so early lay
Prevents the eyelids of the blushing day.
There might you hear her kindle her soft voice
In the close murmur of a sparkling noise;

85 And lay the groundwork of her hopeful song,
     Still keeping in the forward stream so long
     Till a sweet whirlwind, striving to get out,
     Heaves her soft bosom, wanders round about,
     And makes a pretty earthquake in her breast,
90 Till the fledged notes at length forsake their nest,
     Fluttering in wanton shoals, and to the sky
     Winged with their own wild echoes prattling fly.
     She opes the floodgate and lets loose a tide
     Of streaming sweetness which in state doth ride
95 On the waved back of every swelling strain,
     Rising and falling in a pompous train.
     And while she thus discharges a shrill peal
     Of flashing airs she qualifies their zeal
     With the cool epode of a graver note:
100 Thus high, thus low, as if her silver throat
     Would reach the brazen voice of war's hoarse bird,
     Her little soul is ravished, and so poured
     Into loose ecstasies that she is placed
     Above herself, music's enthusiast.
105   Shame now and anger mixed a double stain
     In the musician's face: 'Yet once again,
     Mistress, I come—now reach a strain, my lute,
     Above her mock, or be forever mute.
     Or tune a song of victory to me
110 Or to thyself sing thine own obsequy.'
     So said, his hands sprightly as fire he flings,
     And with a quavering coyness strikes the strings.
     The sweet-lipped sisters, musically frighted,
     Singing their fears are fearfully delighted;
115 Trembling as when Apollo's golden hairs
     Are fanned and frizzled in the wanton airs
     Of his own breath, which, married to his lyre,
     Doth tune the spheres and make heaven's self look higher.
     From this to that, from that to this he flies,
120 Feels music's pulse in all her arteries;
     Caught in a net which there Apollo spreads
     His fingers struggle with the vocal threads;
     Following those little rills he sinks into
     A sea of Helicon; his hand does go
125 Those parts of sweetness which with Nectar drop,
     Softer than that which pants in Hebe's cup.
     The humourous strings expound his learnèd touch
     By various glosses: now they seem to grutch
     And murmur in a buzzing din, then jingle
130 In shrill-tongued accents, striving to be single.
     Every smooth turn, every delicious stroke
     Gives life to some new grace: thus doth h'invoke

Sweetness by all her names; thus, bravely thus,
Fraught with a fury so harmonious,
135 The lute's light genius now does proudly rise,
Heaved on the surges of swollen rhapsodies
Whose flourish, meteor-like, doth curl the air
With flash of high-borne fancies; here and there
Dancing in lofty measures, and anon
140 Creeps on the soft touch of a tender tone,
Whose trembling murmurs, melting in wild airs,
Run to and fro, complaining his sweet cares
Because those precious mysteries that dwell
In music's ravished soul he dare not tell,
145 But whisper to the world: thus do they vary
Each string his note, as if they meant to carry
Their master's blessed soul (snatched out at his ears
By a strong ecstasy) through all the spheres
Of music's heaven, and seat it there on high
150 In the empyraeum of pure harmony.
At length—after so long, so loud a strife
Of all the strings, still breathing the best life
Of blessed variety attending on
His fingers' fairest revolution
155 In many a sweet rise, many as sweet a fall—
A full-mouth diapason swallows all.
    This done he lists what she would say to this,
And she, although her breath's late exercise
Had dealt too roughly with her tender throat,
160 Yet summons all her sweet powers for a note:
Alas, in vain! For while, sweet soul, she tries
To measure all those wild diversities
Of chatt'ring strings by the small size of one
Poor, simple voice, raised in a natural tone,
165 She fails, and failing grieves, and grieving dies.
She dies, and leaves her life the victor's prize,
Falling upon his lute: O fit to have
(That lived so sweetly) dead, so sweet a grave!

OUT OF VIRGIL,
IN THE PRAISE OF THE SPRING

All trees, all leavy groves confess the spring
Their gentlest friend: then, then the lands begin
To swell with forward pride, and seed desire
To generation; heaven's almighty sire
5 Melts on the bosom of his love and pours
Himself into her lap in fruitful showers;

And by a soft insinuation, mixed
With earth's large mass, doth cherish and assist
Her weak conceptions. No lone shade but rings
10 With chattering birds' delicious murmurings.
Then Venus' mild instinct at set times yields
The herds to kindly meetings; then the fields,
Quick with warm zephyrs' lively breath, lay forth
Their pregnant bosoms in a fragrant birth.
15 Each body's plump and juicy, all things full
Of supple moisture: no coy twig but will
Trust his belovèd bosom to the sun,
Grown lusty now; no vine so weak and young
That fears the foul-mouthed Auster or those storms
20 That the south-west wind hurries in his arms,
But hastes her forward blossoms and lays out,
Freely lays out, her leaves. Nor do I doubt
But when the world first out of chaos sprang
So smiled the days and so the tenor ran
25 Of their felicity. A spring was there,
And everlasting spring; the jolly year
Led round in his great circle—no wind's breath
As then did smell of winter or of death.
When life's sweet light first shone on beasts, and when
30 From their hard mother earth sprang hardy men,
When beasts took up their lodging in the wood,
Stars in their higher chambers: never could
The tender growth of things endure the sense
Of such a change but that the heavens' indulgence
35 Kindly supplies sick nature, and doth mould
A sweetly tempered mean, nor hot nor cold.

OUT OF THE GREEK. CUPID'S CRIER

Love is lost, nor can his mother
Her little fugitive discover:
She seeks, she sighs, but nowhere spies him:
Love is lost and thus she cries him.
5   O yes! If any happy eye
This roving wanton shall descry,
Let the finder surely know
Mine is the wag; 'tis I that owe
The wingèd wanderer, and that none
10   May think his labour vainly gone,
The glad descrier shall not miss
To taste the nectar of a kiss

From Venus' lips. But as for him
That brings him to me, he shall swim
15   In riper joys: more shall be his,
Venus assures him, than a kiss.
But lest your eye discerning slide
These marks may be your judgement's guide:
His skin as with a fiery blushing
20   High-coloured is; his eyes still flushing
With nimble flames, and though his mind
Be ne'er so cursed his tongue is kind,
For never were his words in aught
Found the pure issue of his thought.
25   The working bee's soft-melting gold,
That which their waxen mines enfold,
Flow not so sweet as do the tones
Of his tuned accents: but if once
His anger kindle, presently
30   It boils out into cruelty
And fraud. He makes poor mortals' hurts
The objects of his cruel sports.
With dainty curls his froward face
Is crowned about; but O what place,
35   What farthest nook of lowest hell
Feels not the strength, the reaching spell
Of his small hand? Yet not so small
As 'tis powerful therewithall.
Though bare his skin his mind he covers,
40   And like a saucy bird he hovers
With wanton wing, now here, now there,
'Bout men and women, nor will spare
Till at length he perching rest
In the closet of their breast.
45   His weapon is a little bow,
Yet such a one as, Jove knows how,
Ne'er suffered yet his little arrow
Of heaven's high'st arches to fall narrow.
The gold that on his quiver smiles
50   Deceives men's fears with flattering wiles.
But O—too well my wounds can tell—
With bitter shafts 'tis sauced too well.
He is all cruel, cruel all;
His torch, imperious though but small,
55   Makes the sun (of flames the sire)
Worse than sun-burnt in his fire.
Wheresoe'er you chance to find him
Seize him, bring him (but first bind him):
Pity him not but fear thyself—
60   Though thou see the crafty elf

Tell down his silver drops unto thee,
They're counterfeit and will undo thee.
With baited smiles if he display
His fawning cheeks, look not that way;
65   If he offer sug'red kisses
Start, and say the serpent hisses.
Draw him, drag him, though he pray,
Woo, entreat, and crying say
'Prithee, sweet, now let me go:
70   Here's my quiver, shaft and bow—
I'll give thee all, take all'—take heed
Lest his kindness make thee bleed.
     Whate'er it be Love offers, still presume
     That though it shines, 'tis fire and will consume.

OUT OF THE ITALIAN

Would anyone the true cause find
How love came nak'd, a boy, and blind?
'Tis this: list'ning one day too long
To the sirens in my mistress' song,
5   The ecstasy of a delight
So much o'ermast'ring all his might,
To that one sense made all else thrall,
     And so he lost his clothes, eyes, heart and all.

OUT OF CATULLUS

Come and let us live my dear,
Let us love and never fear
What the sourest fathers say:
Brightest Sol that dies today
5   Lives again as blithe tomorrow,
But if we dark sons of sorrow
Set; O then how long a night
Shuts the eyes of our short light!
Then let amorous kisses dwell
10   On our lips, begin and tell
A thousand and a hundred, score
A hundred and a thousand more,
Till another thousand smother
That, and that wipe off another.

15   Thus at last when we have numbered
    Many a thousand, many a hundred,
    We'll confound the reckoning quite
    And lose ourselves in wild delight;
    While our joys so multiply
20   As shall mock the envious eye.

WISHES TO HIS (SUPPOSED) MISTRESS

    Who e'er she be,
    That not impossible she
    That shall command my heart and me;

    Where'er she lie,
5   Locked up from mortal eye
    In shady leaves of destiny,

    Till that ripe birth
    Of studied fate stands forth
    And teach her fair steps to our earth;

10   Till that divine
    Idea take a shrine
    Of crystal flesh through which to shine,

    Meet you her my wishes,
    Bespeak her to my blisses,
15   And be ye called my absent kisses.

    I wish her beauty,
    That owes not all his duty
    To gaudy tire or glistering shoe-tie.

    Something more than
20   Taffeta or tissue can,
    Or rampant feather or rich fan.

    More than the spoil
    Of shop, or silkworm's toil,
    Or a bought blush, or a set smile.

25   A face that's best
    By its own beauty dressed,
    And can alone command the rest.

A face made up
Out of no other shop,
30   Than what nature's white hand sets ope.

A cheek where youth
And blood, with pen of truth,
Write what the reader sweetly ru'th.

A cheek where grows
35   More than a morning rose;
Which to no box his being owes.

Lips where all day
A lover's kiss may play,
Yet carry nothing thence away.

40   Looks that oppress
Their richest tires, but dress
And clothe their simplest nakedness.

Eyes that displaces
The neighbour diamond, and outfaces
45   That sunshine by their own sweet graces.

Tresses that wear
Jewels but to declare
How much themselves more precious are;

Whose native ray
50   Can tame the wanton day
Of gems that in their bright shades play.

Each ruby there,
Or pearl that dare appear,
Be its own blush, be its own tear.

55   A well-tamed heart,
For whose more noble smart
Love may be long choosing a dart.

Eyes that bestow
Full quivers on love's bow,
60   Yet pay less arrows than they owe.

Smiles that can warm
The blood, yet teach a charm,
That chastity shall take no harm.

        Blushes that bin
65   The burnish of no sin,
        Nor flames of aught too hot within.

        Joys that confess
        Virtue their mistress,
        And have no other head to dress.

70   Fears fond and flight,
        As the coy bride's when night
        First does the longing lover right.

        Tears quickly fled,
        And vain as those are shed
75   For a dying maidenhead.

        Days that need borrow
        No part of their good morrow
        From a forspent night of sorrow.

        Days that in spite
80   Of darkness, by the light
        Of a clear mind are day all night.

        Nights sweet as they
        Made short by lovers' play,
        Yet long by the absence of the day.

85   Life that dares send
        A challenge to his end,
        And when it comes say 'Welcome friend'.

        Sidneyan showers
        Of sweet discourse, whose powers
90   Can crown old winter's head with flowers.

        Soft silken hours,
        Open suns, shady bowers
        'Bove all, nothing within that lours.

        Whate'er delight
95   Can make day's forehead bright,
        Or give down to the wings of night.

        In her whole frame
        Have nature all the name,
        Art and ornament the shame.

100   Her flattery
      Picture and poesy,
    Her council her own virtue be.

    I wish her store
    Of worth may leave her poor
105   Of wishes: and I wish—no more.

    Now if time knows
    That her whose radiant brows
    Weave them a garland of my vows;

    Her whose just bays
110   My future hopes can raise
    A trophy to her present praise;

    Her that dares be
    What these lines wish to see:
    I seek no further, it is she.

115   'Tis she, and here
    Lo I unclothe and clear
    My wishes' cloudy character.

    May she enjoy it,
    Whose merit dare apply it,
120   But modesty dares still deny it.

    Such worth as this is
    Shall fix my flying wishes
    And determine them to kisses.

    Let her full glory,
125   My fancies, fly before ye,
    Be ye my fictions, but her story.

UPON TWO GREEN APRICOTS SENT TO COWLEY BY SIR CRASHAW

Take these, time's tardy truants, sent by me
To be chastised, dear friend, and chid by thee.
Pale sons of our Pomona! Whose wan cheeks
Have spent the patience of expecting weeks,

5   Yet are scarce ripe enough, at best, to show
       The red, but of the blush to thee they owe.
       By thy comparison they shall put on
       More summer in their shame's reflection,
       Than e'er the fruitful Phoebus' flaming kisses
10   Kindled on their cold lips. O had my wishes
       And the dear merits of your muse their due,
       The year had found some fruit early as you;
       Ripe as those rich composures time computes
       Blossoms, but our blessed taste confesses fruits.
15   How does thy April-Autumn mock these cold
       Progressions 'twixt whose terms poor time grows old?
       With thee alone he wears no beard: thy brain
       Gives him the morning world's fresh gold again.
       'Twas only paradise, 'tis only thou,
20   Whose fruit and blossoms both bless the same bough.
       Proud in the pattern of thy precious youth,
       Nature, methinks, might easily mend her growth.
       Could she in all her births but copy thee
       Into the public year's proficiency,
25   No fruit should have the face to smile on thee
       (Young master of the world's maturity)
       But such whose sun-born beauties, what they borrow
       Of beams today, pay back again tomorrow,
       Nor need be double gilt. How then must these
30   Poor fruits look pale at thy Hesperides!
       Fain would I chide their slowness, but in their
       Defects I draw mine own dull character.
       Take them, and me in them acknowledging
       How much my summer waits upon thy spring.

EPITAPHS

UPON THE DEATH OF A GENTLEMAN

       Faithless and fond mortality
       Who will ever credit thee?
       Fond and faithless thing, that thus
       In our best hopes beguilest us.
5   What a reckoning hast thou made
       Of the hopes in him we laid?
       For life by volumes lengthenèd,
       A line or two, to speak him dead.
       For the laurel in his verse
10   The sullen cypress o'er his hearse.

For a silver-crownèd head
A dirty pillow in death's bed.
For so dear, so deep a trust,
Sad requital, thus much dust!
15 Now though the blow that snatched him hence
Stopped the mouth of eloquence;
Though she be dumb e'er since his death,
Not used to speak but in his breath,
Yet if at least she not denies
20 The sad language of our eyes
We are contented: for than this
Language none more fluent is.
Nothing speaks our grief so well
As to speak nothing. Come then tell
25 Thy mind in tears whoe'er thou be
That ow'st a name to misery.
Eyes are vocal, tears have tongues,
And there be words not made with lungs:
Sententious showers, O let them fall,
30 Their cadence is rhetorical.
Here's a theme will drink th'expense
Of all thy wat'ry eloquence;
Weep then—only be expressed
Thus much: 'He's dead', and weep the rest.

AN EPITAPH UPON HUSBAND AND WIFE, WHICH DIED AND WERE BURIED TOGETHER

To these whom death again did wed
This grave's the second marriage bed.
For though the hand of fate could force
'Twixt soul and body a divorce,
5 It could not sever man and wife
Because they both lived but one life.
Peace, good reader, do not weep;
Peace, the lovers are asleep.
In the last knot that love could tie.
10 They, sweet turtles, folded lie
Let them sleep, let them sleep on
Till this stormy night be gone,
And th'eternal morrow dawn:
Then the curtains will be drawn,
15 And they awaken with that light
Whose day shall never sleep in night.

UPON MR STANINOUGH'S DEATH

Dear relics of a dislodged soul, whose lack
Makes many a mourning paper put on black,
O stay a while ere thou draw in thy head
And wind thyself up close in thy cold bed;
5   Stay but a little while until I call
A summons worthy of thy funeral.
   Come, then, youth, beauty, and blood, all ye soft powers
Whose silken flatteries swell a few, fond hours
Into a false eternity; come man—
10   Hyperbolized nothing—know thy span.
Take thine own measure here, down, down, and bow
Before thyself in thy idea; thou
Huge emptiness, contract thy bulk and shrink
All thy wild circle to a point! O sink
15   Lower and lower yet, till thy small size
Call heaven to look on thee with narrow eyes;
Lesser and lesser yet, till thou begin
To show a face fit to confess thy kin,
Thy neighbourhood to nothing! Here put on
20   Thyself in this unfeigned reflection;
Here gallant ladies, this unpartial glass
(Through all your painting) shows you your own face.
These death-sealed lips are they dare give the lie
To the proud hopes of poor mortality.
25   These curtained windows, this self-prisoned eye,
Outstares the lids of large-looked tyranny.
This posture is the brave one: this that lies
Thus low stands up, methinks, thus and defies
The world—all-daring dust and ashes, only you
30   Of all interpreters read nature true.

AN EPITAPH UPON MR ASHTON,
A CONFORMABLE CITIZEN

The modest front of this small floor
Believe me, reader, can say more
Than many a braver marble can:
'Here lies a truly honest man'.
5   One whose conscience was a thing
That troubled neither church nor king;

One of those few that in this town
Honour all preachers, hear their own.
Sermons he heard, yet not so many
10   As left no time to practise any.
He heard them reverently and then
His practice preached them o'er again.
His parlour-sermons rather were
Those to the eye than to the ear.
15   His prayers took their price and strength
Not from the loudness nor the length.
He was a protestant at home
Not only in despite of Rome:
He loved his father, yet his zeal
20   Tore not off his mother's veil.
To the church he did allow her dress,
True beauty to true holiness.
Peace, which he loved in life, did lend
Her hand to bring him to his end:
25   When age and death called for the score
No surfeits were to reckon for.
Death tore not, therefore, but sans strife
Gently untwined his thread of life.
What remains, then, but that thou
30   Write these lines, reader, in thy brow,
And by his fair example's light
Burn in thy imitation bright.
So while these lines can but bequeath
A life, perhaps, unto his death,
35   His better epitaph shall be
His life still kept alive in thee.

EPIGRAMS

THE WIDOW'S MITES

Two mites, two drops, yet all her house and land,
Falls from a steady heart, though trembling hand:
The other's wanton wealth foams high and brave,
The other cast away, she only gave.

EASTER DAY

Rise, heir of fresh eternity,
  From thy virgin tomb;
Rise mighty man of wonders, and thy world with thee,
  Thy tomb, the universal east,
5   Nature's new womb,
Thy tomb, fair immortality's perfumèd nest.

Of all the glories make noon gay
  This is the morn.
This rock buds forth the fountain of the streams of day.
10 In joy's white annals live this hour
  When life was born;
No cloud scowl on his radiant lids, no tempest lower.

Life, by this light's nativity,
  All creatures have.
15 Death only by this day's just doom is forced to die:
  Nor is death forced; for may he lie
  Throned in thy grave:
Death will on this condition be content to die.

TO PONTIUS, WASHING HIS HANDS

Thy hands are washed, but O the water's spilt
  That laboured to have washed thy guilt:
The flood, if any can, that can suffice
  Must have its fountain in thine eyes.

MARK 4
'Why are ye afraid, O ye of little faith?'

As if the storm meant him,
Or, cause heaven's face is dim,
  His needs a cloud:
Was ever froward wind
5 That could be so unkind,
  Or wave so proud?
The wind had need be angry, and the water black
That to the mighty Neptune's self dare threaten wrack.

There is no storm but this
10   Of your own cowardice
That braves you out:
You are the storm that mocks
Yourselves; you are the rocks
Of your own doubt:
15   Besides this fear of danger there's no danger here,
And he that here fears danger does deserve his fear.

MATTHEW 27
'*And he answered them nothing*'

O mighty nothing! Unto thee,
Nothing, we owe all things that be.
God spake once when he all things made:
He saved all when he nothing said.
5   The world was made of nothing then:
'Tis made by nothing now again.

MATTHEW 22
'*Neither durst any man from that day ask him any more questions.*'

Midst all the dark and knotty snares
Black wit or malice can or dares,
Thy glorious wisdom breaks the nets
And treads with uncontrollèd steps.
5   Thy quelled foes are not only now
Thy triumphs but thy trophies too:
They, both at once, thy conquests be
And thy conquest's memory.
Stony amazement makes them stand
10   Waiting on thy victorious hand,
Like statues fixèd to the fame
Of thy renown and their own shame:
As if they only meant to breathe
To be the life of their own death.
15   'Twas time to hold their peace when they
Had ne'er another word to say;
Yet is their silence unto thee
The full sound of thy victory.
Their silence speaks aloud and is
20   Thy well-pronouncèd paneg'ris.
While they speak nothing they speak all
Their share in thy memorial;

While they speak nothing they proclaim
Thee with the shrillest trump of fame.
25   To hold their peace is all the ways
These wretches have to speak thy praise.

LUKE 10

'And a certain priest coming that way looked on him and passed by'.

Why dost thou wound my wounds, O thou that passest by,
Handling and turning them with an unwounded eye?
The calm that cools thine eye does shipwrack mine, for O!
Unmoved to see one wretched is to make him so.

TO PONTIUS WASHING HIS BLOODSTAINED HANDS

Is murder no sin? Or a sin so cheap
        That thou need'st heap
A rape upon it? Till thy adulterous touch
        Taught her these sullied cheeks, this blubbered face,
5   She was a nymph—the meadows knew none such—
        Of honest parentage, of unstained race;
The daughter of a fair and well-famed fountain
As ever silver-tipped the side of shady mountain.

See how she weeps and weeps, that she appears
10   Nothing but tears:
Each drop's a tear that weeps for her own waste.
        Hark how at every touch she does complain her;
Hark how she bids her frighted drops make haste,
        And with sad murmurs chides the hands that stain her;
15   Leave, leave for shame or else, good judge, decree
What water shall wash his, when this hath washèd thee.

LUKE 16. DIVES ASKING A DROP

A drop, one drop, how sweetly one fair drop
        Would tremble on my pearl-tipped finger's top.
My wealth is gone, O go it where it will,
        Spare this one jewel; I'll be Dives still.

LUKE 7

'She began to wash his feet with tears and wipe them with the hairs of her head'.

Her eyes' flood licks his feet's fair stain,
Her hair's flame licks up that again.
This flame thus quenched hath brighter beams:
This flood thus stainèd fairer streams.

ON OUR CRUCIFIED LORD, NAKED AND BLOODY

Th'have left thee naked, Lord; O that they had:
This garment too I would they had denied.
Thee with thyself they have too richly clad,
Opening the purple wardrobe of thy side.
   O never could be found garments too good
5   For thee to wear but these of thy own blood

SAMPSON TO HIS DELILAH

Could not once blinding me, cruel, suffice?
When I first looked on thee I lost mine eyes.

OTHER RELIGIOUS POEMS

THE WEEPER

Hail sister springs,
Parents of silver-forded rills!
Ever-bubbling things!
Thawing crystal, snowy hills!
5   Still spending, never spent: I mean
Thy fair eyes, sweet Magdalene.

   Heavens thy fair eyes be,
  Heavens of ever-falling stars:
   'Tis seedtime still with thee,
10   And stars thou sow'st, whose harvest dares
Promise the earth to counter-shine
Whatever makes the heavens' forehead fine.

   But we are deceived all:
  Stars they are indeed too true,
15   For they but seem to fall
  As heaven's other spangles do:
It is not for our earth and us
To shine in things so precious.

   Upwards thou dost weep,
20 Heaven's bosom drinks the gentle stream:
   Where the milky rivers meet
  Thine crawls above and is the cream.
Heaven of such fair floods as this,
Heaven the crystal ocean is.

25   Every morn from hence
  A brisk cherub something sips,
   Whose soft influence
  Adds sweetness to his sweetest lips:
Then too his music and his song
30 Tastes of this breakfast all day long.

   When some new, bright guest
  Takes up among the stars a room,
   And heaven will make a feast,
  Angels with their bottles come,
35 And draw from these full eyes of thine
Their master's water, their own wine.

   The dew no more will weep,
  The primrose's pale cheek to deck,
   The dew no more will sleep,
40 Nuzzled in the lily's neck:
Much rather would it tremble here
And leave them both to be thy tear.

   Not the soft gold which
  Steals from the amber-weeping tree,
45   Makes sorrow half so rich
  As the drops distilled from thee.
Sorrow's best jewels lie in these
Caskets, of which heaven keeps the keys.

When sorrow would be seen
50   In her brightest majesty,
            (For she is a queen)
        Then is she dressed by none but thee:
Then and only then she wears
Her richest pearls (I mean thy tears).

55   Not in the evening's eyes
        When they red with weeping are
            For the sun that dies,
        Sits sorrow with a face so fair:
Nowhere but here did ever meet
60 Sweetness so sad, sadness so sweet.

        Sadness all the while
        She sits in such a throne as this,
            Can do aught but smile,
        Nor believes she sadness is:
65 Gladness itself would be more glad
To be made so sweetly sad.

        There is no need at all
        That the balsam-sweating bough
            So coyly should let fall
        His med'cinable tears, for now
70 Nature hath learnt t'extract a dew
More sovereign and sweet from you.

        Yet let the poor drops weep,
        Weeping is the case of woe,
75   Softly let them creep,
        Sad that they are vanquished so:
They, though to others no relief,
May balsam be for their own grief.

        Golden though he be,
80   Golden Tagus murmurs, though
            Might he flow from thee
        Content and quiet would he go:
Richer far does he esteem
Thy silver than his golden stream.

85   Well does the May that lies
        Smiling in thy cheeks confess
            The April in thine eyes:
        Mutual sweetness they express.
No April e'er lent softer showers,
90 Nor May returnèd fairer flowers.

Thus dost thou melt the year
Into a weeping motion:
Each minute waiteth here,
Takes his tear and gets him gone:
95   By thine eyes' tinct ennobled thus,
Time lays him up: he's precious.

Time, as by thee he passes,
Makes thy ever-wat'ry eyes
His hour-glasses:
100   By them his steps he rectifies.
The sands he used no longer please:
For his own sands he'll use thy seas.

Does thy song lull the air?
Thy tears' just cadence still keeps time.
105   Does thy sweet-breathed prayer
Up in clouds of incense climb?
Still at each sigh (that is each stop),
A bead (that is a tear) doth drop.

Does the night arise?
110   Still thy tears do fall and fall.
Does night lose her eyes?
Still the fountain weeps for all.
Let night or day do what they will
Thou hast thy task: thou weep'st still.

115   Not 'so long she lived'
Will thy tomb report of thee,
But 'so long she grieved':
Thus must we date thy memory.
Others by days, by months, by years,
120   Measure their ages, thou by tears.

Say, wat'ry brothers,
Ye simp'ring sons of those fair eyes,
Your fertile mothers:
What hath our world that can entice
125   You to be born? What is't can borrow
You from her eyes' swol'n wombs of sorrow.

Whither away so fast,
O whither? For the sluttish earth
Your sweetness cannot taste,
130   Nor does the dust deserve your birth.
Whither haste ye then? O say
Why ye trip so fast away.

We go not to seek
The darlings of Aurora's bed,
135   The rose's modest cheek,
Nor the violet's humble head:
No such thing—we go to meet
A worthier object, our Lord's feet.

A HYMN OF THE NATIVITY SUNG BY THE SHEPHERDS

CHORUS Come we shepherds who have seen
Day's king deposèd by night's queen,
Come lift we up our lofty song
To wake the sun that sleeps too long.

5   He in this our general joy
     Slept, and dreamt of no such thing,
While we found out the fair-eyed boy,
     And kissed the cradle of our king.
Tell him he rises now too late
10   To show us aught worth looking at.

Tell him we now can show him more
Than he e'er showed to mortal sight;
Than he himself e'er saw before,
     Which to be seen needs not his light:
15   Tell him, Tityrus, where th'hast been,
Tell him, Thyrsis, what th'hast seen.

TITYRUS Gloomy night embraced the place
     Where the noble infant lay:
The babe looked up and showed his face—
20   In spite of darkness it was day.
It was thy day, sweet, and did rise
Not from the east but from thy eyes.

THYRSIS Winter chid the world and sent
     The angry north to wage his wars;
25   The north forgot his fierce intent
     And left perfumes instead of scars:
By those sweet eyes' persuasive powers,
Where he meant frost he scattered flowers.

BOTH | We saw thee in thy balmy nest,
        Bright dawn of our eternal day;
30

We saw thine eyes break from the east
        And chase the trembling shades away:
We saw thee, and we blessed the sight,
We saw thee by thine own sweet light.

TITYRUS | I saw the curled drops, soft and slow,
35   Come hovering o'er the place's head,
Offering their whitest sheets of snow
        To furnish the fair infant's bed.
Forbear, said I, be not too bold,
40   Your fleece is white, but 'tis too cold.

THYRSIS | I saw th'officious angels bring
        The down that their soft breasts did strow,
For well they now can spare their wings
        When Heaven itself lies here below.
45 Fair youth, said I, be not too rough,
Thy down though soft's not soft enough.

TITYRUS | The babe no sooner 'gan to seek
        Where to lay his lovely head,
But straight his eyes advised his cheek
50   'Twixt mother's breasts to go to bed.
Sweet choice, said I, no way but so
Not to lie cold yet sleep in snow.

ALL | Welcome to our wond'ring sight
        Eternity shut in a span!
55 Summer in winter, day in night!

CHORUS | Heaven in earth and God in man!
Great little one whose glorious birth
Lifts earth to heaven, stoops heaven to earth.

Welcome, though not to gold nor silk,
60   To more than Caesar's birthright is.
Two sister-seas of virgin's milk,
        With many a rarely-tempered kiss
That breathes at once both maid and mother;
Warms in the one, cools in the other.

65 She sings thy tears asleep and dips
        Her kisses in thy weeping eye;
She spreads the red leaves of thy lips
        That in their buds yet blushing lie;

She 'gainst those mother-diamonds tries
70   The points of her young eagle's eyes.

Welcome, though not to those gay flies
  Gilded i'the beams of earthly kings,
Slippery souls in smiling eyes,
  But to poor shepherds, simple things,
75 That use no varnish, no oiled arts,
But lift clean hands full of clear hearts.

Yet when young April's husband-showers
  Shall bless the fruitful Maia's bed,
We'll bring the firstborn of her flowers
80   To kiss thy feet and crown thy head.
To thee, dread lamb, whose love must keep
The shepherds while they feed their sheep.

To thee, meek majesty, soft king,
  Of simple graces and sweet loves,
85 Each of us his lamb will bring
  Each his pair of silver doves:
At last, in fire of thy fair eyes,
We'll burn, our own best sacrifice.

NEW YEAR'S DAY

Rise thou best and brightest morning,
  Rosy with a double red,
With thine own blush thy cheeks adorning
  And the dear drops this day were shed.

5 All the purple pride that laces
  The crimson curtains of thy bed
Gilds thee not with so sweet graces
  Nor sets thee in so rich a red.

Of all the fair-cheeked flowers that fill thee,
10   None so fair thy bosom strows
As the modest maiden lily
  Our sins have shamed into a rose.

Bid thy golden god, the sun,
  Burnished in his best beams rise,
15 Put all his red-eyed rubies on;
  These rubies shall put out their eyes.

Let him make poor the purple east,
   Search what the world's close cabinets keep,
Rob the rich births of each bright nest
20   That flaming in their fair beds sleep.

Let him embrace his own bright tresses
   With a new morning made of gems,
And wear, in those his morning dresses,
   Another day of diadems.

25   When he hàth done all he may
   To make himself rich in his rise,
All will be darkness to the day
   That breaks from one of these bright eyes.

And soon this sweet truth shall appear
30   Dear babe, ere many days be done,
The morn shall come to meet thee here
   And leave her own neglected sun.

Here are beauties shall bereave him
   Of all his eastern paramours;
35   His Persian lovers all shall leave him
   And swear faith to thy sweeter powers.

IN THE GLORIOUS EPIPHANY OF OUR LORD. A HYMN SUNG AS BY THE THREE KINGS

(1) Bright babe, whose awful beauties make
   The morn incur a sweet mistake;
(2) For whom th'officious heavens devise
   To disinherit the sun's rise;
5   (3) Delicately to displace
   The day, and plant it fairer in thy face;
(1) O thou born king of loves,
(2)   Of lights,
(3)   Of joys!
10 (CHORUS) Look up, sweet babe, look up and see
      For love of thee
      Thus far from home
      The east is come
   To seek herself in thy sweet eyes.
15   (1) We, who strangely went astray,
      Lost in a bright
      Meridian night,

  (2) A darkness made of too much day,
  (3)   Beckoned from far
20   By thy fair star,
  Lo, at last have found our way.
(CHORUS) To thee, thou day of night, thou east of west,
  Lo, we at last have found the way
  To thee, the world's great, universal east;
25 The general and indifferent day;
  (1) All-circling point; all-centering sphere;
  The world's one, round, eternal year;
  (2) Whose full and all unwrinkled face
  Nor sinks, nor swells with time or place,
30 (3) But everywhere and every while
  Is one consistent, solid smile,
  (1)   Not vexed and tossed
  (2)   'Twixt spring and frost,
  (3) Nor by alternate shreds of light
35 Sordidly shifting hands with shades and night.
(CHORUS) O little all, in thy embrace
  The world lies warm and likes his place.
  Nor does his full globe fail to be
  Kissed on both his cheeks by thee.
40 Time is too narrow for thy year,
  Nor makes the whole world thy half-sphere.
  (1)   To thee, to thee,
     From him we flee,
  (2) From him, whom by a more illustrious lie
45 The blindness of the world did call the eye;
  (3) To him who by these mortal clouds hast made
  Thyself our sun, though thine own shade.
  (1) Farewell the world's false light;
     Farewell the white
50   Egypt! A long farewell to thee,
     Bright idol, black idolatry;
  The dire face of inferior darkness kissed
  And courted in the pompous mask of a more specious
   mist.
  (2)   Farewell, farewell,
55   The proud and misplaced gates of hell,
     Perched in the morning's way,
  And double-gilded as the doors of day:
  The deep hypocrisy of death and night,
  More desperately dark because more bright.
60 (3)   Welcome the world's sure way,
     Heaven's wholesome ray!
(CHORUS)   Welcome to us; and we,
     Sweet, to ourselves in thee:
  (1) The deathless heir of all thy father's day!

65   (2)   Decently born,
      Embosomed in a much more rosy morn—
      The blushes of thy all-unblemished mother.
    (3)   No more that other
      Aurora shall set ope
70   Her ruby casements, or hereafter hope
      From mortal eyes
      To meet religious welcomes at her rise.
 (CHORUS) We, precious ones, in you have won
      A gentler morn, a juster sun.
75   (1) His superficial beams sun-burnt our skin,
    (2)   But left within
    (3) The night and winter still of death and sin.
 (CHORUS) Thy softer yet more certain darts
      Spare our eyes but pierce our hearts.
80   (1) Therefore with his proud, Persian spoils
    (2) We court thy more concerning smiles.
    (3)   Therefore with his disgrace
      We gild the humble cheek of this chaste place;
 (CHORUS) And at thy feet pour forth his face.
85   (1) The doting nations now no more
      Shall any day but thine adore:
    (2) Nor (much less) shall they leave these eyes
      For cheap Egyptian deities.
    (3) In whatsoe'er more sacred shape
90   Of ram, he-goat, or reverend ape,
      Those beauteous ravishers oppressed so sore
      The too hard-tempted nations.
    (1)   Never more
      By wanton heifer shall be worn
95   (2) A garland or a gilded horn;
      The altar-stalled ox, fat Osiris, now
      With his fair sister cow
    (3) Shall kick the clouds no more, but—lean and tame—
 (CHORUS) See his horned face, and die for shame:
100   And Mithra now shall be no name.
    (1) No longer shall the immodest lust
      Of adulterous, godless dust
    (2) Fly in the face of heaven, as if it were
      The poor world's fault that he is fair.
105   (3) Nor with perverse loves and religious rapes
      Revenge thy bounties in their beauteous shapes,
      And punish best things worst because they stood
      Guilty of being much for them too good.
    (1) Proud sons of death, that durst compel
110   Heaven itself to find them hell!
    (2) And by strange wit of madness wrest
      From this world's east the other's west.

  (3) All-idolizing worms that thus could crowd
   And urge their sun into thy cloud,
115   Forcing his sometimes eclipsed face to be
   A long deliquium to the light of thee.
 (CHORUS) Alas, with how much heavier shade
   The shame-faced lamp hung down his head
    For that one eclipse he made
120   Than all those he sufferèd!
  (1) For this he looked so big, and every morn
   With a red face confessed this scorn,
   Or hiding his vexed cheeks in a hired mist
   Kept them from being so unkindly kissed.
125 (2) It was for this the day did rise
    So oft with blubbered eyes;
   For this the evening wept, and we ne'er knew,
    But called it dew.
   (3) This daily wrong
130   Silenced the morning sons and damped their song.
 (CHORUS) Nor was't our deafness, but our sins, that thus
   Long made th'harmonious orbs all mute to us.
   (1) Time has a day in store
    When this so proudly poor
135   And self-oppressèd spark, that has so long
   By the love-sick world been made
   Not so much their sun as shade,
   Weary of this glorious wrong,
   From them and from himself shall flee
140   For shelter to the shadow of thy tree:
 (CHORUS) Proud to have gained this precious loss
   And changed his false crown for thy cross.
  (2) That dark day's clear doom shall define
   Whose is the master-fire; which sun should shine.
145   That sable judgement shall by new laws
   Decide and settle the great cause
    Of controverted light,
 (CHORUS) And nature's wrongs rejoice to do thee right.
  (3) That forfeiture of noon to night shall pay
150   All the idolatrous thefts done by this night of day,
   And the great penitent press his own pale lips
   With an elaborate love-eclipse,
    To which the low world's laws
    Shall lend no cause
155 (CHORUS) Save those domestic which he borrows
   From our sins and his own sorrows.
  (1) Three sad hours' sackcloth then shall show to us
   His penance, as our fault, conspicuous;
  (2) And he more needfully and nobly prove
160   The nation's terror now than erst their love:

        (3) Their hated loves changed into wholesome fears,
(CHORUS)   The shutting of his eye shall open theirs.
        (1) As by a fair-eyed fallacy of day
        Misled before they lost their way,
165   So shall they, by the seasonable fright
        Of an unseasonable night,
        Losing it once again, stumble on true light:
        (2) And as before his too-bright eye
        Was their more blind idolatry,
170   So his officious blindness now shall be
        Their black but faithful perspective of thee;
        (3)   His new, prodigious night
        Their new and admirable light;
        The supernatural dawn of thy pure day.
175   While wondering they
        (The happy converts now of him
        Whom they compelled before to be their sin)
            Shall henceforth see
        To kiss him only as their rod,
180   Whom they so long courted as God,
(CHORUS)   And their best use of him they worshipped be
        To learn of him at least to worship thee.
        (1) It was their weakness wooed his beauty:
            But it shall be
185   Their wisdom now as well as duty,
        T'enjoy his blot, and as a large, black letter
        Use it to spell thy beauties better,
        And make the night itself their torch to thee.
        (2) By the oblique ambush of this close night
190   Couched in that conscious shade
        The right-eyed areopagite
        Shall with a vigorous guess invade
        And catch thy quick reflex, and sharply see
            On this dark ground
195   To descant thee.
        (3) O prize of the rich spirit! With what fierce chase
            Of his strong soul shall he
            Leap at thy lofty face
        And seize the swift flash in rebound
200   From this obsequious cloud
            Once called a sun,
            Till dearly thus undone;
(CHORUS)   Till thus triumphantly tamed (O ye two
        Twin suns) and taught now to negotiate you.
205   (1) Thus shall that reverend child of light,
        (2) By being scholar first of that new night,
        Come forth great master of the mystic day,
        (3) And teach obscure mankind a more close way

By the frugal, negative light
210   To read more legible thine original ray,
(CHORUS)   And make our darkness serve thy day;
Maintaining 'twixt thy world and ours
A commerce of contrary powers,
A mutual trade
215   'Twixt sun and shade;
By confederate black and white
Borrowing day and lending night.
(1) Thus we who when with all the noble powers
That, at thy cost, are called—not vainly—ours,
220   We vow to make brave way
Upwards, and press on for the pure, intelligential
     prey;
(2)   At least to play
The amorous spies
And peep and proffer at thy sparkling throne,
225   (3) Instead of bringing in the blissful prize
And fastening on thine eyes,
Forfeit our own
And nothing gain
But more ambitious loss, at least of brain:
230   (CHORUS)   Now by abasèd lids shall learn to be
Eagles, and shut our eyes that we may see.

The Close

Therefore to thee and thine auspicious ray
Dread sweet, lo thus
At least by us
235   The delegated eye of day
Does first his sceptre, then himself in solemn tribute
     pay.
Thus he undresses
His sacred, unshorn tresses:
At thy adorèd feet, thus, he lays down
240   (1)   His gorgeous tire
Of flame and fire;
(2) His glittering robe; (3) his sparkling crown;
(1) His gold; (2) his myrrh; (3) his frankincense,
(CHORUS)   To which he now has no pretence.
245   For, being showed by this day's light, how far
He is from sun enough to make thy star,
His best ambition now is but to be
Something a brighter shadow, sweet, of thee;
Or on heaven's azure forehead high to stand
250   Thy golden index, with a duteous hand
Pointing us home to our own sun,
The world's and his Hyperion.

CHARITAS NIMIA: OR THE DEAR BARGAIN

Lord, what is man? Why should he cost thee
So dear? What had his ruin lost thee?
Lord, what is man, that thou hast overbought
    So much a thing of naught?

5   Love is too kind, I see, and can
Make but a simple merchant man.
'Twas for such sorry merchandise
Bold painters have put out his eyes.

Alas, sweet lord, what wer't to thee
10   If there were no such worms as we?
Heaven ne'er the less still heaven would be,
      Should mankind dwell
      In the deep hell.
What have his woes to do with thee?

15   Let him go weep
      O'er his own wounds;
      Seraphims will not sleep
Nor spheres let fall their faithful rounds.

Still would the youthful spirits sing,
20   And still thy spacious palace ring;
Still would those beauteous ministers of light
      Burn all as bright,

And bow their flaming heads before thee;
Still thrones and dominations would adore thee;
25   Still would those ever-wakeful sons of fire
      Keep warm thy praise
      Both nights and days,
And teach thy loved name to their noble lyre.

Let froward dust then do its kind,
30   And give itself for sport to the proud wind.
Why should a piece of peevish clay plead shares
In the eternity of thy old cares?
Why shouldst thou bow thy awful breast to see
What mine own madnesses have done with me?

35   Should not the king still keep his throne
Because some desperate fool's undone?
Or will the world's illustrious eyes
Weep for every worm that dies?

Will the gallant sun
40   E'er the less glorious run?
Will he hang down his golden head
Or e'er the sooner seek his western bed,
Because some foolish fly
Grows wanton and will die?

45   If I were lost in misery
What was it to thy heaven and thee?
What was it to thy precious blood
If my foul heart called for a flood?

What if my faithless soul and I
50   Would needs fall in
With guilt and sin,
What did the lamb that he should die?
What did the lamb that he should need,
When the wolf sins, himself to bleed?

55   If my base lust
Bargained with death and well-beseeming dust,
Why should the white
Lamb's bosom write
The purple name
60   Of my sin's shame?

Why should his unstained breast make good
My blushes with his own heart-blood?
O my saviour make me see
How dearly thou hast paid for me,
65   That, lost again, my life may prove
As then in death, so now in love.

IN THE GLORIOUS ASSUMPTION OF OUR BLESSED LADY

Hark! She is called. The parting hour is come.
Take thy farewell, poor world, heaven must go home.
A piece of heavenly earth, purer and brighter
Than the chaste stars whose choice lamps come to light her,
5   While through the crystal orbs, clearer than they,
She climbs, and makes a far more milky way.
She's called. Hark how the dear, immortal dove
Sighs to his silver mate 'Rise up, my love!
Rise up, my fair, my spotless one!'

10 The winter's past, the rain is gone,
  The spring is come, the flowers appear:
 No sweets but thou are wanting here.
   Come away, my love!
   Come away, my dove! Cast off delay:
15   The court of heaven is come
    To wait upon thee home: come, come away!
   The flowers appear,
 Or quickly would wert thou once here.
 The spring is come, or if it stay,
20 'Tis to keep time with thy delay.
 The rain is gone, except so much as we
 Detain in needful tears to weep the want of thee.
   The winter's past,
   Or if he make less haste,
25 His answer is, why she does so:
 If summer come not, how can winter go?
   Come away, come away:
 The shrill winds chide, the waters weep thy stay,
 The fountains murmur, and each loftiest tree
30 Bows low his heavy top to look for thee.
   Come away, my love,
   Come away, my dove! (etc.)
 She's called again; and will she go?
 When heaven bids come who can say no?
35 Heaven calls her and she must away:
 Heaven will not and she cannot stay.
 Go then, go glorious
   On the golden wings
 Of the bright youth of heaven that sings
40 Under so sweet a burthen. Go
 Since thy dread son will have it so.
 And while thou goest our song and we
 Will, as we may, reach after thee.
 Hail holy queen of humble hearts!
45 We in thy praise will have our parts.
   Thy precious name shall be
   Thyself to us, and we
   With holy care will keep it by us.
   We to the last
50   Will hold it fast
   And no assumption shall deny us.
   All the sweetest showers
   Of our fairest flowers
   Will we strow upon it.
55   Though our sweets cannot make
   It sweeter, they can take
   Themselves new sweetness from it.

Maria, men and angels sing,
Maria, mother of our king.
60   Live, rosy princess, live, and may the bright
Crown of a most incomparable light
Embrace thy radiant brows. O may the best
Of everlasting joys bathe thy white breast.
Live, our chaste love, the holy mirth
65   Of heaven, the humble pride of earth.
Live, crown of women, queen of men.
Live, mistress of our song. And when
Our weak desires have done their best,
Sweet angels, come and sing the rest.

ON A PRAYER BOOK SENT TO MRS M. R.

Lo, here a little volume but large book—
        Fear it not, sweet,
        It is no hypocrite,
Much larger in itself than in its look.

5   It is, in one rich handful, heaven and all
        Heaven's royal hosts encamped, thus small,
        To prove that true schools use to tell,
A thousand angels in one point can dwell.

It is love's great artillery
10   Which here contracts itself and comes to lie
Close-couched in your white bosom, and from thence,
As from a snowy fortress of defence,
Against the ghostly foe to take your part,
And fortify the hold of your chaste heart.

15   It is the armoury of light,
Let constant use but keep it bright
        You'll find it yields
To holy hands and humble hearts,
        More swords and shields
20   Than sin hath shares or hell hath darts.

        Only be sure
        The hands be pure
That hold these weapons, and the eyes
Those of turtles chaste and true;
25   Wakeful and wise
Here is a friend shall fight for you,
Hold but this book before your heart,
Let prayer alone to play his part.

But O, the heart
30   That studies this high art
Must be a sure housekeeper,
And yet no sleeper.

Dear soul be strong,
Mercy will come ere long
35   And bring her bosom full of blessings;
Flowers of never-fading graces,
To make immortal dressings
For worthy souls, whose wise embraces
Store up themselves for him who is alone
40   The spouse of virgins and the virgin's son.
But if the noble bridegroom when he comes
        Shall find the wand'ring heart from home,
            Leaving her chaste abode
                To gad abroad

45   Amongst the gay mates of the god of flies
            To take her pleasures, and to play
                And keep the devil's holiday;
        To dance in the sunshine of some smiling
                But beguiling
50   Sphere of sweet and sug'red lies,
            Some slippery pair
            Of false, perhaps, as fair,
        Flattering but forswearing eyes—

Doubtless some other heart
55   Will get the start,
            And stepping in before,
        Will take possession of the sacred store
            Of hidden sweets and holy joys,
            Words which are not heard with ears,
60   (These tumultuous shops of noise)
            Effectual whispers whose still voice
        The soul itself more feels than hears.

Amorous languishments, luminous trances,
        Sights which are not seen with eyes,
65   Spiritual and soul-piercing glances,
            Whose pure and subtle lightning flies
        Home to the heart and sets the house on fire,
        And melts it down in sweet desire,
                Yet doth not stay
70   To ask the window's leave to pass that way.

Delicious deaths, soft exhalations
Of soul—dear and divine annihilations;
    A thousand unknown rites
    Of joys and rarified delights;

75 An hundred thousand loves and graces,
    And many a mystic thing
    Which the divine embraces
Of the dear spouse of spirits with them will bring:
    For which it is no shame
80 That dull mortality must not know a name.

Of all this hidden store
Of blessings, and ten thousand more,
    If when he come
He find the heart from home,
85   Doubtless he will unload
Himself some other where,
    And pour abroad
    His precious sweets
On the fair soul whom first he meets.

90 O fair, O fortunate, O rich, O dear!
    O happy and thrice happy she,
    Dear silver-breasted dove
     Whoe'er she be
     Whose early love
95   With wingèd vows
Makes haste to meet her morning spouse,
And close with his immortal kisses.
    Happy soul who never misses
    To improve that precious hour,
100   And every day
     Seize her sweet prey,
All fresh and fragrant as he rises,
Dropping with a balmy shower
A delicious dew of spices.

105 O let that happy soul hold fast
Her heavenly armful, she shall taste
At once ten thousand paradises:
    She shall have power
    To rifle and deflower
110 The rich and roseal spring of those rare sweets,
Which with a swelling bosom there she meets,
Boundless and infinite . . . .
. . . . bottomless treasures
      Of pure, inebriating pleasures;

115   Happy soul she shall discover
   What joy, what bliss,
    How many heavens at once it is
  To have a God become her lover.

IN MEMORY OF THE VIRTUOUS AND LEARNÈD LADY MADRE DE TERESA THAT SOUGHT AN EARLY MARTYDOM

  Love, thou art absolute, sole lord
  Of life and death. To prove the word
  We need to go to none of all
  Those thy old soldiers, stout and tall,
5 Ripe and full-grown, that could reach down
  With strong arms their triumphant crown;
  Such as could with lusty breath
  Speak loud unto the face of death
  Their great lord's glorious name; to none
10 Of those whose large breasts built a throne
  For love their Lord, glorious and great:
  We'll see him take a private seat,
  And make a mansion in the mild
  And milky soul of a soft child.

15 Since she had learnt to lisp a name
  Of martyr, yet she thinks it shame
  Life should so long play with that breath,
  Which, spent, can buy so brave a death.

  She never undertook to know
20 What death with love should have to do;
  Nor hath she e'er yet understood
  Why to show love she should shed blood;
  Yet though she cannot tell you why,
  She can love and she can die.

25 Scarce had she blood enough to make
  A guilty sword blush **for** her sake,
  Yet has she a heart **dares** hope to prove
  How much less strong is death than love.

  Be love but there, let poor six years
30 Be posed with the maturest fears
  Man trembles at, we straight shall find
  Love knows no nonage, nor the mind.

'Tis love, not years or limbs, that can
Make the martyr or the man.
35   Love touched her heart, and lo it beats
High, and burns with such brave heats,
Such thirst to die as dare drink up
A thousand cold deaths in one cup.
Good reason for she breathes all fire:
40   Her weak breast heaves with strong desire
Of what she may with fruitless wishes
Seek for amongst her mother's kisses.

Since 'tis not to be had at home
She'll travel to a martyrdom.
45   No home for her confesses she
But where she may a martyr be.
She'll to the Moors, and trade with them
For this unvalued diadem:
She offers them her dearest breath,
50   With Christ's name in't, in change for death.
She'll bargain with them and will give
Them God, and teach them how to live
In him; or if they this deny
For him she'll teach them how to die.
55   So shall she leave amongst them sown
Her Lord's blood, or at least her own.

Farewell then all the world, adieu,
Teresa is no more for you.
Farewell all pleasures, sports and joys,
60   Never till now esteemèd toys.
Farewell whatever dear may be—
Mother's arms or father's knee.
Farewell house and farewell home,
She's for the Moors and martyrdom.

65   Sweet, not so fast, lo thy fair spouse,
Whom thou seek'st with so swift vows,
Calls thee back and bids thee come
T'embrace a milder martyrdom.

Blessed powers forbid thy tender life
70   Should bleed upon a barbarous knife,
Or some base hand have power to race
Thy breast's chaste chamber and uncase
A soul kept there so sweet. O no,
Wise heaven will never have it so.

75   Thou art Love's victim and must die
        A death more mystical and high:
        Into Love's hand thou shalt let fall
        A still surviving funeral.

        His is the dart must make the death,
80   Whose stroke shall taste thy hallowed breath;
        A dart thrice dipped in that rich flame
        Which writes thy spouse's radiant name
        Upon the roof of heaven, where ay
        It shines, and with a sovereign ray
85   Beats bright upon the burning faces
        Of souls, which in that name's sweet graces

        Find everlasting smiles. So rare,
        So spiritual, pure and fair
        Must be the immortal instrument
90   Upon whose choice point shall be spent
        A life so loved; and that there be
        Fit executioners for thee,
        The fairest and the first-born loves of fire,
        Blessed seraphims, shall leave their choir
95   And turn Love's soldiers upon thee
        To exercise their archery.

        O how oft shalt thou complain
        Of a sweet and subtle pain?
        Of intolerable joys?
100   Of a death in which who dies
        Loves his death and dies again
        And would forever be so slain?
        And lives and dies and knows not why
        To live, but that he still may die.

105   How kindly will thy gentle heart
        Kiss the sweetly-killing dart;
        And close in his embraces keep
        Those delicious wounds that weep
        Balsam, to heal themselves with. Thus
110   When these thy deaths so numerous
        Shall all at last die into one,
        And melt thy soul's sweet mansion—
        Like a soft lump of incense, hasted
        By too hot a fire and wasted
115   Into perfuming clouds—so fast
        Shalt thou exhale to heaven at last
        In a dissolving sigh, and then

O what? Ask not the tongues of men:
Angels cannot tell. Suffice
120 Thyself shalt feel thine own full joys,
And hold them fast forever there
As soon as thou shalt first appear,
The moon of maiden stars; thy white
Mistress, attended by such bright
125 Souls as thy shining self, shall come
And in her first ranks make thee room;
Where 'mongst her snowy family
Immortal welcomes wait on thee.
O what delight when she shall stand
130 And teach thy lips heaven with her hand,
On which thou now mayst to thy wishes
Heap up thy consecrated kisses.
What joy shall seize thy soul when she,
Bending her blessèd eyes on thee
135 Those second smiles of heaven shall dart,
Her mild rays, through thy melting heart.

Angels, thy old friends, there shall greet thee,
Glad at their own home now to meet thee.
All thy good works which went before,
140 And waited for thee at the door,
Shall own thee there, and all in one
Weave a constellation
Of crowns, with which the king thy spouse
Shall build up thy triumphant brows.

145 All thy old woes shall now smile on thee,
And thy pains set bright upon thee;
All thy sorrows here shall shine,
And thy sufferings be divine.
Tears shall take comfort and turn gems,
150 And wrongs repent to diadems.
Even thy deaths shall live, and new-
Dress the soul which late they slew.
Thy wounds shall blush to such bright scars
As keep account of the Lamb's wars.
155 Those rare works, where thou shalt leave writ
Love's noble history, with wit
Taught thee by none but him, while here
They feed our souls, shall clothe thine there.

Each heavenly word, by whose hid flame
160 Our hard hearts shall strike fire, the same
Shall flourish on thy brows, and be
Both fire to us and flame to thee;

Whose light shall live bright, in thy face
By glory, in our hearts by grace.

165 Thou shalt look round about, and see
Thousands of crowned souls throng to be
Themselves thy crown, sons of thy vows:
The virgin births with which thy spouse
Made fruitful thy fair soul: go now
170 And with them all about thee bow
To him. Put on (he'll say) put on
My rosy love, that thy rich zone,
Sparkling with the sacred flames
Of thousand souls whose happy names
175 Heaven keeps upon thy score (thy bright
Life, brought them first to kiss the light

That kindled them to stars), and so
Thou with the Lamb thy Lord shall go;
And wheresoe'er he sets his white
180 Steps, walk with him those ways of light:
Which who in death would live to see
Must learn in life to die like thee.

AN APOLOGY FOR THE PRECEDENT HYMN

Thus have I back again to thy bright name,
Fair sea of holy fires, transfused the flame
I took from reading thee. 'Tis to thy wrong
I know, that in my weak and worthless song
5 Thou here art set to shine, where thy full day
Scarce dawns. O pardon if I dare to say
Thine own dear books are guilty, for from thence
I learnt to know that love is eloquence.
That heavenly maxim gave me heart to try
10 If what to other tongues is tuned so high,
Thy praise might not speak English too; forbid
(By all thy mysteries that there lie hid)
Forbid it, mighty love, let no fond hate
Of names and words so far prejudicate.
15 Souls are not Spaniards too, one friendly flood
Of baptism blends them all into one blood.
Christ's faith makes but one body of all souls
And loves that body's soul: no law controls

Our free traffic for heaven—we may maintain
20 Peace sure with piety though it dwell in Spain.
What soul soever in any language can
Speak heaven like hers is my soul's countryman.
O 'tis not Spanish but 'tis heaven she speaks,
'Tis heaven that lies in ambush there, and breaks
25 From thence into the wond'ring reader's breast,
Who finds his warm heart hatched into a nest
Of little eagles and young loves, whose high
Flights scorn the lazy dust and things that die.
There are enow whose draughts as deep as hell
30 Drink up all Spain in sack: let my soul swell
With thee, strong wine of love; let others swim
In puddles, we will pledge this seraphim
Bowls full of richer blood than blush of grape
Was ever guilty of. Change we our shape,
35 My soul, some drink from men to beasts: O then
Drink we till we prove more, not less, than men,
And turn not beasts but angels. Let the king
Me ever into these his cellars bring,
Where flows such wine as we can have of none
40 But him who trod the wine-press all alone.
Wine of youth's life and the sweet deaths of love,
Wine of immortal mixture, which can prove
Its tincture from the rosy nectar; wine
That can exalt weak earth, and so refine
45 Our dust that in one draught mortality
May drink itself up and forget to die.

ON HOPE. BY WAY OF QUESTION AND ANSWER BETWEEN A. COWLEY AND R. CRASHAW

Cowley

Hope, whose weak being ruined is
Alike if it succeed and if it miss;
Whom ill and good doth equally confound,
And both the horns of fate's dilemma wound.
5   Vain shadow, that doth vanish quite
Both at full noon and perfect night.
The fates have not a possibility
Of blessing thee.
If things then from their ends we happy call,
10 'Tis hope is the most hopeless thing of all.

Crashaw

Dear hope! Earth's dowry and heaven's debt,
The entity of things that are not yet.
Subtlest but surest being! Thou by whom
Our nothing hath a definition.
15   Fair cloud of fire, both shade and light,
      Our life in death, our day in night.
      Fates cannot find out a capacity
         Of hurting thee.
From thee their thin dilemma with blunt horn
20   Shrinks, like the sick moon at the wholesome morn.

Cowley

Hope, thou bold taster of delight,
Who instead of doing so devour'st it quite.
Thou bring'st us an estate, yet leav'st us poor
By clogging it with legacies before.
25   The joys which we entire should wed
      Come deflowered virgins to our bed.
      Good fortunes without gain imported be,
         So mighty custom's paid to thee:
For joy, like wine kept close, doth better taste—
30   If it take air before its spirits waste.

Crashaw

Thou art love's legacy under lock
Of faith, the steward of our growing stock.
Our crown lands lie above, yet each meal brings
A seemly portion for the sons of kings.
35   Nor will the virgin-joys we wed
      Come less unbroken to our bed
      Because that from the bridal cheek of bliss
         Thou thus steal'st down a distant kiss:
Hope's chaste kiss wrongs no more joy's maidenhead
40   Than spousal rites prejudge the marriage bed.

Cowley

Hope, fortune's cheating lottery,
Where for one prize an hundred blanks there be.
Fond archer Hope, who tak'st thine aim so far
That still or short or wide thine arrows are.
45   Thine empty cloud the eye itself deceives
      With shapes that our own fancy gives;
      A cloud, which gilt and painted now appears,
         But must drop presently in tears.
When thy false beams o'er reason's light prevail
50   By *ignes fatui*, not north stars, we sail.

Crashaw

Fair Hope, our earlier heaven! By thee
Young time is taster to eternity.
The generous wine with age grows strong, not sour,
Nor need we kill thy fruit to smell thy flower.
55   Thy golden head never hangs down
    Till in the lap of Love's full noon
    It falls and dies—oh, no, it melts away
      As doth the dawn into the day;
As lumps of sugar lose themselves, and twine
60 Their subtle essence with the soul of wine.

Cowley

Brother of fear! More gaily clad,
The merrier fool o'the two, yet quite as mad.
Sire of repentance, shield of fond desire!
That blows the chemic's and the lover's fire;
65   Still leading them insensibly on
    With the strange witchcraft of 'anon'.
    By thee the one doth changing nature through
      Her endless labyrinths pursue,
And th'other chases woman while she goes
70 More ways and turns than hunted nature knows.

Crashaw

Fortune, alas, above the world's law wars:
Hope kicks the curled head of conspiring stars.
Her keel cuts not the waves, where our winds stir,
And fate's whole lottery is one blank to her.
75   Her shafts and she fly far above,
    And forage in the fields of light and love.
    Sweet hope, kind cheat, fair fallacy! By thee
      We are not where or what we be,
But what and where we would be: thus art thou
80 Our absent presence and our future now.

Crashaw

Faith's sister! Nurse of fair desire,
Fear's antidote! A wise and well-stayed fire
Tempered 'twixt cold despair and torrid joy;
Queen regent in young love's minority.
85   Though the vexed chemic vainly chases
    His fugitive gold through all her faces,
    And love's more fierce, more fruitless fires assay,
      One face more fugitive than all they:
True Hope's a glorious huntress and her chase
90 The God of nature in the field of grace.

TO THE NOBLEST AND BEST OF LADIES, THE COUNTESS OF DENBIGH

(Persuading her to resolution in religion and to render herself without further delay into the communion of the Catholic church)

What heaven-entreated heart is this
Stands trembling at the gate of bliss;
Holds fast the door, yet dares not venture
Fairly to open it and enter?
5   Whose definition is a doubt
'Twixt life and death, 'twixt in and out?
Say, ling'ring fair, why comes the birth
Of your brave soul so slowly forth?
Plead your pretences, O you strong
10   In weakness, why you choose so long
In labour of yourself to lie,
Nor daring quite to live nor die.
Ah linger not, loved soul, a slow
And late consent was a long no:
15   Who grants at last, long time tried
And did his best to have denied.
What magic bolts, what mystic bars
Maintain the will in these strange wars!
What fatal yet fantastic bands
20   Keep the free heart from its own hands!
So when the year takes cold we see
Poor waters their own prisoners be:
Fettered and locked up fast they lie
In a sad self-captivity.
25   Th'astonished nymphs their flood's strange fate deplore
To see themselves their own securer shore.
Thou that alone canst thaw this cold
And fetch the heart from its stronghold:
Almighty love! End this long war
30   And of a meteor make a star.
O fix this fair indefinite;
And 'mongst thy shafts of sovereign light
Choose out that sure, decisive dart
Which has the key of this close heart,
35   Knows all the corners of't and can control
The self-shut cabinet of an unsearched soul.
O let it be at last love's hour;
Raise this tall trophy of thy power;
Come once the conquering way; not to confute
40   But kill this rebel word 'Irresolute'

That so, in spite of all this peevish strength
Of weakness she may write 'Resolved' at length.
Unfold at last, unfold fair flower,
And use the season of love's shower,
45 Meet his well-meaning wounds, wise heart,
And haste to drink the wholesome dart:
That healing shaft which heav'n till now
Hath in love's quiver hid for you.
O dart of love, arrow of light!
50 O happy you if it hit right.
It must not fall in vain, it must
Not mark the dry, regardless dust.
Fair one it is your fate, and brings
Eternal worlds upon its wings.
55 Meet it with widespread arms and see
Its seat your soul's just centre be.
Disband dull fears, give faith the day.
To save your life kill your delay:
It is love's siege, and sure to be
60 Your triumph, though his victory.
'Tis cowardice that keeps this field,
And want of courage not to yield.
Yield then, O yield, that love may win
The fort at last and let life in.
65 Yield quickly: lest perhaps you prove
Death's prey before the prize of love.
This fort of your fair self, if't be not won
He is repulsed indeed—but you are undone.

TO THE NAME ABOVE EVERY NAME, THE NAME OF JESUS, A HYMN

I sing the name which none can say
But touched with an interior ray:
The name of our new peace, our good,
Our bliss, and supernatural blood:
5 The name of all our lives and loves.
Hearken and help, ye holy doves!
The high-born brood of day, you bright
Candidates of blissful light,
The heirs elect of love, whose names belong
10 Unto the everlasting life of song.
All ye wise souls, who in the wealthy breast
Of this unbounded name build your warm nest.
Awake, my glory. Soul (if such thou be

And that fair word at all refer to thee)
15   Awake and sing
        And be all wing:
Bring hither thy whole self and let me see
What of thy parent heaven yet speaks in thee.
        O thou art poor
20   Of noble powers, I see,
And full of nothing else but empty me,
Narrow and low and infinitely less
Than this great morning's mighty business.
        One little world or two
25   Alas, will never do:
        We must have store.
Go, soul, out of thyself and seek for more.
        Go and request
        Great nature for the key of her huge chest
30 Of heavens, the self-involving set of spheres
(Which dull mortality more feels than hears)
        Then rouse the nest
Of nimble art and traverse round
The airy shop of soul-appeasing sound:
35 And beat a summons in the same
        All-sovereign name
To warn each several kind
And shape of sweetness, be they such
        As sigh with supple wind
40   Or answer artful touch,
That they convene and come away
To wait at the love-crowned doors of
        This illustrious day.
Shall we dare this my soul? We'll do't and bring
45 No other note for't but the name we sing:
        Wake lute and harp
        And very sweet-lipped thing
        That talks with tuneful string;
Start into life and leap with me
50 Into a hasty, fit-tuned harmony.
        Nor must you think it much
        T'obey my bolder touch:
I have authority in Love's name to take you
And to the work of Love this morning wake you:
55   Wake—in the name
Of Him who never sleeps, all things that are,
        Or, what's the same,
        Are musical;
        Answer my call
60   And come along;
Help me to meditate mine immortal song.

Come ye soft ministers of sweet, sad mirth,
Bring all your household stuff of heaven on earth.
O you, my soul's most certain wings,
65   Complaining pipes and prattling strings,
        Bring all the store
Of sweets you have, and murmur that you have no more.
        Come, ne'er to part,
        Nature and art!
70   Come, and come strong
To the conspiracy of our spacious song.
Bring all your lutes and harps of heaven and earth,
Whate'er cooperates to the common mirth—
        Vessels of vocal joys,
75   Or you more noble architects of intellectual noise,
Cymbals of heaven or human spheres,
Solicitors of souls or ears.
        And when you are come, with all
That you can bring or we can call,
80   O may you fix
        For ever here, and mix
        Yourselves into the long
And everlasting series of a deathless song;
Mix all your many worlds above
85   And loose them into one of love.
        Cheer thee, my heart,
        For thou too hast played thy part
        And place in the great throng
Of this unbounded, all-embracing song.
90   Powers of my soul be proud,
        And speak loud
To all the dear-bought nations this redeeming name,
And in the wealth of one rich word proclaim
New similes to nature.
95   May it be no wrong
Blessed heavens, to you and your superior song,
That we, dark sons of dust and sorrow,
        A while dare borrow
The name of your delights and our desires,
100   And fit it to so far inferior lyres.
Our murmurs have their music too,
Ye mighty orbs, as well as you;
        Nor yields the noblest nest
Of warbling seraphim to the ears of love
105   A choicer lesson than the joyful breast
        Of a poor, panting turtle-dove.
And we, low worms, have leave to do
The same bright business, ye third heavens, with you.
Gentle spirits, do not complain:

110 We will have care
To keep it fair
And send it back to you again.
Come, lovely name! Appear from forth the bright
Regions of peaceful light,
115 Look from thine own illustrious home,
Fair king of names, and come.
Leave all thy native glories in their gorgeous nest
And give thyself a while, the gracious guest
Of humble souls that seek to find
120 The hidden sweets
Which man's heart meets
When thou art master of the mind.
Come lovely name; life of our hope!
Lo we unlock our hearts wide ope!
125 Unlock thy cabinet of day,
Dearest sweet, and come away.
Lo how the thirsty lands
Gasp for thy golden showers! With long-stretched hands
Lo how the labouring earth,
130 That hopes to be
All heaven by thee,
Leaps at thy birth.
Th'attending world, to wait thy rise,
First turned to eyes,
135 And then, not knowing what to do,
Turned them to tears and spent them too.
Come royal name, and pay th'expense
Of all this precious patience.
O come away
140 And kill the death of this delay.
O see, so many worlds of barren years
Melted and measured out in seas of tears.
O see, the weary lids of wakeful hope,
Love's eastern windows, all wide ope
145 With curtains drawn
To catch the daybreak of thy dawn.
O dawn at last, long looked for day,
Take thine own wings and come away.
Lo, where aloft it comes! It comes among
150 The conduct of adoring spirits, that throng
Like diligent bees and swarm about it.
O they are wise
And know what sweets are sucked from out it.
It is the hive
155 By which they thrive,
Where all their hoard of honey lies.
Lo where it comes, upon the snowy dove's

Soft back, and brings a bosom big with loves.
Welcome to our dark world thou
160   Womb of day!
Unfold thy fair conceptions and display
The birth of our bright joys.
         O thou compacted
Body of blessings; spirit of souls extracted!
165 O dissipate thy spicy powers,
Cloud of condensed sweets, and break upon us
        In balmy showers.
        O fill our senses and take from us
All forces of so profane a fallacy
170 To think aught sweet but that which smells of thee.
Fair, flowery name: in none but thee,
And thy nectareal fragrancy,
        Hourly there meets
An universal synod of all sweets,
175 By whom it is definèd thus
          That no perfume
          For ever shall presume
To pass for odoriferous,
But such alone whose sacred pedigree
180 Can prove itself some kin, sweet name, to thee.
Sweet name, in thy each syllable
A thousand blessed Arabias dwell;
A thousand hills of frankincense;
Mountains of myrrh and beds of spices
185 And ten thousand paradises
The soul that tastes thee takes from thence.
How many unknown worlds there are
Of comforts, which thou hast in keeping!
How many thousand mercies there
190 In pity's lap lie asleeping!
Happy he who has the art
        To awake them,
        And to take them
Home and lodge them in his heart.
195 O that it were as it was wont to be!
When thy old friends of fire, all full of thee,
Fought against frowns with smiles, gave glorious chase
To persecutions, and against the face
Of death and fiercest dangers durst with brave
200 And sober pace march on to meet a grave.
On their bold breasts about the world they bore thee,
And to the teeth of hell stood up to teach thee;
In centre of their inmost souls they wore thee,
Where racks and torments strived in vain to reach thee.
205   Little, alas, thought they

Who tore the fair breasts of thy friends,
            Their fury but made way
For thee—and served therein thy glorious ends.
What did their weapons but with wider pores
210   Enlarge thy flaming-breasted lovers,
            More freely to transpire
            That impatient fire,
The heart that hides thee hardly covers?
What did their weapons but set wide the doors
215   For thee? Fair, purple doors, of love's devising;
The ruby windows which enriched the east
Of thy so oft repeated rising.
Each wound of theirs was thy new morning,
And re-enthroned thee in thy rosy nest,
220   With blush of thine own blood thy day adorning:
It was the wit of love o'er-flowed the bounds
Of wrath, and made thee way through all those wounds.
Welcome dear, all-adorèd name!
            For sure there is no knee
225   That knows not thee:
Or if there be such sons of shame,
            Alas what will they do
            When stubborn rocks shall bow
And hills hang down their heaven-saluting heads
230   To seek for humble beds
Of dust, where in the bashful shades of night
Next to their own low nothing they may lie
And couch before the dazzling light of thy dread majesty.
They that by love's mild dictate now
235   Will not adore thee,
Shall then with just confusion bow
            And break before thee.

Abraham Cowley (1618–67)

THE REQUEST

I have often wished to love: what shall I do?
  Me still the cruel boy does spare,
  And I a double task must bear:
First to woo him and then a mistress too.
5   Come at last and strike for shame,
If thou art anything besides a name.
  I'll think thee else no god to be,
But poets rather gods, who first created thee.

I ask not one in whom all beauties grow;
10   Let me but love, whate'er she be
  She cannot seem deformed to me,
And I would have her seem to others so.
  Desire takes wings and straight does fly,
It stays not dully to enquire the why.
15   That happy thing, a lover, grown,
I shall not see with others' eyes, scarce with mine own.

If she be coy and scorn my noble fire,
If her chill heart I cannot move,
  Why I'll enjoy the very love
20 And make a mistress of my own desire.
  Flames their most vigorous heat do hold,
And purest light, if compassed round with cold:
  So when sharp winter means most harm
The springing plants are by the snow itself kept warm.

25 But do not touch my heart and so be gone;
  Strike deep thy burning arrows in.
  Lukewarmness I account a sin
As great in love as in religion.
  Come armed with flames for I would prove
30 All the extremities of mighty love.
  Th'excess of heat is but a fable:
We know the torrid zone is now found habitable.

Among the woods and forests thou art found;
　　There boars and lions thou dost tame:
35　　Is not my heart a nobler game?
Let Venus men and beasts Diana wound
　　Thou dost the birds thy subjects make;
　　Thy nimble feathers do their wings o'ertake.
　　Thou all the spring their songs dost hear;
40　Make me love too, I'll sing to thee all the year.

What service can mute fishes do to thee?
　　Yet against them thy dart prevails,
　　Piercing the armour of their scales,
And still thy sea-born mother lives i'the sea.
45　　Dost thou deny only to me
The no-great privilege of captivity?
　　I beg or challenge here thy bow:
Either thy pity to me or else thine anger show.

Come, or I'll teach the world to scorn that bow,
50　　I'll teach them thousand wholesome arts
　　Both to resist and cure thy darts;
More than thy skilful Ovid e'er did know.
　　Music of sighs thou shalt not hear,
　　Nor drink one wretchèd lover's tasteful tear.
55　　Nay, unless soon thou woundest me
My verses shall not only wound but murder thee.

THE THRALDOM

I came, I saw and was undone,
Lightning did through my bones and marrow run,
　　A pointed pain pierced deep my heart,
A swift, cold trembling seized on every part:
5　　My head turned round, nor could it bear
　　The poison that was entered there.

So a destroying angel's breath
Blows in the plague and with it hasty death.
　　Such was the pain, did so begin
10　To the poor wretch when Legion entered in.
　　'Forgive me God', I cried, for I
　　Flattered myself I was to die.

But quickly, to my cost, I found
'Twas cruel love, not death, had made the wound.

15 Death a more generous rage does use:
Quarters to all he conquers does refuse.
 Whilst love with barbarous mercy saves
 The vanquished lives to make them slaves.

 I am thy slave then: let me know,
20 Hard master, the great task I have to do.
 Who pride and scorn do undergo
In tempests and rough seas thy galleys row:
 They pant and groan and sigh, but find
 Their sighs increase the angry wind.

25 Like an Egyptian tyrant, some
Thou weariest out in building but a tomb;
 Others with sad and tedious art
Labour i'the quarries of a stony heart:
 Of all the works thou dost assign
30 To all the several slaves of thine,
Employ me, mighty love, to dig the mine.

THE GIVEN LOVE

 I'll on, for what should hinder me
 From loving and enjoying thee?
 Thou canst not those exceptions make
 Which vulgar, sordid mortals take,
5 That my fate's too mean and low.
 'Twere pity I should love thee so
 If that dull cause could hinder me
 In loving and enjoying thee.

 It does not me a whit displease
10 That the rich all honours seize;
 That you all titles make your own;
 Are valiant, learnèd, wise alone—
 But if you claim o'er women too
 The power which over men you do;
15 If you alone must lovers be,
 For that, sirs, you must pardon me.

 Rather than lose what does so near
 Concern my life and being here,
 I'll some such crooked ways invent
20 As you or your forefathers went.
 I'll flatter or oppose the king,
 Turn puritan or anything;

I'll force my mind to arts so new,
Grow rich and love as well as you.

25   But rather thus let me remain
As man in paradise did reign,
When perfect love did so agree
With innocence and poverty.
Adam did no jointure give:
30   Himself was jointure to his Eve.
Untouched with avarice yet, or pride,
The rib came freely back to his side.

A curse upon the man who taught
Women that love was to be bought.
35   Rather dote only on your gold
And that with greedy avarice hold:
For if woman too submit
To that and sell herself for it,
Fond lover, you a mistress have
40   Of her that's but your fellow-slave.

What should those poets mean of old
That made their god to woo in gold?
Of all men sure they had no cause
To blind love to such costly laws;
45   And yet I scarcely blame them now,
For who, alas, would not allow
That women should such gifts receive
Could they, as he, be what they give.

If thou, my dear, thyself shouldst prize
50   Alas, what value would suffice?
The Spaniard could not do't though he
Should to both Indies jointure thee.
Thy beauties, therefore, wrong will take
If thou shouldst any bargain make:
55   To give all will befit thee well,
But not at under-rates to sell.

Bestow thy beauty then on me,
Freely, as nature gave it to thee:
'Tis an exploded Popish thought
60   To think that heaven may be bought.
Prayers, hymns, and praises are the way,
And those my thankful muse shall pay:
Thy body in my verse enshrined
Shall grow immortal as thy mind.

65 I'll fix thy title next in fame
 To Sacharissa's well-sung name.
 So faithfully will I declare
 What all thy wondrous beauties are
 That when, at the last, great assize,
70 All women shall together rise,
 Men straight shall cast their eyes on thee
 And know at first that thou art she.

THE SPRING

Though you be absent here I needs must say
The trees as beauteous are, and flowers as gay,
 As ever they were wont to be:
 Nay, the birds' rural music too
5 Is as melodious and free
 As if they sung to pleasure you.
I saw a rosebud ope this morn: I'll swear
The blushing morning opened not more fair.

How could it be so fair and you away?
10 How could the trees be beauteous, flowers so gay?
 Could they remember but last year,
 How you did them, they you delight,
 The sprouting leaves which you saw here,
 And called their fellows to the sight,
15 Would, looking round for the same sight in vain,
Creep back into their silent barks again.

Where e'er you walked trees were as reverend made
As when of old gods dwelt in every shade.
 Is't possible they should not know
20 What loss of honour they sustain,
 That thus they smile and flourish now
 And still their former pride retain?
Dull creatures! 'Tis not without cause that she
Who fled the god of wit was made a tree.

25 In ancient times sure they much wiser were
 When they rejoiced the Thracian verse to hear;
 In vain did nature bid them stay
 When Orpheus had his song begun:
 They called their wond'ring roots away
30 And bad them silent to him run.
How would those learnèd trees have followed you?
You would have drawn them and their poet too.

But who can blame them now? For, since you're gone,
They're here the only fair and shine alone.
35   You did their natural rights invade:
      Wherever you did walk or sit
      The thickest boughs could make no shade,
      Although the sun had granted it;
The fairest flowers could please no more, near you,
40 Than painted flowers set next to them could do.

Whene'er then you come hither, that shall be
The time which this to others is, to me.
      The little joys which here are now
      The names of punishments do bear,
45   When by their sight they let us know
      How we deprived of greater are.
'Tis you the best of seasons with you bring:
This is for beasts and that for men the spring.

WRITTEN IN JUICE OF LEMON

Whilst what I write I do not see
I dare thus, even to you, write poetry.
    Ah foolish muse which dost so high aspire,
      And know'st her judgement well,
5   How much it does thy power excel,
Yet dar'st be read by thy just doom, the fire.

Alas, thou think'st thyself secure
Because thy form is innocent and pure,
Like hypocrites, which seem unspotted here—
10   But when they sadly come to die,
      And the last fire their truth must try,
Scrawled o'er like thee and blotted they appear.

Go then, but reverently go,
And since thou needs must sin, confess it too;
15 Confess't and with humility clothe thy shame,
      For thou, who else must burnèd be
      An heretic, if she pardon thee
Mayst like a martyr then enjoy the flame.

But if her wisdom grow severe
20 And suffer not her goodness to be there;
If her large mercies cruelly it restrain,
      Be not discouraged, but require
      A more gentle ordeal fire
And bid her by love's flames read it again.

25   Strange power of heat, thou yet dost show
Like winter earth, naked or clothed with snow;
But as the quickening sun approaching near
      The plants arise up by degrees,
      A sudden paint adorns the trees
30   And all kind nature's characters appear.

      So nothing yet in thee is seen,
But when a genial heat warms thee within
A new-born wood of various lines there grows:
      Here buds an A and there a B,
35   Here sprouts a V and there a T,
And all the flourishing letters stand in rows.

      Still silly paper thou wilt think
That all this might as well be writ with ink:
O no—there's sense in this and mystery.
40   Thou now mayst change thy author's name
      And to her hand lay noble claim,
For as she reads she makes the words in thee.

      Yet if thine own unworthiness
Will still, that thou art mine, not hers, confess,
45   Consume thyself with fire before her eyes
      And so her grace or pity move:
      The gods, though beasts they do not love,
Yet like them when they're burnt in sacrifice.

INCONSTANCY

Five years ago, says story, I loved you,
For which you call me most inconstant now:
Pardon me, madam, you mistake the man,
For I am not the same that I was then.
5   No flesh is now the same 'twas then in me,
And that my mind is changed yourself may see.
The same thoughts to retain still and intents
Were more inconstant far, for accidents
Must of all things most strangely inconstant prove
10 If from one subject they t'another move.
My members, then, the father-members were
From whence these take their birth which now are here.
If, then, this body love what th'other did
'Twere incest, which by nature is forbid.

15   You might as well this day inconstant name
        Because the weather is not still the same
        That it was yesterday; or blame the year
        'Cause the spring flowers, and autumn fruit does bear.
        The world's a scene of changes and to be
20   Constant, in nature were inconstancy;
        For 'twere to break the laws herself has made.
        Our substances themselves do fleet and fade;
        The most fixed being still does move and fly
        Swift as the wings of time 'tis measured by.
25   T'imagine then that love should never cease—
        Love, which is but the ornament of these—
        Were quite as senseless as to wonder why
        Beauty and colour stays not when we die.

NOT FAIR

        'Tis very true I thought you once as fair
            As women in th'idea are.
        Whatever here seems beauteous seemed to be
            But a faint metaphor of thee.
5   But then, methoughts, there something shined within
            Which cast this lustre o'er thy skin;
        Nor could I choose but count it the sun's light
            Which made this cloud appear so bright.
        But since I knew thy falsehood and thy pride
10   And all thy thousand faults beside,
        A very Moor, methinks, placed near to thee
            White as his teeth would seem to be.
        So men, they say, by hell's delusion led
            Have ta'en a succubus to bed,
15   Believe it fair and themselves happy call,
            Till the cleft foot discovers all:
        Then they start from it, half ghosts themselves with fear,
            And devil as 'tis it does appear.
        So since against my will I found thee foul,
20   Deformed and crooked in thy soul,
        My reason straight did to my senses show
            That they might be mistaken too:
        Nay, when the world but knows how false you are,
            There's not a man will think you fair:
25   Thy shape will monstrous in their fancies be—
            They'll call their eyes as false as thee.
        Be what thou wilt, hate will present thee so
        As puritans do the pope and papists Luther do.

PLATONIC LOVE

Indeed I must confess
When souls mix 'tis an happiness—
But not complete till bodies too combine
And closely as our minds together join.
5   But half of heaven the souls in glory taste,
    Till by love in heaven at last
      Their bodies too are placed.

In thy immortal part
Man, as well as I, thou art.
10   But something 'tis that differs thee and me,
And we must one even in that difference be.
I thee both as a man and woman prize,
    For a perfect love implies
      Love in all capacities.

15   Can that for true love pass
When a fair woman courts her glass?
Something unlike must in love's likeness be,
His wonder is one and variety;
For he whose soul naught but a soul can move
20   Does a new Narcissus prove
      And his own image love.

That souls do beauty know
'Tis to the body's help they owe:
If when they know't they straight abuse that trust
25   And shut the body from't, 'tis as unjust
As if I brought my dearest friend to see
    My mistress, and at th'instant he
      Should steal her quite from me.

CLAD IN ALL WHITE

Fairest thing that shines below
Why in this robe dost thou appear?
Wouldst thou a white most perfect show
Thou must at all no garment wear.
5   Thou wilt seem much whiter so
Than winter when 'tis clad with snow.

'Tis not the linen shows so fair:
Her skin shines through and makes it bright.
So clouds themselves like suns appear
10   When the sun pierces them with light.
So lilies in a glass enclose,
The glass will seem as white as those.

Thou now one heap of beauty art;
Naught outwards or within is foul:
15   Condensèd beams make every part;
Thy body's clothèd like thy soul:
Thy soul which does itself display
Like a star placed i'the milky way.

Such robes the saints departed wear,
20   Woven all with light divine;
Such their exalted bodies are
And with such full glory shine.
But they regard not mortals' pain:
Men pray, I fear, to both in vain.

25   Yet seeing thee so gently pure
My hopes will needs continue still:
Thou wouldst not take this garment sure,
When thou hadst an intent to kill:
Of peace and yielding who would doubt
30   When the white flag he sees hung out?

ANSWER TO THE PLATONICS

So angels love; so let them love for me:
When I am all soul such shall my love too be.
Who nothing here but like a spirit would do,
In a short time, believe't, will be one too:
5   But shall our love do what in beasts we see?
Even beasts eat too, but not so well as we.
And you as justly might in thirst refuse
The use of wine because beasts water use.
They taste those pleasures as they do their food—
10   Undressed they take it, devour it raw and crude:
But to us men love cooks it at his fire
And adds the poignant sauce of sharp desire.
Beasts do the same 'tis true, but ancient fame
Says gods themselves turned beasts to do the same.

15   The thunderer who, without the female bed,
Could goddesses bring forth from out his head,
Chose rather mortals this way to create:
So much he esteemed his pleasure 'bove his state.
Ye talk of fires which shine but never burn:
20   In this cold world they'll hardly serve our turn;
As useless to despairing lovers grown
As lambent flames to men i'the frigid zone.
The sun does his pure fires on earth bestow
With nuptial warmth to bring forth things below:
25   Such is love's noblest and divinest heat
That warms like his and does like his beget.
Lust you call this—a name to yours more just
If an inordinate desire be lust.
Pygmalion, loving what none can enjoy,
30   More lustful was than the hot youth of Troy.

THE WISH

Well then, I now do plainly see
This busy world and I shall ne'er agree:
The very honey of all earthly joy
    Does, of all meats, the soonest cloy;
5   And they, methinks, deserve my pity,
Who for it can endure the stings,
The crowd and buzz and murmurings
    Of this great hive the city.

Ah yet, ere I descend to the grave,
10   May I a small house and large garden have,
And a few friends and many books, both true,
    Both wise and both delightful too!
And since love ne'er will from me flee,
A mistress moderately fair,
15   And good as guardian angels are,
    Only beloved and loving me!

Oh fountains, when in you shall I
Myself, eased of unpeaceful thoughts, espy?
O fields, O woods, when, when shall I be made
20   The happy tenant of your shade?
    Here's the spring-head of pleasure's flood,
Where all the riches lie that she
    Has coined and stamped for good.

Pride and ambition here
25 Only in far-fetched metaphors appear;
Here naught but winds can hurtful murmurs scatter,
    And naught but echo flatter.
The gods, when they descended hither
From heaven, did always choose their way;
30 And therefore we may boldly say
    That 'tis the way too thither.

How happy here should I
And one dear she live and, embracing, die!
She who is all the world and can exclude,
35   In deserts, solitude.
I should have then this only fear,
Lest men, when they my pleasures see,
Should hither throng to live like me,
    And so make a city here.

MY DIET

Now by my love, the greatest oath that is,
    None loves you half so well as I.
    I do not ask your love for this,
But for heaven's sake believe me or I die.
5   No servant e'er but did deserve
His master should believe that he does serve;
And I'll ask no more wages though I starve.

'Tis no luxurious diet this, and sure
    I shall not by't too lusty prove,
10   Yet shall it willingly endure
If't can but keep together life and love.
    Being your prisoner and your slave
I do not feasts and banquets look to have—
A little bread and water's all I crave.

15 On a sigh of pity I a year can live:
    One tear will keep me twenty at least,
    Fifty a gentle look will give,
A hundred years on one kind word I'll feast;
    A thousand more will added be
20 If you an inclination have for me—
And all beyond is vast eternity.

THE THIEF

Thou robb'st my days of business and delights;
  Of sleep thou robb'st my nights.
  Ah, lovely thief, what wilt thou do?
  What, rob me of heaven too?
5   Thou even my prayers dost steal from me,
  And I with wild idolatry
Begin to God and end them all to thee.

Is it a sin to love that it should thus
  Like an ill conscience torture us?
10   Whate'er I do, where e'er I go—
  None guiltless e'er was haunted so—
  Still, still, methinks thy face I view
  And still thy shape does me pursue,
As if not you me but I had murdered you.

15 From books I strive some remedy to take
  But thy name all the letters make:
  Whate'er 'tis writ I find that there,
  Like points and commas everywhere.
  Me blessed for this let no man hold,
20   For I, as Midas did of old,
Perish by turning everything to gold.

What do I seek, alas, or why do I
  Attempt in vain from thee to fly?
  For making thee my deity
25   I gave thee then ubiquity.
  My pains resemble hell in this:
  The divine presence there too is
But to torment men, not to give them bliss.

THE BARGAIN

Take heed, take heed, thou lovely maid,
  Nor be by glittering ills betrayed.
Thyself for money? O, let no man know
  The price of beauty fall'n so low.
5   What dangers ought'st thou not to dread
When love that's blind is by blind fortune led?

The foolish Indian that sells
His precious gold for beads and bells
Does a more wise and gainful traffic hold
10   Than thou who sell'st thyself for gold.
What gains in such a bargain are?
He'll in thy mines dig better treasures far.

Can gold, alas, with thee compare?
The sun that makes it's not so fair;
15   The sun which can nor make nor ever see
A thing so beautiful as thee,
In all the journeys he does pass,
Though the sea served him for a looking-glass.

Bold was the wretch that cheapened thee:
20   Since Magus none so bold as he.
Thou'rt so divine a thing that thee to buy
Is to be counted simony:
Too dear he'll find his sordid price—
H'as forfeited that and the benefice.

25   If it be lawful thee to buy
There's none can pay that rate but **I**:
Nothing on earth a fitting price can be
But what on earth's most like to thee.
And that my heart does only bear,
30   For there thyself, thy very self is there.

So much thyself does in me live
That when it for thyself I give,
'Tis but to change that piece of gold for this
Whose stamp and value equal is.
35   And that full weight too may be had
My soul and body—two grains more—I'll add.

COUNSEL

Gently, ah gently, madam, touch
The wound which you yourself have made:
That pain must needs be very much
Which makes me of your hand afraid.
5   Cordials of pity give me now,
For I too weak for purgings grow.

Do but a while with patience stay,
    For counsel yet will do no good,
Till time and rest and heaven allay
10   The violent burnings of my blood:
For what effect from this can flow
To chide men drunk for being so?

Perhaps the physic's good you give,
    But ne'er to me can useful prove:
15 Medicines may cure but not revive,
    And I'm not sick but dead in love.
In love's hell, not his world, am I—
At once I live, am dead and die.

What new-found rhetoric is thine?
20   Even thy dissuasions me persuade,
And thy great power does clearest shine
    When thy commands are disobeyed.
In vain thou bid'st me to forbear:
Obedience were rebellion here.

25 Thy tongue comes in as if it meant
    Against thine eyes t'assist my heart;
But different far was his intent,
    For straight the traitor took their part;
And by this new foe I'm bereft
30 Of all that little which was left.

The act, I must confess, was wise
    As a dishonest act could be:
Well knew the tongue, alas, your eyes
    Would be too strong for that and me;
35 And part o'the triumph chose to get
Rather than be a part of it.

RESOLVED TO BE BELOVED

'Tis true I have loved already three or four
    And shall three or four hundred more:
    I'll love each fair one that I see
Till I find one at last that shall love me.

5 That shall my Canaan be, the fatal soil
    That ends my wand'rings and my toil.
    I'll settle there and happy grow:
The country does with milk and honey flow.

The needle trembles so and turns about
10   Till it the northern point find out,
        But constant then and fixed does prove:
Fixed, that his dearest pole as soon may move.

Then may my vessel torn and shipwrecked be
        If it put forth again to sea:
15   It never more abroad shall roam
Though't could next voyage bring the Indies home.

But I must sweat in love, and labour yet
        Till I a competency get.
        They're slothful fools who leave a trade
20 Till they a moderate fortune by't have made.

Variety I ask not; give me one
        To live perpetually upon.
        The person love does to us fit,
Like manna has the taste of all in it.

THE SAME

        For heaven's sake what do you mean to do?
        Keep me or let me go, one of the two.
        Youth and warm hours let me not idly lose,
                The little time that love does choose.
5   If always here I must not stay
                Let me be gone whilst yet 'tis day,
        Lest I faint and benighted lose my way.

                'Tis dismal one so long to love
        In vain, till to love more as vain must prove:
10   To hunt so long on nimble prey till we
                Too weary to take others be.
                Alas 'tis folly to remain
                And waste our army thus in vain,
        Before a city which will ne'er be ta'en.

15   At several hopes wisely to fly
        Ought not to be esteemed inconstancy:
        'Tis more inconstant always to pursue
                A thing that always flies from you;
                For that at last may meet a bound
20   But no end can to this be found:
        'Tis nought but a perpetual, fruitless round.

When it does hardness meet and pride
My love does then rebound t'another side,
But if it aught that's soft and yielding hit
25   It lodges there and stays in it.
    Whatever 'tis shall first love me,
    That it my heaven may truly be,
I shall be sure to give't eternity.

THE DISCOVERY

By heaven, I'll tell her boldly that 'tis she:
    Why should she ashamed or angry be
      To be beloved by me?
    The gods may give their altars o'er—
5   They'll smoke but seldom any more
If none but happy men must them adore.

The lightning which tall oaks oppose in vain,
    To strike sometimes does not disdain
      The humble furzes of the plain.
10   She being so high and I so low
Her power by this does greater show,
Who at such distance gives so sure a blow.

Compared with her all things so worthless prove
    That naught on earth can towards her move
15   Till't be exalted by her love.
    Equal to her, alas, there's none:
    She like a deity is grown,
That must create or else must be alone.

If there be man who thinks himself so high
20   As to pretend equality,
      He deserves her less than I,
    For he would cheat for his relief;
    And one would give with lesser grief
To an undeserving beggar than a thief.

AGAINST FRUITION

No, thou'rt a fool I'll swear if e'er thou grant:
Much of my veneration thou must want,
When once thy kindness puts my ignorance out:
For a learned age is always least devout.

5   Keep still thy distance, for at once to me
    Goddess and woman too thou canst not be.
    Thou'rt queen of all that sees thee, and as such
    Must neither tyrannize nor yield too much.
    Such freedoms give as may admit command,
10 But keep the forts and magazines in thine hand.
    Thou'rt yet a whole world to me and dost fill
    My large ambition, but 'tis dangerous still,
    Lest I like the Pellaean prince should be,
    And weep for other worlds having conquered thee.
15 When love has taken all thou hast away
    His strength by too much riches will decay.
    Thou in my fancy dost much higher stand
    Than women can be placed by nature's hand;
    And I must needs, I'm sure, a loser be
20 To change thee as thou'rt there for very thee.
    Thy sweetness is so much within me placed
    That shouldst thou nectar give 'twould spoil the taste.
    Beauty at first moves wonder and delight:
    'Tis nature's juggling trick to cheat the sight.
25 We admire it whilst unknown, but after more
    Admire ourselves for liking it before.
    Love, like a greedy hawk, if we give way
    Does over-gorge himself with his own prey.
    Of very hopes a surfeit he'll sustain,
30 Unless by fears he cast them up again.
    His spirit and sweetness dangers keep alone:
    If once he lose his sting he grows a drone.

THE GIVEN HEART

I wonder what those lovers mean who say
    They have given their hearts away.
    Some good, kind lover tell me how,
For mine is but a torment to me now.

5   If so it be one place both hearts contain
        For what do they complain?
        What courtesy can love do more
    Than to join hearts that parted were before?

    Woe to her stubborn heart if once mine come
10   Into the self-same room:
        'Twill tear and blow up all within,
    Like a granado shot into a magazine.

15
20

Then shall love keep the ashes and torn parts
  Of both our broken hearts:
    Shall out of both one new one make—
From hers the alloy, from mine the metal take.

For of her heart he from the flames will find
  But little left behind:
    Mine only will remain entire—
No dross was there to perish in the fire.

THE PROPHET

Teach me to love? Go, teach thyself more wit:
  I chief professor am of it.
    Teach craft to Scots and thrift to Jews;
    Teach boldness to the stews;
In tyrants' courts teach supple flattery;
Teach Jesuits, that have travelled far, to lie;
    Teach fire to burn and winds to blow;
    Teach restless fountains how to flow;
    Teach the dull earth, fixed, to abide;
Teach womankind inconstancy and pride.
See if your diligence here will useful prove:
    But, prithee, teach not me to love.

The god of love, if such a thing there be,
  May learn to love from me.
    He who does boast that he has bin
    In every heart since Adam's sin,
I'll lay my life, nay mistress on't (that's more)
I'll teach him things he never knew before.
    I'll teach him a receipt to make
    Words that weep and tears that speak;
    I'll teach him sighs like those in death,
At which the souls go out too with the breath:
Still the soul stays, yet still does from me run,
    As light and heat does with the sun.

'Tis I who love's Columbus am; 'tis I
  Who must new worlds in it descry:
    Rich worlds that yield of treasure more
    Than all that has been known before.
And yet like his, I fear, my fate must be
To find them out for others, not for me.
    Me times to come, I know it, shall
    Love's last and greatest prophet call.

But, ah, what's that if she refuse
To hear the wholesome doctrines of my muse?
35   If to my share the prophet's fate must come,
      Hereafter fame, here martyrdom.

WOMEN'S SUPERSTITION

Or I'm a very dunce or womankind
Is a most unintelligible thing:
I can no sense nor no contexture find,
      Nor their loose parts to method bring:
5   I know not what the learned may see
      But they're strange Hebrew things to me.

By customs and traditions they live,
And foolish ceremonies of antique date:
We lovers new and better doctrines give,
10   Yet they continue obstinate:
      Preach we, love's prophets, what we will,
      Like Jews they keep their old law still.

Before their mother's gods they fondly fall,
Vain idol-gods that have no sense nor mind:
15   Honour's their Ashtaroth and pride their Baal—
      The thundering Baal of womankind;
      With twenty other devils more
      Which they, as we do them, adore.

But then, like men both covetous and devout,
20   Their costly superstition loth t'omit,
And yet more loth to issue monies out
      At their own charge to furnish it.
      To these expensive deities
      The hearts of men they sacrifice.

THE SOUL

Some dull philosopher when he hears me say
      My soul is from me fled away,
Nor has of late informed my body here
      But in another breast does lie,
5   That neither is nor will be I,
As a form servient and assisting there—

Will cry 'Absurd!' and ask me how I live,
   And syllogisms against it give.
A curse on all your vain philosophies,
    Which on weak nature's law depend,
    And know not how to comprehend
Love and religion, those great mysteries.

Her body is my soul: laugh not at this,
   For by my life I swear it is.
'Tis that preserves my being and my breath:
    From that proceeds all that I do,
    Nay all my thoughts and speeches too,
And separation from it is my death.

LOVE'S INGRATITUDE

I little thought, thou fond, ingrateful sin,
   When first I let thee in,
   And gave thee but a part
   In my unwary heart,
    That thou wouldst e'er have grown
So false or strong to make it all thine own.

At mine own breast with care I fed thee still,
   Letting thee suck thy fill;
   And daintily I nourished thee
   With idle thoughts and poetry!
    What ill returns dost thou allow?
I fed thee then and thou dost starve me now.

There was a time when thou wast cold and chill,
   Nor hadst the power of doing ill:
   Into my bosom did I take
   This frozen and benumbèd snake,
    Not fearing from it any harm—
But now it stings that breast which made it warm.

What cursèd weed's this love! But one grain sow
   And the whole field 'twill overgrow:
   Straight will it choke up and devour
   Each wholesome herb and beauteous flower:
    Nay, unless something soon I do
'Twill kill, I fear, my very laurel too.

25   But now all's gone I now, alas, complain,
            Declare, protest and threat in vain,
            Since by my own unforced consent
            The traitor has my government,
            And is so settled in the throne
30   That 'twere rebellion now to claim mine own.

LOVE'S VISIBILITY

With much of pain and all the art I knew
        Have I endeavoured hitherto
To hide my love and yet all will not do.

The world perceives it and it may be she,
5   Though so discreet and good she be,
By hiding it to teach that skill to me.

Men without love have oft so cunning grown
        That something like it they have shown,
But none who had it ever seemed t'have none.

10   Love's of a strangely open, simple kind,
            Can no arts or disguises find,
But thinks none sees it 'cause itself is blind.

The very eye betrays our inward smart:
        Love of himself left there a part
15   When through it he passed into the heart.

Or if by chance the face betray not it
        But keep the secret wisely, yet
Like drunkenness into the tongue 'twill get.

RESOLVED TO LOVE

I wonder what the grave and wise
        Think of all us that love:
Whether our pretty fooleries
        Their mirth or anger move.
5   They understand not breath, that words does want;
Our sighs to them are unsignificant.

One of them saw me th'other day
  Touch the dear hand which I admire:
My soul was melting straight away
10   And dropped before the fire.
This silly wiseman who pretends to know
Asked why I looked so pale and trembled so.

Another from my mistress' door
  Saw me with eyes all wat'ry come,
15 Nor could the hidden cause explore,
    But thought some smoke was in the room.
Such ignorance from unwounded learning came:
He knew tears made from smoke but not by flame.

If learned in other things you be
20   And have in love no skill,
For God's sake keep your arts from me,
    For I'll be ignorant still.
Study or action others may embrace:
My love's my business and my books her face.

25 These are but trifles, I confess,
    Which me—weak mortal—move;
Nor is your busy seriousness
    Less trifling than my love:
The wisest king who from his sacred breast
30 Pronounced all vanity chose it for the best.

MY FATE

Go, bid the needle his dear north forsake,
  To which with trembling reverence it does bend;
Go, bid the stones a journey upwards make;
  Go, bid th'ambitious flame no more ascend—
5 And when these false to their old motions prove
Then shall I cease thee, thee alone, to love.

The fast-linked chain of everlasting fate
  Does nothing tie more strong than me to you;
My fixed love hangs not on your love or hate,
10   But will be still the same whate'er you do.
You cannot kill my love with your disdain:
Wound it you may and make it live in pain.

Me, mine example, let the stoics use
 Their sad and cruel doctrine to maintain;
15 Let all predestinators me produce
 Who struggle with eternal bonds in vain.
This fire I'm born to, but 'tis she must tell
Whether't be beams of heaven or flames of hell.

You who men's fortunes in their faces read,
20 To find out mine look not, alas, on me;
But mark her face and all the features heed,
 For only there is writ my destiny:
Or if stars show it gaze not on the skies,
But study the astrology of her eyes.

25 If thou find there kind and propitious rays,
 What Mars or Saturn threaten I'll not fear:
I well believe the fate of mortal days
 Is writ in heaven, but O my heaven is there.
What can men learn from stars they scarce can see?
30 Two great lights rule the world, and her two me.

THE USURPATION

Thou hadst to my soul no title or pretence:
 I was mine own and free
 Till I had given myself to thee—
But thou hast kept me slave and prisoner since.
5 Well, since so insolent thou'rt grown,
Fond tyrant I'll depose thee from thy throne:
Such outrages must not admitted be
 In an elective monarchy.

Part of my heart by gift did to thee fall.
10 My country, kindred and my best
 Acquaintance were to share the rest:
But thou, their covetous neighbour, drav'st out all,
 Nay more: thou mak'st me worship thee
And wouldst the rule of my religion be.
15 Was ever tyrant claimed such power as you,
 To be both emperor and pope too?

The public miseries and my private fate
 Deserve some tears, but greedy thou,
 Insatiate maid, wilt not allow
20 That I one drop from thee should alienate:

Nor wilt thou grant my sins a part,
Though the sole cause of most of them thou art,
Counting my tears thy tribute and thy due
    Since first mine eyes I gave to you.

25 Thou all my joys and all my hopes dost claim,
    Thou ragest like a fire in me,
    Converting all things into thee.
Naught can resist or not increase the flame.
    Nay every grief and every fear
30 Thou dost devour unless thy stamp it bear.
Thy presence, like the crowned basilisk's breath,
    All other serpents puts to death.

As men in hell are from diseases free
    So from all other ills am I—
35   Free from their known formality;
But all pains eminently lie in thee.
    Alas, alas, I hope in vain
My conquered soul from out thine hands to gain,
Since all the natives there thou'st overthrown
40   And planted garrisons of thine own.

MAIDENHEAD

Thou worst estate even of the sex that's worst;
    Therefore by nature made at first
    T'attend the weakness of our birth.
Slight, outward curtain to the nuptial bed,
5 Thou case to buildings not yet finishèd!
    Who like the centre of the earth
    Dost heaviest things attract to thee
Though thou a point imaginary be.

A thing God thought for mankind so unfit
10   That his first blessing ruined it,
    Cold, frozen nurse of fiercest fires,
Who, like the parchèd plains of Afric's sand,
A sterile and a wild, unlovely land,
    Art always scorched with hot desires,
15   Yet, barren quite, didst thou not bring
Monsters and serpents forth thyself to sting.

Thou that bewitchest men, whilst thou dost dwell
    Like a close conjurer in his cell,

And fear'st the day's discovering eye!
20   No wonder 'tis at all that thou shouldst be
Such tedious and unpleasant company,
      Who liv'st so melancholily!
      Thou thing of subtle, slippery kind
Which women lose and yet no man can find.

25   Although I think thou never found wilt be,
      Yet I'm resolved to search for thee.
      The search itself rewards the pains:
So, though the chemic his great secret miss
(For neither it in art nor nature is)
30   Yet things well worth his toil he gains,
      And does his charge and labour pay
With good unsought experiments by the way.

Say what thou wilt chastity is no more
      Thee than a porter is his door.
35   In vain to honour they pretend
Who guard themselves with ramparts and with walls:
Them only fame the truly valiant calls
      Who can an open breach defend.
      Of thy quick loss can be no doubt,
40   Within so hated and so loved without.

WEEPING

See where she sits and in what comely wise
      Drops tears more fair than others' eyes.
Ah, charming maid let not ill fortune see
      Th'attire thy sorrow wears,
5   Nor know the beauty of thy tears—
For she'll still come to dress herself in thee.

As stars reflect on waters so I spy
      In every drop, methinks, her eye.
The baby which lives there and always plays
10   In that illustrious sphere
      Like a Narcissus does appear,
Whilst in his flood the lovely boy did gaze.

Ne'er yet did I behold so glorious weather
      As this sunshine and rain together.
15   Pray heaven her forehead, that pure hill of snow,
      (For some such fountain we must find
      To waters of so fair a kind)
Melt not to feed that beauteous stream below.

20   Ah, mighty love, that it were inward heat
        Which made this precious limbeck sweat!
     But what, alas, ah what does it avail
       That she weeps tears so wondrous cold
       As scarce the ass' foot can hold:
     So cold that I admire they fall not hail.

DISCRETION

Discreet? What means this word discreet?
    A curse on all discretion!
This barbarous term you will not meet
    In all love's lexicon.

5   Jointure, portion, gold, estate,
      Houses, household stuff, or land—
The low conveniences of fate—
      Are Greek no lovers understand.

Believe me, beauteous one, when love
10   Enters into a breast,
The two first things it does remove
    Are friends and interest.

Passion's half-blind, nor can endure
    The careful, scrup'lous eyes,
15 Or else I could not love I'm sure
     One who in love were wise.

Men in such tempests tossed about
     Will, without grief or pain,
Cast all their goods and riches out,
20   Themselves their port to gain.

As well might martyrs who do choose
    That sacred death to take
Mourn for the clothes which they must lose
    When they're bound naked to the stake.

THE CURE

Come doctor, use thy roughest art,
    Thou canst not cruel prove;
Cut, burn and torture every part
    To heal me of my love.

5   There is no danger if the pain
         Should me to a fever bring:
       Compared with heats I now sustain
         A fever is so cool a thing
         (Like drink which feverish men desire)
10   That I should hope 'twould almost quench my fire.

THE SEPARATION

       Ask me not what my love shall do or be
       (Love which is soul to body, and soul of me)
         When I am separated from thee.
         Alas I might as easily show
5   What after death the soul will do—
       'Twill last, I'm sure, and that is all we know.

       The thing called soul will never stir nor move,
       But all that while a lifeless carcass prove,
         For 'tis the body of my love:
10   Not that my love will fly away,
       But still continue as—they say—
       Sad, troubled ghosts about their graves do stray.

HER UNBELIEF

       'Tis a strange kind of ignorance this in you,
         That you your victories should not spy,
         Victories gotten by your eye!
       That your bright beams, as those of comets do,
5   Should kill but know not how nor who.

       That truly you my idol might appear;
         Whilst all the people smell and see
         The odorous flames I offer thee,
       Thou sit'st and dost not see, nor smell, nor hear
10   Thy constant, zealous worshipper.

       They see't too well who at my fires repine,
         Nay th'unconcerned themselves do prove
         Quick-eyed enough to spy my love:
       Nor does the cause in thy face clearlier shine
15   Than the effect appears in mine.

Fair infidel, by what unjust decree
   Must I, who with such restless care
   Would make this truth to thee appear,
Must I, who preach it and pray for it, be
20   Damned by thy incredulity?

I by thy unbelief am guiltless slain.
   O have but faith and then that you
   May know that faith for to be true,
It shall itself by a miracle maintain
25   And raise me from the dead again.

Meanwhile my hopes may seem to be o'erthrown:
   But lovers' hopes are full of art,
   And thus dispute, that since my heart,
Though in thy breast, yet is not by thee known,
30   Perhaps thou mayst not know thine own.

THE INCURABLE

I tried if books would cure my love but found
   Love made them nonsense all.
I applied receipts of business to my wound,
   But stirring did the pain recall.

5 As well might men who in a fever fry
   Mathematic doubts debate;
As well might men who mad in darkness lie
   Write the dispatches of a state.

I tried devotion, sermons, frequent prayer,
10   But those did worse than useless prove:
For prayers are turned to sin in those who are
   Out of charity or in love.

I tried in wine to drown the mighty care,
   But wine, alas, was oil to the fire;
15 Like drunkards' eyes my troubled fancy there
   Did double the desire.

I tried what mirth and gaiety would do,
   And mixed with pleasant companies:
My mirth did graceless and insipid grow
20   And 'bove a clinch it could not rise.

Nay—God forgive me for't—at last I tried
   'Gainst this some new desire to stir
And loved again, but 'twas where I espied
   Some faint resemblances of her.

25   The physic made me worse with which I strove
   This mortal ill t'expel,
As wholesome medicines the disease improve
   There where they work not well.

THE INNOCENT ILL

Though all thy gestures and discourses be
   Coined and stamped by modesty;
   Though from thy tongue ne'er slipped away
One word which nuns at th'altar might not say,
5   Yet such a sweetness, such a grace
   In all thy speech appear,
   That what to th'eye a beauteous face,
   That thy tongue is to the ear;
So cunningly it wounds the heart,
10   It strikes such heat through every part,
That thou a tempter worse than Satan art.

Though in thy thoughts scarce any tracks have bin
   So much as of original sin,
   Such charms thy beauty wears as might
15   Desires in dying saints excite.
   Thou with strange adultery
   Dost in each breast a brothel keep:
   Awake, all men do lust for thee
   And some enjoy thee when they sleep.
20   Ne'er before did woman live
   Who to such multitudes did give
The root and cause of sin, but only Eve.

Though in thy breast so quick a pity be
   That a fly's death's a wound to thee.
25   Though savage and rock-hearted those
Appear that weep not even romance's woes,
   Yet ne'er before was tyrant known
   Whose rage was of so large extent:
   The ills thou dost are whole thine own;
30   Thou'rt principal and instrument.

In all the deaths that come from you
You do the treble office do
Of judge, of torturer and of weapon too.

Thou lovely instrument of angry fate
35   Which God did for our faults create;
    Thou pleasant, universal ill,
Which sweet as health, yet like a plague dost kill;
    Thou kind, well-natured tyranny;
    Thou chaste committer of a rape;
40   Thou voluntary destiny
    Which no man can or would escape!
So gentle and so glad to spare,
    So wondrous good and wondrous fair,
We know, even the destroying angels are.

DIALOGUE

She   What have we done? What cruel passion moved thee
    Thus to ruin her that loved thee?
Me thou hast robbed but what art thou
Thyself the richer now?
5   Shame succeeds the short-lived pleasure,
So soon is spent and gone, this thy ill-gotten treasure.

He   We have done no harm, nor was it theft in me
    But noblest charity in thee.
    I'll the well-gotten pleasure
10   Safe in my memory treasure.
    What though the flower itself do waste?
The essence from it drawn does long and sweeter last.

She   No, I'm undone: my honour thou hast slain
    And nothing can restore't again.
15   Art and labour to bestow
    Upon the carcass of it now
    Is but t'embalm a body dead:
The figure may remain; the life and beauty's fled.

He   Never, my dear, was honour yet undone
20   By love, but indiscretion.
    To the wise it all things does allow,
    And cares not what we do but how.
    Like tapers shut in ancient urns
Unless it let in air forever shines and burns.

25 *She*   Thou first, perhaps, who didst the fault commit
            Wilt make thy wicked boast of it.
        For men, with Roman pride, above
        The conquest do the triumph love,
           Nor think a perfect victory gained
30   Unless they through the streets their captive lead enchained.

    He   Whoe'er his secret joys has open laid
            The bawd to his own wife is made.
        Beside what boast is left for me
        Whose whole wealth's a gift from thee?
35   'Tis you the conqueror are; 'tis you
   Who have not only ta'en but bound and gagged me too.

   She   Though public punishment we escape, the sin
            Will rack and torture us within:
        Guilt and sin our bosom bears;
40   And though fair yet the fruit appears,
        That worm which now the core does waste
   When long 't has gnawed within will break the skin at last.

    He   That thirsty drink, that hungry food I sought,
            That wounded balm, is all my fault.
45   And thou in pity didst apply
        The kind and only remedy.
        The cause absolves the crime, since me
   So mighty force did move, so mighty goodness thee.

   She   Curse on thine arts! Methinks I hate thee now—
50   And yet I'm sure I love thee too!
        I'm angry but my wrath will prove
        More innocent than did thy love.
        Thou hast this day undone me quite,
   Yet wilt undo me more shouldst thou not come at night.

LOVE GIVEN OVER

It is enough: enough of time and pain
      Hast thou consumed in vain.
      Leave wretched Cowley leave
      Thyself with shadows to deceive.
5 Think that already lost which thou must never gain.

Three of thy lustiest and thy freshest years
   Tossed in storms of hopes and fears,
     Like helpless ships that be
     Set on fire i'the midst o'the sea,
10 Have all been burnt in love and all been drowned in tears.

Resolve then on it and by force or art
   Free thy unlucky heart,
     Since fate does disapprove
     Th'ambition of thy love,
15 And not one star in heaven offers to take thy part.

If e'er I clear my heart from this desire,
   If e'er it home to its breast retire,
     It ne'er shall wander more about
     Though thousand beauties called it out.
20 A lover burnt like me forever dreads the fire.

The pox, the plague, and every small disease
   May come as oft as ill fate please,
     But death and love are never found
     To give a second wound:
25 We're by those serpents bit but we're devoured by these.

Alas, what comfort is't that I am grown
   Secure of being again o'erthrown?
     Since such an enemy needs not fear
     Lest anyone should quarter there,
30 Who has not only sacked but quite burnt down the town.

ODES

OF WIT

Tell me, O tell, what kind of thing is wit,
   Thou who master art of it.
For the first matter loves variety less;
Less women love't, either in love or dress.
5   A thousand different shapes it bears,
     Comely in thousand shapes appears.
Yonder we saw it plain, and here 'tis now,
Like spirits in a place, we know not how.

London, that vents of false ware so much store,
10   In no ware deceives us more:
For men led by the colours and the shape
Like Zeuxis' birds fly to the painted grape.
               Some things do through our judgement pass
               As through a multiplying glass;
15   And sometimes, if the object be too far,
We take a falling meteor for a star.

Hence 'tis a wit, that greatest word of fame,
               Grows such a common name,
And wits by our creation they become
20   Just so as tit'lar bishops made at Rome.
               'Tis not a tale, 'tis not a jest
               Admired with laughter at a feast,
Nor florid talk which can that title gain:
The proofs of wit forever must remain.

25   'Tis not to force some lifeless verses meet
               With their five gouty feet.
All everywhere like man's must be the soul,
And reason the inferior powers control.
               Such were the numbers which could call
30   The stones into the Theban wall.
Such miracles are ceased, and now we see
No towns or houses raised by poetry.

Yet 'tis not to adorn and gild each part:
               That shows more cost than art.
35   Jewels at nose and lips but ill appear—
Rather than all things wit, let none be there.
               Several lights will not be seen
               If there be nothing else between.
Men doubt, because they stand so thick i'the sky,
40   If those be stars which paint the galaxy.

'Tis not when two like words make up one noise:
               Jests for Dutch men and English boys—
In which who finds out wit the same may see
In anagrams and acrostics poetry.
45   Much less can that have any place
               At which a virgin hides her face:
Such dross the fire must purge away; 'tis just
The author blush there where the reader must.

'Tis not such lines as almost crack the stage
50   When Bajazet begins to rage

Nor a tall metaphor in the bombast way;
Nor the dry chips of short-lunged Seneca,
  Nor upon all things to obtrude
  And force some odd similitude.
55 What is it then, which like the power divine
We only can by negatives define?

In a true piece of wit all things must be
  Yet all things there agree.
As in the ark, joined without force or strife,
60 All creatures dwelt, all creatures that had life;
  Or as the primitive forms of all
  (If we compare great things with small)
Which without discord or confusion lie
In that strange mirror of the deity.

65 But love that moulds one man up out of two
  Makes me forget and injure you.
I took you for myself sure when I thought
That you in anything were to be taught.
  Correct my error with thy pen,
70   And if any ask me then
What thing right wit and height of genius is,
I'll only show your lines and say 'tis this.

UPON HIS MAJESTY'S RESTORATION
AND RETURN

(Virgil: Quod optanti divum promittere nemo Auderet, volvenda dies,
en, attulit ultro)

Now blessings on you all, ye peaceful stars
Which meet at last so kindly, and dispense
Your universal, gentle influence
To calm the stormy world and still the rage of wars.
5   Nor whilst around the continent
Plenipotentary beams ye sent,
  Did your pacific lights disdain
  In their large treaty to contain
The world apart, o'er which do reign
10 Your seven fair brethren, of great Charles his wain.
No star amongst ye all did, I believe,
  Such vigorous assistance give
  As that which thirty years ago
  At Charles his birth did, in despite
15   Of the proud sun's meridian light,

His future glories and this year foreshow:
   No less effects than these we may
   Be assured of from that powerful ray,
Which could outface the sun and overcome the day.

20   Auspicious star again arise
And take thy noontide station in the skies;
Again all heaven prodigiously adorn,
   For lo thy Charles again is born!
   He then was born with and to pain:
25   With and to joy he's born again.
   And wisely for this second birth,
   By which thou certain wert to bless
The land with full and flourishing happiness,
   Thou mad'st of that fair month thy choice
30   In which heaven, air, and sea, and earth,
And all that's in them all does smile and does rejoice.
'Twas a right season, and the very ground
Ought with a face of paradise to be found,
   Then when we were to entertain
35   Felicity and innocence again.

Shall we again, good heaven, that blessèd pair behold
Which the abusèd people fondly sold
For the bright fruit of the forbidden tree,
   By seeking all like gods to be?
40   Will peace her Halcyon nest venture to build
   Upon a shore with shipwrecks filled?
And trust that sea where she can hardly say
   Sh'has known these twenty years one calmy day?
   Ah, mild and gall-less dove
45   Which dost the pure and candid dwellings love,
   Canst thou in Albion still delight,
   Still canst thou think it white?
Will ever fair religion appear
In these deformèd ruins? Will she clear
50   Th'Augean stables of her churches here?
   Will justice hazard to be seen
Where a High Court of Justice e'er has been?
   Will not the tragic scene
And Bradshaw's bloody ghost affright her there,
55   Her who shall never fear?
Then may Whitehall for Charles his seat be fit,
If justice shall endure at Westminster to sit.

   Of all, methinks, we least should see
The cheerful looks again of liberty.

60   That name of Cromwell which does freshly still
The curses of so many sufferers fill,
    Is still enough to make her stay
    And jealous for a while remain,
Lest, as a tempest carried him away,
65   Some hurricane should bring him back again.
    Or she might justlier be afraid
Lest that great serpent, which was all a tail
(And in his pois'nous folds whole nations prisoners made)
    Should a third time perhaps prevail
70   To join again and with worse sting arise,
As it had done when cut in pieces twice.
    Return, return, ye sacred four,
And dread your perished enemies no more:
    Your fears are causeless all, and vain
75   Whilst you return in Charles his train,
For God does him that he might you restore,
    Nor shall the world him only call
Defender of the faith, but of ye all.

    Along with you plenty and riches go,
80   With a full tide to every port they flow;
With a warm, fruitful wind o'er all the country blow.
Honour does as ye march her trumpet sound
    The arts encompass you around,
    And against all alarms of fear
85   Safety itself brings up the rear:
And in the head of this angelic band,
Lo, how the goodly prince at last does stand,
O righteous God, on his own happy land.
'Tis happy now, which could, with so much ease
90   Recover from so desperate a disease;
    A various, complicated ill
Whose every symptom was enough to kill;
    In which one part of three frenzy possessed
    And lethargy the rest.
95   'Tis happy which no bleeding does endure
    A surfeit of such blood to cure.
    'Tis happy, which beholds the flame
In which by hostile hands it ought to burn,
    Or that which if from heaven it came
100   It did but well deserve all into bonfire turn.

    We feared, and almost touched the black degree
    Of instant expectation,
    That the three dreadful angels we
Of famine, sword, and plague should here established see;

105 God's great triumvirate of desolation
      To scourge and to destroy the sinful nation.
      Justly might heaven protectors such as those
      And such committees for their safety impose
      Upon a land which scarcely better chose.
110   We feared that the fanatic war
      Which men against God's houses did declare
      Would from th'almighty enemy bring down
          A sure destruction on our own.
      We read th'instructive histories which tell
115   Of all those endless mischiefs that befell
      The sacred town which God had loved so well,
      After that fatal curse had once been said
      'His blood be upon ours and on our children's head'.
      We knew, though there a greater blood was spilt
120   'Twas scarcely done with greater guilt.
      We know those miseries did befall
      Whilst they rebelled against that prince whom all
      The rest of mankind did the love and joy of mankind call.

          Already was the shaken nation
125   Into a wild and deformed chaos brought,
          And it was hasting on, we thought,
      Even to the last of ills, annihilation,
      When in the midst of this confusèd night,
      Lo, the blessed spirit moved and there was light.
130   For in the glorious general's previous ray
          We saw a new-created day.
      We by it saw, though yet in mists it shone,
      The beauteous work of order moving on.
      Where are the men who bragged that God did bless,
135   And with the marks of good success
      Sign his allowance of their wickedness?
      Vain men, who thought the divine power to find
      In the fierce thunder and the violent wind.
          God came not till the storm was past,
140   In the still voice of peace he came at last.
      The cruel business of destruction
      May by the claws of the great fiend be done.
      Here, here we see th'Almighty's hand indeed,
      Both by the beauty of the work we see't and by the speed.

145   He who had seen the noble British heir,
      Even in that ill, disadvantageous light,
      With which misfortune strives t'abuse our sight;
      He who had seen him in his cloud so bright;
          He who had seen the double pair
150   Of brothers heavenly good and sisters heavenly fair,

Might have perceived, methinks, with ease—
But wicked men see only what they please—
That God had no intent t'extinguish quite
    The pious king's eclipsèd right.
155 He who had seen how by the power divine
All the young branches of this royal line
Did in their fire without consuming shine;
How through a rough red sea they had been led,
By wonders guarded and by wonders fed;
160 How many years of trouble and distress
They'd wandered in their fatal wilderness,
And yet did never murmur or repine;
    Might, methinks, plainly understand
    That after all these conquered trials past
165 Th'almighty mercy would at last
Conduct them with a strong, unerring hand
    To their own promised land.
    For all the glories of the earth
    Ought to be entailed by right of birth,
170   And all heaven's blessings to come down
Upon his race, to whom alone was given
The double royalty of earth and heaven,
Who crowned the kingly with the martyr's crown.

The martyr's blood was said of old to be
175   The seed from whence the church did grow.
The royal blood which dying Charles did sow
Becomes no less the seed of royalty.
    'Twas in dishonour sown;
    We find it now in glory grown:
180 The grave could but the dross of it devour;
'Twas sown in weakness and 'tis raised in power.

We now the question well decided see
    Which eastern wits did once contest
        At the great monarch's feast—
185 Of all on earth what things the strongest be:
And some for women, some for wine did plead,
    (That is for folly and for rage)
Two things which we have known indeed
        Strong in this latter age.
190   But as 'tis proved by heaven at length
    The king and truth have greatest strength
    When they their sacred force unite
        And twine into one right.
No frantic commonwealths or tyrannies,
195   No cheats and perjuries and lies,
    No nets of human policies,

No stores of arms or gold (though you could join
Those of Peru to the great London mine),
No towns, no fleets by sea or troops by land,
200　No deeply entrenched islands can withstand,
　　　　Or any small resistance bring
Against the naked truth and the unarmèd king.

The foolish lights which travellers beguile
　　End the same night when they begin;
205　No art so far can upon nature win
As e'er to put out stars or long keep meteors in.
Where's now that *ignis fatuus* which e'erwhile
　　Misled our wand'ring isle?
　　Where's that impostor Cromwell gone?
210　Where's now that falling star his son?
Where's the large comet now whose raging flame
So fatal to our monarchy became?
Which o'er our heads in such proud horror stood,
Insatiate with our ruin and our blood?
215　The fiery tail did to vast length extend,
And twice for want of fuel did expire
　　And twice renewed the dismal fire,
Though long the tail, we saw at last its end.
　　The flames of one triumphant day,
220　　Which like an anti-comet here
　　Did fatally to that appear,
　　For ever frighted it away.
Then did th'allotted hour of dawning right
　　First strike our ravished sight,
225　Which malice or which art no more could stay
Than witch's charms can a retardment bring
　　To the resuscitation of the day
　　Or resurrection of the spring.
We welcome both and with improved delight
230　Bless the preceding winter and the night.

Man ought his future happiness to fear:
　　If he be always happy here
　　He wants the bleeding mark of grace,
The circumcision of the chosen race.
235　　If no one part of him supplies
　　The duty of a sacrifice,
　　He is, we doubt, reserved entire
　　As a whole victim for the fire:
Besides, even in this world below,
240　To those who never did ill fortune know,
The good does nauseous or insipid grow.

Consider man's whole life and you'll confess
The sharp ingredient of some bad success
Is that which gives the taste to all his happiness.
245   But the true method of felicity
      Is when the worst
      Of human life is placed the first,
And when the child's correction proves to be
      The cause of perfecting the man.
250   Let our weak days lead up the van;
    Let the brave second and triarian band
      Firm against all impression stand:
      The first we may defeated see—
The virtue and the force of these are sure of victory.

255   Such are the years, great Charles, which now we see
      Begin their glorious march with thee:
Long may their march to heaven and still triumphant be.
      Now thou art gotten once before
    Ill fortune never shall o'ertake thee more.
260   To see't again and pleasure in it find
      Cast a disdainful look behind:
Things which offend when present, and affright,
    In memory, well painted, move delight.
      Enjoy then all thy afflictions now;
265   Thy royal father's came at last;
      The martyrdom's already past,
      And different crowns to both ye owe.
No gold did e'er the kingly temples bind
    Than thine more tried and more refined.
270   As a choice medal for heaven's treasury
God did stamp first upon one side of thee
The image of his suffering humanity;
On th'other side, turned now to sight, does shine
The glorious image of his power divine.

275   So when the wisest poets seek
    In all their liveliest colours to set forth
      A picture of heroic worth—
    The pious Trojan or the prudent Greek—
    They choose some comely prince of heavenly birth
280   (No proud, gigantic son of earth
    Who strives t'usurp the gods' forbidden seat)
    They feed him not with nectar and the meat
      That cannot without joy be ate,
    But in the cold of want and storms of adverse chance
285   They harden his young virtue by degrees:
    The beauteous drop first into ice does freeze
    And into solid crystal next advance.

His murdered friends and kindred he does see
    And from his flaming country flee.
290   Much is he tossed at sea and much at land
Does long the force of angry gods withstand.
He does long troubles and long wars sustain
    Ere he his fatal birthright gain.
    With no less time or labour can
295   Destiny build up such a man,
    Who's with sufficient virtue filled
    His ruined country to rebuild.

    Nor without cause are arms from heaven
To such a hero by the poets given.
300   No human metal is of force t'oppose
    So many and so violent blows.
    Such was the helmet, breastplate, shield,
    Which Charles in all attacks did wield.
And all the weapons malice e'er could try,
305   Of all the several makes of wicked policy,
Against this armour struck, but at the stroke,
Like swords of ice, in thousand pieces broke.
To angels and their brethren spirits above
No show on earth can sure so pleasant prove
310   As when they great misfortunes see
    With courage borne and decency.
So were they borne when Worcester's dismal day
Did all the terrors of black fate display;
So were they borne when no disguise's cloud
315   His inward royalty could shroud;
And one of th'angels whom just God did send
    To guard him in his nobler flight—
A troop of angels did him then attend—
Assured me in a vision th'other night
320   That he (and who could better judge than he?)
    Did then more greatness in him see,
    More lustre and more majesty,
Than all his coronation pomp can show to human eye.

Him and his royal brothers when I saw
325   New marks of honour and of glory
    From their affronts and sufferings draw,
And look like heavenly saints even in their purgatory;
Methoughts I saw the three Judaean youths
(Three unburnt martyrs for the noblest truths)
330   In the Chaldean furnace walk:
How cheerfully and unconcerned they talk!
No hair is singed, no smallest beauty blasted:
    Like painted lamps they shine unwasted.

The greedy fire itself dares not be fed
335 With the blessed oil of an anointed head.
    The honourable flame—
Which rather light we ought to name—
Does like a glory compass them around,
And their whole body's crowned.
340 What are these two bright creatures which we see
    Walk with the royal three
    In the same ordeal fire,
    And mutual joys inspire?
    Sure they the beauteous sisters are,
345   Who whilst they seek to bear their share,
Will suffer no affliction to be there.
Less favour to those three of old was shown,
    To solace with their company
    The fiery trials of adversity:
350 Two angels join with these, the others had but one.

Come forth, come forth, ye men of God beloved,
    And let the power now of that flame
Which against you so impotent became
    On all your enemies be proved.
355 Come, mighty Charles, desire of nations, come;
    Come, you triumphant exile, home.
He's come; he's safe at shore; I hear the noise
Of a whole land which does at once rejoice;
I hear th'united people's sacred voice.
360   The sea which circles us around
    Ne'er sent to land so loud a sound:
The mighty shout sends to the sea a gale
    And swells up every sail:
The bells and guns are scarcely heard at all,
365 The artificial joy's drowned by the natural.
All England but one bonfire seems to be,
One Etna shooting flames into the sea.
The starry worlds which shine to us afar
    Take ours at this time for a star.
370 With wine all rooms, with wine the conduits flow,
And we, the priests of a poetic rage,
    Wonder that in this Golden Age
    The rivers too should not do so.
There is no stoic sure who would not now
375   Even some excess allow,
And grant that one wild fit of cheerful folly
Should end our twenty years of dismal melancholy.

Where's now the royal mother, where,
    To take her mighty share

380   In this so ravishing sight,
  And with the part she takes to add to the delight?
   Ah, why art thou not here,
  Thou always best, and now the happiest queen,
  To see our joy and with new joy be seen?
385 God has a bright example made of thee
   To show that womankind may be
  Above that sex which her superior seems,
  In wisely managing the wide extremes
  Of great affliction, great felicity.
390 How well those different virtues thee become,
  Daughter of triumphs, wife of martyrdom!
  Thy princely mind with so much courage bore
  Affliction that it dares return no more;
  With so much goodness used felicity
395 That it cannot refrain from coming back to thee—
  'Tis come, and seen today in all its bravery.

  Who's that heroic person leads it on
   And gives it like a glorious bride
   (Richly adorned with nuptial pride)
400   Into the hands now of thy son?
  'Tis the good general, the man of praise,
   Whom God at last in gracious pity
   Did to the enthrallèd nation raise
   Their great Zerubbabel to be,
405 To loose the bonds of long captivity
  And to rebuild their temple and their city.
  For ever blessed may he and his remain,
  Who with a vast though less-appearing gain
  Preferred the solid great above the vain,
410 And to the world this princely truth has shown
  That more 'tis to restore than to usurp a crown.
  Thou worthiest person of the British story
   (Though 'tis not small, the British glory)
  Did I not know my humble verse must be
415 But ill-proportioned to the heighth of thee,
   Thou and the world should see
  How much my muse, the foe of flattery,
  Does make true praise her labour and design—
  An *Iliad* or an *Aeneid* should be thine.

420 And ill should we deserve this happy day
   If no acknowledgements we pay
   To you, great patriots of the two
   Most truly other Houses now,
  Who have redeemed from hatred and from shame
425 A parliament's once venerable name;

And now the title of a House restore
To that which was but slaughter-house before.
If my advice, ye worthies, might be ta'en
    Within those reverend places,
430   Which now your living presence graces,
Your marble statues always should remain
To keep alive your useful memory
And to your successors th'example be
Of truth, religion, reason, loyalty.
435   For though a firmly settled peace
May shortly make your public labours cease,
The grateful nation will with joy consent
    That in this sense you should be said
    (Though yet the name sounds with some dread)
440 To be the Long, the Endless, Parliament.

ANACREONTICS

I
LOVE

I'll sing of heroes and of kings:
In mighty numbers, mighty things,
Begin, my muse—but, lo, the strings
To my great song rebellious prove;
5   The strings will sound of nought but love.
I broke them all and put on new;
'Tis this or nothing sure will do.
These sure, said I, will me obey,
These sure heroic notes will play.
10   Straight I began with thund'ring Jove
And all th'immortal powers but love.
Love smiled and from my enfeebled lyre
Came gentle airs, such as inspire
Melting love, soft desire.
15   Farewell then heroes, farewell kings,
And mighty numbers, mighty things:
Love tunes my heart just to my strings.

II
DRINKING

The thirsty earth soaks up the rain
And drinks and gapes for drink again.

The plants suck in the earth and are
With constant drinking fresh and fair.
5   The sea itself, which one would think
Should have but little need of drink,
Drinks ten thousand rivers up,
So filled that they o'erflow the cup.
The busy sun—and one would guess
10   By's drunken, fiery face no less—
Drinks up the sea and when h'as done
The moon and stars drink up the sun.
They drink and dance by their own light,
They drink and revel all the night.
15   Nothing in nature's sober found,
But an eternal health goes round.
Fill up the bowl then, fill it high,
Fill all the glasses there; for why
Should every creature drink but I,
20   Why, man of morals, tell me why?

V
AGE

Oft am I by the women told
Poor Anacreon thou grow'st old.
Look how thy hairs are falling all,
Poor Anacreon how they fall!
5   Whether I grow old or no
By th'effects I do not know.
This I know without being told:
'Tis time to live if I grow old;
'Tis time short pleasures now to take,
10   Of little life the best to make
And manage wisely the last stake.

VI
THE ACCOUNT

When all the stars are by thee told
(The endless sums of heavenly gold)
Or when the hairs are reckoned all
From sickly Autumn's head that fall,
5   Or when the drops that make the sea,
Whilst all her sands thy counters be:

Thou then and thou alone mayst prove
Th'arithmetician of my love.
An hundred loves at Athens score,
10   At Corinth write an hundred more.
Fair Corinth does such beauties bear
So few is an escaping there.
Write then at Chios seventy three;
Write then at Lesbos—let me see—
15   Write me at Lesbos ninety down,
Full ninety loves, and half a one.
And next to these let me present
The fair Ionian regiment;
And next the Carian company—
20   Five hundred both, effectively.
Three hundred more at Rhodes and Crete:
Three hundred 'tis I'm sure, complete;
For arms at Crete each face does bear
And every eye's an archer there.
25   Go on, this stop why dost thou make?
Thou think'st perhaps that I mistake.
Seems this to thee too great a sum?
Why, many thousands are to come.
The mighty Xerxes could not boast
30   Such different nations in his host.
On, for my love if thou be'st weary
Must find some better secretary.
I have not yet my Persian told,
Nor yet my Syrian loves enrolled,
35   Nor Indian, nor Arabian,
Nor Cyprian loves, nor African,
Nor Scythian nor Italian flames:
There's a whole map behind of names.
Of gentle love i'the temperate zone
40   And cold ones in the frigid one—
Cold, frozen loves with which I pine
And parchèd loves beneath the line.

X
THE GRASSHOPPER

Happy insect, what can be
In happiness compared to thee?
Fed with nourishment divine,
The dewy morning's gentle wine!
5   Nature waits upon thee still
And thy verdant cup does fill:

'Tis filled wherever thou dost tread,
Nature's self's thy Ganymed.
Thou dost drink and dance and sing,
10   Happier than the happiest king!
All the fields which thou dost see,
All the plants, belong to thee;
All that summer hours produce,
Fertile made with early juice.
15   Man for thee does sow and plough:
Farmer he and landlord thou!
Thou dost innocently joy,
Nor does thy luxury destroy.
The shepherd gladly heareth thee
20   More harmonious than he;
Thee country hinds with gladness hear,
Prophet of the ripened year!
Thee Phoebus loves and does inspire;
Phoebus is himself thy sire.
25   To thee of all things upon earth
Life is no longer than thy mirth.
Happy insect, happy thou,
Dost neither age nor winter know:
But when thou'st drunk and danced and sung
30   Thy fill the flowery leaves among
(Voluptuous and wise withall,
Epicurean animal!)
Sated with thy summer feast
Thou retirest to endless rest.

MISCELLANEOUS

IN IMITATION OF MARTIAL'S EPIGRAM
(*Si tecum mihi chare Martialis*, &. L.5. Ep.21)

If, dearest friend, it my good fate might be
T'enjoy at once a quiet life and thee;
If we for happiness could leisure find
And wand'ring time into a method bind,
5   We should not, sure, the great men's favour need
Nor on long hopes the court's thin diet feed.
We should not patience find daily to hear
The calumnies and flatteries spoken there.
We should not the lords' tables humbly use
10   Or talk in ladies' chambers love and news;

But books and wise discourse, gardens and fields,
And all the joys that unmixed nature yields.
Thick summer shades where winter still does lie,
Bright winter fires that summer's part supply.
15 Sleep not controlled by cares, confined to night,
Or bound to any rule but appetite.
Free but not savage or ungracious mirth,
Rich wines to give it quick and easy birth.
A few companions, which ourselves should choose,
20 A gentle mistress and a gentler muse.
Such, dearest friend, such without doubt should be
Our place, our business and our company.
Now, to himself alas does neither live,
But sees good suns, of which we are to give
25 A strict account, set and march thick away:
Knows a man how to live and does he stay?

THE CHRONICLE
(A ballad)

Margarita first possessed,
    If I remember well, my breast;
Margarita first of all,
But when a while the wanton maid
5 With my restless heart had played,
    Martha took the flying ball.

Martha soon it did resign
    To the beauteous Catherine;
    Beauteous Catherine gave place
10 (Though both lothe and angry she to part
With the possession of my heart)
    To Elisa's conqu'ring face.

Elisa till this hour might reign
    Had she not evil councils ta'en.
15   Fundamental laws she broke
And still new favourites she chose,
Till up in arms my passions rose
    And cast away her yoke.

Mary then and gentle Ann
20   Both to reign at once began:
    Alternately they swayed,
And sometimes Mary was the fair
And sometimes Ann the crown did wear,
    And sometimes both I obeyed.

25   Another Mary then arose
          And did rigorous laws impose:
          A mighty tyrant she!
      Long, alas, I should have been
      Under that iron-sceptered queen,
30   Had not Rebecca set me free.

      When fair Rebecca set me free
          'Twas then a golden time with me;
          But soon those pleasures fled,
      For the gracious princess died
35   In her youth and beauty's pride,
          And Judith reignèd in her stead.

      One month, three days and half an hour
          Judith held the sovereign power.
          Wondrous beautiful her face,
40   But so weak and small her wit
      That she to govern was unfit,
          And so Susanna took her place.

      But when Isabella came,
          Armed with a resistless flame
45   And th'artillery of her eye;
      Whilst she proudly marched about
      Greater conquests to find out,
          She beat out Susan by the by.

      But in her place I then obeyed
50   Black-eyed Bess, her viceroy-maid,
          To whom ensued a vacancy.
      Thousand worse passions then possessed
      The interregnum of my breast:
          Bless me from such an anarchy!

55   Gentle Henrietta then,
          And a third Mary next began,
          Then Joan and Jane and Audria;
      And then a pretty Thomasine,
      And then another Catherine,
60   And then a long *et cetera*.

      But should I now to you relate
          The strength and riches of their state,
          The powder, patches and the pins,
      The ribbons, jewels and the rings,
65   The lace, the paint and warlike things
          That make up all their magazines:

If I should tell the politic arts
   To take and keep men's hearts;
   The letters, embassies and spies,
70 The frowns and smiles and flatteries,
The quarrels, tears and perjuries,
   Numberless, nameless mysteries!

And all the little lime-twigs laid
   By Matchavil the waiting-maid;
75 I more volomnious should grow
(Chiefly if I like them should tell
All change of weathers that befell)
   Than Holinshed or Stow.

But I will briefer with them be,
80 Since few of them were long with me.
   A higher and a nobler strain
My present empress does claim:
Helenora, first o'the name,
   Whom God grant long to reign!

PROMETHEUS ILL-PAINTED

How wretchèd does Prometheus' state appear,
Whilst he his second misery suffers here!
Draw him no more lest as he tortured stands
He blames great Jove's less than the painter's hands.
5 It would the vultures' cruelty outgo
If once again his liver thus should grow.
Pity him, Jove, and his bold theft allow,
The flames he once stole from thee grant him now.

TO THE BISHOP OF LINCOLN,
UPON HIS ENLARGEMENT OUT OF THE TOWER

Pardon, my lord, that I am come so late
T'express my joy for your return of fate.
So when injurious chance did you deprive
Of liberty, at first I could not grieve:
5 My thoughts a while like you imprisoned lay—
Great joys as well as sorrows make a stay.

They hinder one another in the crowd
And none are heard whilst all would speak aloud.
Should every man's officious gladness haste
10   And be afraid to show itself the last,
The throng of gratulations now would be
Another loss to you of liberty.
When of your freedom men the news did hear,
Where it was wished for—that is everywhere—
15   'Twas like the speech which from your lips does fall—
As soon as it was heard it ravished all,
So Tully did from exile come:
Thus longed for he returned, and cherished Rome,
Which could no more his tongue and councils miss:
20   Rome, the world's head, was nothing without his.
Wrong to those sacred ashes I should do
Should I compare any to him but you:
You, to whom art and nature did dispense
The consulship of wit and eloquence.
25   Nor did your fate differ from his at all
Because the doom of exile was his fall,
For the whole world without a native home
Is nothing but a prison of larger room.
But like a melting woman suffered he,
30   He who before outdid humanity:
Nor could his spirit constant and steadfast prove,
Whose art 't had been and greatest end to move.
You put ill fortune in so good a dress
That it outshone other men's happiness:
35   Had your prosperity always clearly gone
As your high merits would have led it on,
You had half been lost, and an example then
But for the happy, the least part of men.
Your very sufferings did so graceful show
40   That some straight envied your affliction too.
For a clear conscience and heroic mind
In ills their business and their glory find.
So though less worthy stones are drowned in night
The faithful diamond keeps his native light,
45   And is obliged to darkness for a ray
That would be more oppressed than helped by day.
Your soul then most showed her unconquered power,
Was stronger and more armèd than the tower.
Sure unkind fate will tempt your spirit no more:
50   Sh'has tried her weakness and your strength before.
T'oppose him still who once has conquered so
Were now to be your rebel not your foe.
Fortune henceforth will more of Providence have
And rather be your friend than be your slave.

THE TREE OF KNOWLEDGE
THAT THERE IS NO KNOWLEDGE
(Against the dogmatists)

The sacred tree midst the fair orchard grew;
   The phoenix truth did on it rest
   And built his perfumed nest.
That right Porphyrian tree which did true logic show
5   Each leaf did learnèd notions give,
   And the apples were demonstrative:
   So clear their colour and divine
The very shade they cast did other lights outshine.

Taste not, said God, 'Tis mine and angels' meat:
10   A certain death does sit
   Like an ill worm i'the core of it.
Ye cannot know and live, nor live or know and eat.
   Thus spoke God, yet man did go
   Ignorantly on to know;
15   Grew so more blind, and she
Who tempted him to this grew yet more blind than he.

The only science man by this did get
   Was but to know he nothing knew:
   He straight his nakedness did view,
20   His ignorant, poor estate, and was ashamed of it.
   Yet searches probabilities
   And rhetoric and fallacies,
   And seeks by useless pride
With slight and withering leaves that nakedness to hide.

25   Henceforth, said God, the wretched sons of earth
   Shall sweat for food in vain
   That will not long sustain,
And bring with labour forth each fond abortive birth.
   That serpent too, their pride,
30   Which aims at things denied;
   That learned and eloquent lust
Instead of mounting high shall creep upon the dust.

REASON:
THE USE OF IT IN DIVINE MATTERS

Some blind themselves 'cause possibly they may
   Be led by others a right way:
They build on sands, which if unmoved they find,
   'Tis but because there was no wind.

5   Less hard 'tis not to err ourselves than know
       If our forefathers erred or no.
     When we trust men concerning God we then
       Trust not God concerning men.

     Visions and inspirations some expect
10   Their course here to direct;
     Like senseless chemists their own wealth destroy
       Imaginary gold t'enjoy.
     So stars appear to drop to us from sky
       And gild the passage as they fly:
15   But when they fall and meet th'opposing ground
       What but a sordid slime is found?

     Sometimes their fancies they 'bove reason set
       And fast that they may dream of meat.
     Sometimes ill spirits their sickly souls delude
20   And bastard forms obtrude.
     So Endor's wretched sorceress, although
       She Saul through his disguise did know,
     Yet when the devil comes up disguised she cries
       Behold the gods arise.

25   In vain, alas, these outward hopes are tried:
       Reason within's our only guide.
     Reason which (God be praised!) still walks, for all
       Its old, original fall.
     And since itself the boundless Godhead joined
30   With a reasonable mind,
     It plainly shows that mysteries divine
       May with our reason join.

     The Holy Book, like the eighth sphere, does shine
       With thousand lights of truth divine:
35   So numberless the stars that to the eye
       It makes but all one galaxy.
     Yet reason must assist too for in seas
       So vast and dangerous as these
     Our course by stars above we cannot know
40   Without the compass too below.

     Though reason cannot through faith's mysteries see,
       It sees that there and such they be;
     Leads to heaven's door and there does humbly keep,
       And there through chinks and keyholes peep.
45   Though it, like Moses, by a sad command
       Must not come into the Holy Land
     Yet thither it infallibly does guide
       And from afar 'tis all descried.

Notes

EDMUND WALLER

1. SONG. l. 11. Waller's *Sacharissa* is Dorothy Spencer (1617–84), Countess of Sunderland.
l. 20. *Lethe*   the classical underworld river of oblivion.

2. TO AMORET. l. 7. *strook*   struck.

3. THE STORY OF PHOEBUS AND DAPHNE APPLIED. See Ovid, *Metamorphoses* I.

4. TO A LADY IN RETIREMENT. l. 6. *Helen*   wife of Menelaus, abducted to Troy by Paris.   *the Egyptian queen*   Cleopatra.

5. SONG. l. 4. *resemble*   compare.

7. TO THE MUTABLE FAIR. l. 13. See Motteux's translation of *Don Quixote*, I. i. 8.
l. 16. *make a stoop*   swoop down (hawking term).
l. 21. *formal*   having a regular motion.
ll. 32f. Waller gives Juno a more active rôle than usual; in most versions it is Jove who fashions a cloud in Juno's likeness to save her from Ixion.

8. PUERPERIUM.   Latin for 'lying in', 'confinement'. The poem relates to the birth of Charles I's fourth son, Henry.
l. 6. *The god of rage*   Mars, god of war.
l. 16. *halcyon*   literally a kingfisher, figuratively a bringer of peace.
l. 17. *Gloriana*   Henrietta Maria

10. THE FALL. ll. 15–16. See Gen. 3:19.

13. THE NIGHT-PIECE. l. 5. *Lely*   Sir Peter Lely (1618–80), Dutch by birth, was in England by 1647 and was, from 1661, Charles II's Principal Painter.
l. 26. *idea*   in the Platonic sense of 'form', 'ideal'.

14. TO MR HENRY LAWES. Henry Lawes (1596–1662), younger brother of William Lawes; best remembered for his association with *Comus*; a prolific song-writer.
l. 1. a renaissance commonplace.
l. 15. *Noye*   William Noye (1577–1662), Attorney-General from 1631.
l. 27. *ut, re, mi*   notes in a musical scale.

14. TO VANDYCK. Sir Anthony Vandyck (1599–1641), born at Antwerp; in England from 1632; favoured by Charles I; famous as a portrait painter.
l. 25. *rehearse*   tell, repeat.
l. 27. *assay*   attempt.
l. 50. *Prometheus*   son of the Titan Iapetus, stole fire from heaven for man's use.

16. TO MY LORD OF LEICESTER. Robert Sidney (1595–1677), 2nd Earl of Leicester, was ambassador in France between 1636 and 1641.
l. 19. *Thetis*   mother to Achilles and husband of Peleus.
l. 21. *Ajax*   (called Telamon to distinguish him from Ajax, son of Oileus) competed with Odysseus for Achilles' armour after the latter's death. When the armour was awarded to Odysseus Ajax killed himself.
l. 23. *Achave*   Argive (from Argos)—Homer uses 'Argive'='Greek'.
l. 28. *Syrius*   the Dog-star (Sirius).

16. TO MY YOUNG LADY LUCY SIDNEY. Lucy Sidney was a younger sister of Waller's Sacharissa.

17. TO MY LORD NORTHUMBERLAND. . . . Algernon Percy (1602–68), 10th earl. His wife, Lady Anne Cecil, died in 1637.
l. 17. *Emilius*   Lucius Aemilius Paullus (d. 160 B.C.) finished the Rome/Macedon war with his victory at Pydna.
l. 29. *then*   than (a common seventeenth-century variant).

18. ON MY LADY ISABELLA. . . . ll. 15–16. Nero was emperor A.D. 54–68: this traditional story lacks real evidence.

18. UPON BEN JONSON. l. 17. *Narcissus*   the beautiful youth who, falling in love with his own reflection in a pool, wasted away because of this unrequitable love.
l. 24. *colours*   rhetorical devices.
l. 30. *Proteus*   sea god and archetypal shape-changer.

19. TO MY LADY MORTON. . . . Ann, Countess of Morton, was daughter of Sir Edward Villiers and wife of Lord Dalkeith, later Earl of Morton.
ll. 13–14. To save Bethulia from Holofernes, who was besieging the city, Judith entered his camp and killed him in his drunken sleep.
ll. 17–18. Ann Morton escaped from England to France in 1646 with Princess Henriette-Anne.
ll. 21–2. See *Aeneid* II.

20. A PANEGYRIC TO MY LORD PROTECTOR. ll. 9–10. Neptune saved Aeneas and his followers by calming a storm raised by Juno to destroy them (see *Aeneid* I).
l. 15. Cromwell conquered Ireland in 1649–50.
l. 16. Cromwell defeated the Scots in the campaigns that started in 1650 and culminated in the 1654 Act of Union.
ll. 67–8. Aulus Plautius' landing in Kent (A.D. 43) began the Roman invasion of Britain, but the island was never wholly subdued.
l. 69. *the Black Prince*   Edward, son of Edward III and Philippa of Hainault, defeated the French at Poitiers.
l. 70. *Henry*   Henry V.
l. 73. *the Macedonian*   Alexander.
l. 74. *Thetis*   see above, p. 245.
ll. 77–9. When Alexander invaded Persia (334 B.C.) he was opposed by King Darius, far from his military equal. After being defeated at Gaugamele Darius fled to Media where he was killed by his kinsman Bessus.
l. 85. *Roman wall*   Hadrian's wall, built to keep the Celts at bay.
l. 92. as a result of the 1654 Act of Union.
l. 93. *Preferred*   favoured.
ll. 101–4. This stanza presumably refers to the peace treaty with Holland in 1654.
l. 106. *Preventing*   anticipating, 'sending news before . . .'
l. 125. Cromwell's father was a gentleman. The family history goes back to Richard Williams (said to have come to England in 1485 with Henry VII) who adopted the surname of his uncle Sir Thomas Cromwell.
l. 136. See I Sam. 16:11.
l. 170. Octavian (later the Emperor Augustus) reunited the Roman empire by defeating Antony at Actium. His reign was marked by political and military reorganization and relatively stable conditions.
l. 188. See Gen. 37:7.

25. OF THE DANGER HIS MAJESTY (BEING PRINCE) ESCAPED. . . . The poem

describes events which occurred in September 1623 when Prince Charles reached the coast at Santander on his way back from Spain.

l. 10. *Bacchus*   god of wine; son of Zeus (the thunderer) and Semele.

l. 11. *Arion*   a semi-mythical poet whose singing was so beautiful that when he was thrown overboard on a journey from Italy to Corinth he was saved by a dolphin.

ll. 13–24. Edward IV seized the throne in 1461 and defeated the Lancastrians at Towton. Henry VI was captured in 1465 and murdered in 1471. Edward owed much of his success to Richard Neville, Earl of Warwick. Warwick negotiated a match for Edward with Bona, daughter of the Duke of Savoy, but the king married Elizabeth Woodville and Warwick later switched his allegiance to Henry.

l. 64. This Titan must be Hyperion, the sun-god whose son Phäethon tried to drive his father's chariot ('car') across the sky but died in the attempt.

ll. 85ff. Virgil tells in *Aeneid* I how Juno tried to destroy the Trojans by raising a storm at sea.

l. 96. *Priam*   King of Troy during the Trojan War.

l. 107. *Thetis*   see above, p. 245.

l. 121. *Aurora*   goddess of dawn.

l. 135. *Jason*   led the Argonauts in search of the Golden Fleece.
Theseus   best remembered for killing the Cretan Minotaur.

l. 138. *Musaeus*   poet of the sixth century A.D. who wrote about Hero and Leander.

ll. 141–2. *Leander*   Hero's lover: he drowned in the Hellespont, which he habitually swam to visit her.

ll. 163–4. Claudian, *Epithalamium de nuptiis Honorii Augusti*, 247–50.

ll. 165ff. See *Iliad* VII, 19f.

l. 169. *depends*   hangs.

29. AT PENSHURST. Penshurst was the family seat in Kent.

l. 26. Orpheus was so skilled in music that his singing and lyre-playing could move even trees and stones.   *numerous*   harmonious.

l. 34. Apollo is, *inter alia*, god of poetry.

30. AT PENSHURST. l. 1. *Dorothea*   see above, p. 245.

l. 17. *Amphion*   according to legend, built the walls of Thebes by playing so beautifully that the stones moved into place without other help.

ll. 26–7. Sir Philip Sidney was born in November 1554: a tree in Penshurst Park is known as Sidney's oak, although it is doubtful if it was planted to celebrate the birth.

31. OF SALLE. Pirates from Salle troubled the English coast in the early years of Charles I's reign. In 1637 an English fleet helped the king of Morocco to regain control over the rebels from Salle.

l. 1. See above.

ll. 13ff. See I Sam. 15:33.

ll. 29–30. Hercules was the son of Alcmena by Zeus, and his tenth labour was to bring Geryon's cattle to Mycenae. While he was doing this some were stolen by the giant Cacus, but Hercules recovered them and killed Cacus.

ll. 33ff. The Moroccan king sent his ambassador on board the English fleet mentioned above.

l. 40. *manumized*   freed (usually used of slaves),

32. OF A WAR WITH SPAIN AND A FIGHT AT SEA. Spain declared war on England in February 1656. An English fleet under Blake and Montague went to the Mediterranean and in September Captain Richard Stayner captured or destroyed eight Spanish galleons.

l. 9. *Electors*   those princes who could vote for the election of a Holy Roman Emperor.

l. 61. This Mount Ida is near Troy: from it Jove could watch the Trojan War.

l. 73. *Thetis*   see above, p. 245.

l. 77. *the marquis*   the Marquis of Badajoz, Viceroy of Mexico.

l. 84. The phoenix incarcerated itself in a nest of aromatic spices.

l. 101. Although Montague was not directly involved in Stayner's exploit he had custody of the prisoners and treasure ('half Peru') gained by this victory over the plate-fleet.

34. INSTRUCTIONS TO A PAINTER. Thorn Drury (*Poems* II, p. 208) suggests that Waller derived the painter device from the Italian Businello. It became a popular seventeenth-century genre.

l. 22. *Batavians*   the Dutch.

ll. 43–4, It is commonplace to refer to the Dutch and Belgians as heavy drinkers: Waller's phrasing recalls 'Dutch courage', a term still in use.

l. 82. *Thetis*   see above, p. 245.

l. 83. *Paphian queen*   Venus: Paphos, on Cyprus, was a cult-centre for her.

ll. 92ff. The English Hamburg fleet set sail by mistake and was almost wholly captured by the Dutch.

l. 114. *Actium*   the naval battle in which Octavian defeated Antony and Cleopatra.

ll. 127ff. See *Iliad* XVIII.

l. 130. Phrygia was a district in Asia Minor. 'Phrygian' often='Trojan', frequently with overtones of effeminacy.

l. 137. Opdam commanded the joint Dutch-Danish fleet which defeated Sweden in 1658.

ll. 157–8. See Gen. 37:31f.

l. 184. *earnest*   indication, omen.

l. 192. See above, p. 247.

l. 223. *Boreas*   the north wind.

l. 241ff. See above, ll. 43–4n.

l. 258. *Charon*   ferried the souls of the dead across Styx to the underworld.

l. 269. *comet's hair*   the tail of a comet (Latin 'cometa' literally='long-haired').

l. 301. *Augustus*   Octavian Caesar, later known as Augustus, the victor of Actium.

41. ON THE STATUE OF KING CHARLES I. This statue was cast *c.* 1630 by Le Sœur but was not erected at Charing Cross until 1674.

l. 4. *wanted*   lacked.

41. TO ONE MARRIED TO AN OLD MAN. Waller gives a witty twist to a common epitaph *topos* which goes back at least to Martial and is best known in English in Jonson's 'Which cover lightly, gentle earth' (*Epigrammes* XXII).

42. OF ENGLISH VERSE. l. 5. Waller's concern over the durability of the vernacular echoes sixteenth-century controversy in England and earlier Italian debates.

43. OF TEA, COMMENDED BY HER MAJESTY. l. 1. The myrtle was sacred to Venus, the bay to Apollo.

43. EPITAPH ON SIR GEORGE SPEKE. Speke represented Bath and Chippenham in Parliament and died in 1682; his mother was related to Waller.

l. 15. See Prov. 31:1ff.

l. 34. See following poem, ll. 3–4 n.

44. LONG AND SHORT LIFE. The root idea occurs in Seneca, *Epistles* xciii.2:

'Longa est vita si plena est' ('A life is long if it is fulfilled'). See also Jonson, *Underwood* LXX.

HENRY VAUGHAN

45. TO MY INGENUOUS FRIEND R.W. The friend has not been identified.
l. 2. *score*   debt.
l. 4. *niggard*   mean.
l. 13. *maze*   Martin suggests the meaning 'dissipation'.
l. 17. *mulcts*   fines.
l. 22. *affect*   'are in the habit of doing'.
l. 26. *Elysian fields*   the home of the blessed in the afterlife.
l. 33. *Randolph*   Thomas Randolph (1605–35), poet and dramatist. *Amyntas* and *The Jealous Lovers* are two of his plays.
l. 40. *Lethe*   see above, p. 245.
46. TO AMORET GONE FROM HIM. l. 20. *influence*   the influence of the stars acting on them.
l. 22. *element*   constitute.
47. A RHAPSODY. l. 5. *sack*   used in the seventeenth century to designate strong white wines as against Rhenish and red wines.
l. 19. *clown*   shepherd.
l. 29. *Endymion*   was loved by the moon-goddess Selene.
l. 36. *catchpoles*   sheriff's officers with the power of arrest.
l. 44. *Cymbeline and Lud*   both early British kings (according to Geoffrey of Monmouth): statues of such kings were placed on Ludgate in 1260 and removed in 1586.
ll. 47–8. Caligula.
l. 53. Julius Caesar crossed the river Rubicon on his way to assume power in Rome.
l. 56. *Brundisium*   Roman city on the east coast of Italy.
l. 57. *Sylla* (138–78 B.C.)   a leader of the Roman aristocracy who defeated the 'popular' party in the civil war of 83–2 and became dictator.
l. 63. *pregnant*   (*a*) completely full; (*b*) conducive to wit.
48. TO HIS FRIEND. The friend has not been identified.
l. 2. *entails*   here in the general sense of 'inheritances'.
l. 24. *rout*   mob.
l. 38. *pilgrim-shoe*   a shoe worn out by walking.
l. 52. *piece*   silver coin, often specifically a silver 4*d.* piece.
50. UPON A CLOAK LENT HIM BY MR J. RIDSLEY. Nothing is known of this Ridsley.
l. 2. *even*   'one and the same thing'.
l. 18. *shag*   a rough cloth with a long, hairy nap.
l. 20. Beeston Castle, near Chester, fell to Parliamentary forces on 16 November, 1645 (see F. E. Hutchinson, *Henry Vaughan*, p. 65).
l. 31. *good-wife*   strictly 'woman of the house'; here perhaps 'nurse'.
l. 36. *circuit beast*   horse used by a judge on his circuit around a given area to deal with court cases.
l. 40. Cicero (*Paradox* i. 8) attributes the saying 'Omnia mecum porto mea' to Bias of Priene.
l. 41. *pure Adamite*   the Adamites were a religious sect which originated in Africa in the second century A.D. and sought to revive the primitive simplicity of Adam by, for example, abandoning clothes.

l. 44. *microcosmography*   the study of man as the 'little world' or microcosm as reflecting the great world (macrocosm).

l. 46. The number seven occurs several times in the Genesis account of the flood (7:13f.), but there is no mention of pillars, although Prov. 9:1 refers to the seven pillars of wisdom.

l. 49. *cerecloth*   wax-coated linen used to wrap corpses.   *Bedlam*   the lunatic hospital of St Mary of Bethlehem in London.

l. 52. *Speed*   John Speed (1552?–1629), cartographer and author of a *History of Great Britain*.

l. 56. *Arras*   tapestry with figures woven into it.

l. 60. *Fetter Lane*   according to Martin the allusion is to the stone-cutter Edward Marshall, who lived in the lane.

l. 64. *herbal*   book describing plants.

l. 84. *Brownist*   follower of Robert Brown (*c.* 1550–1633): 'Brownist' was often used=puritan.

l. 90. *Lapland lease*   the phrase is obscure but the context and the next couplet provide two clues. Lapland was often thought of as a home of witches, while one meaning of 'lease' is as a weaving term, so the phrase may mean 'a magic coat or cloak from Lapland'.

54. POEMS FROM SILEX SCINTILLANS. *Silex Scintillans*   (Latin) 'shining flint'.

54. REGENERATION. l. 28. *Jacob's bed*   See Gen. 28:11f.

l. 68. *ray*   (*a*) the sun's rays; (*b*) the rays of God's grace. (The reference *Cant. Cap. 5. ver. 17.* should be to 4:16.)

56. RESURRECTION AND IMMORTALITY. l. 9. *ray*   see note above.

l. 21. *recruits*   fresh supplies.

l. 26. *incorporates*   'forms into a body or substance'.

l. 51. See I Cor. 13:12.

58. THE SEARCH. cf. Herbert, 'Redemption'.

l. 21. *Sychar*   see John 4:5–6.

l. 26. *white*   auspicious.

l. 38. *Ideas*   images.

ll. 45–6. See Matt. 27:60.

ll. 55f. See Matt. 4:1f.; Luke 4:1f.

61. MOUNT OF OLIVES. ll. 9–10. Both Jonson and Randolph wrote poems celebrating the Cotswold Games; Cooper's Hill was celebrated by Denham.

l. 16. *sheep-ward*   shepherd.

62. 'THOU THAT KNOW'ST FOR WHOM I MOURN'. l. 44. *tares*   weeds.

65. THE MORNING WATCH. ll. 18ff. See Herbert, 'Prayer'.

66. 'SILENCE AND STEALTH OF DAYS! TIS NOW'. l. 19. *snuff*   the charred part of a candle-wick.

67. 'SURE THERE'S A TIE OF BODIES, AND AS THEY'. l. 9. *Absents. . . conspire*   Martin suggests this means 'persons absent from each other, though not dead, feel a mutual sympathy'.

l. 17. See John 11:1f.

68. PEACE. l. 17. *ranges*   wanderings.

68. 'AND DO THEY SO? HAVE THEY A SENSE'. l. 2. *influence*   heavenly control.

69. THE RELAPSE. l. 13. See Exodus 10:21–2.

l. 18. *yew*   often associated with death and graveyards.

l. 23f. See Herbert. 'Affliction I' ('My days were strawed with flowers and happiness').

71. CORRUPTION. l. 25. *lieger*   'as subjects'.

72. IDLE VERSE. l. 4. *on the score*   in debt.

l. 13. *purls*   decorative borders on clothing: the image is picked up in 'robes' and here means 'excessive luxury'.

l. 19. *cypress*   a commonplace symbol of mourning.

73. THE DAWNING. l. 21. *pursy*   swelling.

74. AFFLICTION l. 3. *accessions*   attacks (of disease).

l. 11. Vaughan may have in mind any of several texts in Job (e.g. 10:9; 33:6).

75. LOVE AND DISCIPLINE. l. 5. *spill*   kill (OE 'spillan').

76. THE WORLD. ll. 1–2. The association of eternity with a ring is not uncommon: see, e.g., Thomas Philipott's 'Considerations upon Eternity' and Bunyan's *Book for Boys and Girls* LXXII.

77. THE MUTINY. l. 10. *coil*   tumult.

l. 18. *Babel*   see Gen. 11:3f.

78. MAN. l. 9. *staidness*   settledness, stability.

ll. 12ff. See Luke 12:24, 27.

82. COCK-CROWING. l. 12. *tinned*   presumably 'set in a tin holder'.

l. 29. See above, p. 150, 'The Relapse', l. 13n.

84. THE GARLAND. l. 19. *lists*   borders.

l. 27. *abear*   behaviour.

84. THE BIRD. l. 28. *satyrs*   classical countryside deities associated with Bacchus; usually given small horns and (in Roman legend) goat-like lower bodies.

89. CHILDHOOD. ll. 21ff. Vaughan probably had in mind Matt. 4:5–6 or Luke 4:9–11.

90. ABEL'S BLOOD. See Gen. 4.

l. 16. See Psalms 42:7.

92. THE AGREEMENT. l. 15. *ascendants*   rising beams.

96. THE WATERFALL. l. 5. *retinue*   accompaniment.

JOHN DENHAM

99. COOPER'S HILL. Denham's poem is an important example of English 'local' poetry, pointing backwards to Jonson's 'To Penshurst' and Carew's 'To Saxham' and forwards to Pope's 'Windsor Forest'. The text used here is based on that of 1688: see O Hehir, *Expans'd Hieroglyphicks*.

l. 19. St Paul's Cathedral was the subject of Waller's 'Upon his majesty's repairing of Paul's'.

l. 39. *Mars . . . Venus*   Charles I, Henrietta Maria.

l. 50. *pompous*   weighty, dignified.

l. 56. *prevent*   anticipate.

l. 60. *god's great mother*   Cybele, whom the Romans called the mother of the gods.

ll. 67–8. Julius Caesar invaded Britain in A.D. 55 and 54; Albanact was an early British king, killed by Humber, king of the Huns (according to Geoffrey of Monmouth); Brutus was the eponymous founder of Britain, having fled the sack of Troy; Cnut ruled A.D. 1016–35.

l. 70. Many cities have claimed to be Homer's birthplace, but Smyrna and Chios seem the most probable candidates. (Camoens speaks of the seven cities in Canto 5 of *The Lusiads*.)

l. 77. Edward III and his son, the Black Prince, who extended his father's French conquests.

l. 79. *Bellona*   the Roman goddess of war—Edward's wife was Philippa of Hainault.

l. 83. *that order*   of St George.

l. 92. *royal pair*   Charles and Henrietta Maria.

l. 101. *patron*   St George.

l. 103. *azure circle*   the silver star of the Garter knights has in its middle the red cross of St George, with a surrounding blue garter.

l. 113. *neighbouring hill*   St Anne's Hill.

l. 115. *abbey*   Chertsey Abbey.

l. 118. Henry VIII is the king referred to.

l. 119. *luxury*   lasciviousness.

l. 132. *stiles*   pens.

l. 138. In Aesop's fable the stork nourishes its young by pecking sustenance from its own breast.

l. 144. *calenture*   a delirium caused by excessive heat.

l. 172. *overlay*   suffocate.

l. 193. *Eridanus*   the river into which Phäethon fell from the sun's chariot.

l. 214. *self-enamoured youth*   Narcissus.

l. 235. Faunus and Sylvanus are both Roman woodland gods and both are at times identified with Pan.

l. 329. *charter*   Magna Carta, signed by King John at Runnymede.

106. A SONG. l. 1. *Morpheus*   god of sleep and dreams.

l. 8. See above, p. 245.

107. NEWS FROM COLCHESTER. l. 5. *stone-horse*   stallion.

l. 6. Francis Woodcock was a Parliamentarian and member of the Assembly of Divines; George Fox founded the Quakers; James Naylor was another Quaker.

l. 10. In England buggery was often considered 'the Italian vice'.

l. 16–17. The reference is to the ordinance of December 1644 commanding that Christmas should be a time of fasting not feasting.

l. 22. *cates*   foods.

ll. 26–7. See Mark 5:13 and Luke 8:32f.

l. 33. *mayor*   presumably Sir Isaac Pennington (1587–1660), Lord Mayor of London from 1642.

l. 47. *vailed*   taken off.

l. 50. *Sister*   mocking use of the Puritan habit of speaking of brothers and sisters in God.

l. 61. *our masters*   the Jesuits.

l. 63. *trepan*   trap, ensnare.

109. THE PROLOGUE TO HIS MAJESTY. l. 15. *muses' well*   Aganippe, on Mount Helicon.

l. 22. *peculiar*   particular.

l. 27. *tiring-house*   dressing-room in a theatre.

l. 37. i.e. beheaded Charles I (the lion is a common symbol of monarchy).

110. FRIENDSHIP AND SINGLE LIFE. . . . l. 8. *sally ports*   gates from which besieged forces issued to attack the besiegers.

l. 32. *The Trojan Hero*   Aeneas.

l. 44. Venus, Cupid's mother, was born from the union of the sea's foam with the severed genitals of Uranus.

ll. 70–2. Solomon's son was Rehoboam: see I Kings 11 and 12 for the general context.

l. 75. *Secure*   content (Latin securus').
l. 91. *amorous boy*   Paris.

113. NATURA NATURATA. l. 12. *engines*   devices.
l. 17. by an act of August 1649.
l. 19. *nice*   sensitive.
l. 23. *tropes*   rhetorical devices.

114. ON MY LORD CROFTS' AND MY JOURNEY INTO POLAND. . . . William, Lord Crofts, held various posts under Charles II and was created baron in 1658, dying in 1677. Denham and Crofts were sent to Poland in 1650 to raise money for Charles, and as a result of Crofts' eloquence the Polish Diet voted money for him, this being levied from British merchants in Poland.
l. 6. Sir John Cockram went to Poland before Denham and Crofts on a similar mission.
l. 32. *the Constitution*   this is the name for a general act passed at the end of each session of the Polish Diet.
l. 36. Almost nothing is known of Molleson or his activities, but he was probably a Parliamentary agent acting against such missions as this of Crofts and Denham.
l. 65. Banks quotes from a letter of Daniel O'Neill in 1651, which speaks of a 'Mr Sands' being entrusted to convey £1,000 of the Polish money to the Marquis of Ormonde. This does not fully explain Denham's lines but the poet may have been content to have the pun even at the expense of clarity.

116. THE PROGRESS OF LEARNING. l. 2. Circe was an Homeric enchantress who tempted travellers, then turned them into swine.
l. 5. See *Aeneid* VI.
ll. 21–2. Abraham lived in Chaldea before moving to Canaan.
ll. 29–30. Jason recovered the Golden Fleece from Colchis: Denham is allegorizing the myth to image the gradual movement of cultural leadership from Afro-Asia to Greece.
l. 31. *Musaeus*   a legendary early Greek poet-musician.   *Orpheus*   son of the muse Calliope, and the greatest musician of legend.
ll. 41–2. Denham seems to be referring to the fact that one of the Greek words for 'creator' is also a word for 'poet'.
l. 48. *novelists*   followers of Bacon's anti-Aristotelian position.
l. 67. *Latium*   Italy.
l. 73. According to legend Minerva was born from Jove's head.
l. 77. *Anacreon*   Greek lyric poet (*c.* 563–478 B. C.).   *Hesiod*   eighth-century Greek poet of *Works and Days* and *Theogony*.   *Theocritus*   third-century Greek poet, regarded as inventor of the pastoral.
l. 80. *the Mantuan swan*   Virgil.
l. 81. *Augustus*   Augustus Caesar.
l. 86. Latin 'vates' can mean either prophet or poet.
l. 92. *Typhis*   see Seneca, *Medea*, 375ff.
l. 94. *Thule*   a northern land discovered by the third-century B.C. Greek navigator Pytheas; often identified with Norway or Iceland; came to be regarded as the northernmost land on earth.
l. 113. Referring to Christ's pun on Peter's name (Greek 'petros'='rock'); see Matt. 16:18.
l. 117. *the fisher*   Peter (see Matt. 4:18).
l. 123. *the old giants*   these must be the sons of Ge who rebelled against Zeus. Denham is referring to the kind of medieval biblical criticism which perverted text to uphold papal claims.
l. 135. *Hildebrand*   Gregory VII (Pope, 1073–85).

l. 151. Ignatius Loyola (1491–1556), founder of the Jesuits; Martin Luther (1483–1546) and John Calvin (1509–64) were the two great founders of protestantism.

l. 159. *Aaron's rod*   for Aaron as prototype-priest see Exod. 28, and for specific references to his rod see Exod. 7:12, Num. 17: 3, 10, and Heb. 9: 4.

l. 165. *calcined*   a chemical term, here meaning 'converted' (in a divisive sense).

l. 168. *fatuous fires   ignes fatui*, will-o'-the-wisps.

ll. 171–2. See above, p. 245, 'To the Mutable Fair', ll. 32ff n.

l. 173. *chimera*   a monster with a lion's head, goat's body, dragon's tail.

l. 178. *cyclops*   these one-eyed giants lived on an island and made thunderbolts for Zeus.

l. 188. *resumes*   reassimilates.

ll. 195–6. Arachne challenged Athene to a weaving contest. Athene tore up Arachne's weaving: the latter hanged herself but Athene turned her into a spider.

l. 212. *Cham*   Ham, son of Noah.

l. 224. William Harvey's *De Motu Cordis et Sanguinis* was published in 1628.

ll. 233–4. The quotation has not been traced.

121. TO HIS MISTRESS. l. 8. See above, p. 245, 'To Vandyck', l. 50n.

121. A SPEECH AGAINST PEACE. . . . The 'speaker' of this satire seems to be John Hampden, one of Charles I's main Parliamentary opponents. The Close Committee is presumably the Committee of Safety set up in 1642.

l. 7. *the Bishop's Bill*   in June 1641 the Lords rejected a bill for the exclusion of bishops from the House of Lords.

ll. 13–15. Royalists suspected Hampden and William Fiennes, Viscount Saye and Sele (1582–1662), of aiding the Scottish invasion of 1646.

l. 26. *their knight*   Sir John Hotham, who refused to surrender Hull to Charles at the start of the war.

l. 30. It is impossible to say just what petition Denham is referring to.

l. 36. A Parliamentary committee to collect monies for the war met at Haberdashers' Hall.

ll. 37ff. The Irish Catholics rebelled against the English garrisons in October 1641 : Parliament spread rumours that Charles was sympathetic to the rebels.

124. A WESTERN WONDER. This refers to a military incident in the west in 1643. Sir Ralph Hopton led a small royalist force in Cornwall at the start of the war. In April 1643 James Chudleigh defeated Hopton at Stourton Down, but at Stratton in May Hopton beat Chudleigh and his commander, the first Earl of Stamford.

l. 21. The Earl of Essex successfully besieged Reading in April 1643, but it was not until May that Parliament provided him with the money to follow up his success.

l. 25. *Peters and Case*   Hugh Peters was a prominent nonconformist preacher; Thomas Case was a similar figure.

l. 27. See above, p. 252, 'News from Colchester', l. 33n. The reference to digging is to the fortifications thrown up around London in 1643 because of Charles's approach.

125. A SECOND WESTERN WONDER. After Hopton's Stratton victory, Parliament sent Sir William Waller to contain him. Waller, after besieging Hopton at Devizes, was defeated by Hopton and Lord Wilmot on 13th July.

l. 4. *firkin*   a measure of quantity, usually a fourth part (here of a powder barrel).

l. 6. *Sir Ralph*   Hopton.
l. 7. *the Vies*   Devizes. The line refers to injuries Hopton received in the battle of Lansdown (5th July), after which he withdrew to Devizes. The book of l. 9. is the journal *Mercurius Civicus* and the 'preaching lady' is Lady Waller.

126. TO SIR RICHARD FANSHAW. . . . Fanshaw (1608–66) was a follower of Charles. His main claim to literary fame is this translation (pub. 1648) of Guarini's play.
l. 36. *outfaced*   convinced.

127. AN ELEGY UPON THE DEATH OF THE LORD HASTINGS. Henry, Lord Hastings (1630–49), son of the sixth Earl of Huntingdon.
l. 21. *victim*   Charles I.
l. 31. *smoke*   I prefer this reading (from *Lachrymae Musarum*, 1650) to the alternative 'stroke' because it fits better with 'inflamed' and 'choke'.

128. A PANEGYRIC ON HIS EXCELLENCY, THE LORD GENERAL MONK. This poem is usually attributed to Denham and there is no reason to question his authorship. George Monk (1608–74) was primarily a soldier. He fought for Charles until 1644 when he was captured; served Parliament in Ireland until 1649; went to Scotland with Cromwell; was general of the fleet 1652–3. Monk was instrumental in negotiating the restoration.
l. 13. *Fabius*   Fabius Cunctator ('the delayer') became dictator in 217 B.C. after Rome's defeat at Lake Trasimene: his nickname was earned by his tactics of harassing Hannibal without being drawn into battle.
l. 16. *conscious*   living.
ll. 35–6. The oracle at Delphi issued prophecies in the name of Apollo.
l. 37. *tripos*   the Delphi priestess gave out prophecies while seated on a tripos (three-legged stool).
ll. 46f. The palladium was said to be Pallas' image: while Troy held the image the city was invulnerable so it was stolen by Diomedes. The point of Denham's lines seems to be that the palladium not only protected Troy but was protected by the city, since after the theft the image was carried from place to place before settling in Rome.
ll. 58f. This refers to Monk's activities as general of the fleet against the Dutch.

129. ON MR ABRAHAM COWLEY. . . . l. 7. *Aurora*   goddess of dawn.
l. 38. *garb*   manner, style (as distinct from material, 'clothes').
l. 40. *Jason*   undertook the task of regaining the Golden Fleece so that he could gain the throne of Iolcos from Pelius.
l. 43. *Flaccus*   Horace.
l. 47. Cowley's *Pindarique Odes*, the first sustained English attempt at Pindar's manner, were published in 1648.
ll. 67–8. *Pythagoras* (*c.* 580 B.C.)   Greek philosopher-mathematician, taught the idea of metempsychosis.

132. ON THE EARL OF STRAFFORD'S TRIAL AND DEATH. Thomas Wentworth, Earl of Strafford, was impeached and executed in May 1641.
l. 26. *precedent*   this refers to a restoration decision which, in effect, meant that partial guilt could not be held equivalent to full treason.

132. TO THE FIVE MEMBERS OF THE HONOURABLE HOUSE OF COMMONS. Charles came in person to Parliament (January 1642) to demand the arrest of five members—John Pym, William Strode, Arthur Haselrig, John Hampden, Denzil Holles.
l. 20. *pursuivant*   here an officer who executes warrants.

l. 56. This must refer to the king-Parliament correspondence preceding the outbreak of war.

134. VERSES ON THE CAVALIERS. . . . Probably, but not certainly, by Denham. The poem is based upon the arrests of royalists following the outbreak of royalist feeling in 1655.

l. 9. *Petre*   William, 4th Baron Petre of Writtle.

l. 10. *legem pone*   The phrase derives from Psalm CXIX (Vulgate) and came to be associated with 25th March, a pay-day. Humorously, the phrase came to mean 'ready money'. Denham thus seems to be saying that Petre was imprisoned merely for not paying some Parliamentary demand. His wife was Lady Elizabeth Petre, from whom he separated.

l. 14. *Maynard*   probably Sir John Maynard (d. 1658).

l. 17. *Coventry*   Sir William Coventry (1628?–86). His father, Thomas Lord Coventry, was Lord Keeper of the Seal from 1625 to 1640.

l. 21. *Byron*   Richard, 2nd Lord Byron, fought at Edgehill.

l. 25. *Lucas*   Sir John Lucas, who became Baron Lucas of Shenfield in 1645.

l. 29. *St. John*   probably Charles Paulet (1625–99), 1st Duke of Bolton. The wife referred to was his second, Mary, daughter of the Earl of Sunderland.

l. 33. *Russell*   John Russell, son of the 4th Earl of Bedford.

l. 35. *Caulier*   unidentified.

l. 37. *Cornwallis*   went into exile with Charles; created Baron Cornwallis of Eye at the restoration.

l. 41. *Progers*   Edward Progers was equerry to James I and page to Charles I.

l. 45. *Shirley*   Sir Robert Shirley, royalist conspirator, died in the Tower in 1656.

ll. 47–8. *rooks*   here='cheats'. Shirley had been released in 1650 on payment of surety but was later re-arrested: 'under the line' is clearly meant to suggest that the payment had been made to a corrupt authority.

l. 49. *Nichols*   Richard Nichols was later groom of the bedchamber to James, Duke of York.   *Lyttleton*   Sir Charles Lyttleton, an active royalist, died in 1716.

l. 53. *Paston*   Colonel John Paston, son of Edward Paston of Norfolk.

l. 57. *Panton*   Colonel Thomas Panton.

ll. 63–4. Waller's 'Panegyric to my Lord Protector' was published 1655 (see p. 20).

l. 69. *Argonauts*   the men who sailed with Jason in the 'Argo'.

ll. 73–4. Penn and Venables led the Commonwealth fleet of 1655 to attack Spanish possessions in the West Indies. Venables unsuccessfully attacked Santo Domingo in April but took Jamaica in May.

l. 76. *Cullen*   Cologne. Charles II was there from 1654 to 1656 and the reference here is to royalist plots of this time.

ll. 81–2. *act/Of pardon*   the Act of Oblivion (1652) granted pardon for all treasons prior to the battle of Worcester, but many royalists were excepted.

136. MARTIAL. EPIGRAM OUT OF AN EPIGRAM BY MARTIAL. From Martial, XI. civ.

l. 29. *pap*   soft, pliable.

137. SARPEDON'S SPEECH TO GLAUCUS. . . . l. 10. *Xanthus* of Lydia; one of the early Greek chroniclers.

l. 13. *Lycians*   inhabitants of Lycia in Asia Minor.

RICHARD CRASHAW

139. MUSIC'S DUEL. Based on a Latin poem by Famianus Stroda (1572–1649).
l. 3. *plat*   plot of ground.
l. 39. *point*   introduce a major theme.
l. 64. *lubric*   voluble.
l. 77. *Helicon*   mountain in Boeotia, sacred to the Muses.
l. 78. *Prefer*   offer.
l. 82. *Prevents*   anticipates.
l. 99. *epode*   (a) lyric metre in which a long line is followed by a shorter; (b) the third stanza in a lyric structure, differing metrically from the other two.
l. 103. *ecstasies*   the mystical sense of the word, as defined by those which follow.
l. 126. *Hebe*   daughter of Zeus and Hera; handmaiden to the gods.
l. 128. *grutch*   complain.
l. 150. *empyraeum*   the outermost sphere and home of the saints.
l. 156. *diapason*   the voice's entire range.

142. OUT OF VIRGIL . . . *Georgics* ii. 323–45.
l. 19. *Auster*   the south wind.

143. OUT OF THE GREEK. CUPID'S CRIER. From Moschus (*Moschi Reliquiae* ii).
l. 5. *O yes*   Oyez ('Hear ye')—the town-crier's cry.

145. OUT OF THE ITALIAN. Origin unknown.

145. OUT OF CATULLUS. Catullus V, often translated in this period.

146. WISHES TO HIS (SUPPOSED) MISTRESS. l. 11. *Idea*   in the Platonic sense of 'ideal'.
l. 18. *tire*   attire.
l. 20. *tissue*   cloth of gold.

149. UPON TWO GREEN APRICOTS. . . . l. 3. *Pomona*   Roman fruit-goddess.
l. 30. *Hesperides*   ('daughters of evening') lived near the Atlas mountains guarding a tree that produced golden apples.

151. AN EPITAPH UPON HUSBAND AND WIFE. . . . l. 9. *turtles*   turtle-doves.

152. UPON MR STANINOUGH'S DEATH. James Staninough, fellow of Queens' College, died 1635.

152. AN EPITAPH UPON MR ASHTON. . . . *conformable*   here 'religious conformist'.
l. 27. *sans*   without.

153. THE WIDOW'S MITES. See Mark 12:41–4; Luke 21:1–4.

154. TO PONTIUS, WASHING HIS HANDS. See Matt. 27:24.

154. MARK 4. See Mark 4:40 (also Matt. 8:26).

155. MATTHEW 27. See Matt. 27:12.

155. MATTHEW 22. See Matt. 22:46.
l. 20. *panegyris*   eulogy.

156. LUKE 10. See Luke 10:31.

156. LUKE 16. DIVES ASKING A DROP. See Luke 16:24 (Dives is not named by Luke).

157. LUKE 7. See Luke 7:38.

157. THE WEEPER. For analogues see Martin pp. 432–4, to which should be added Sarbiewski's 'Oculi B. Aloysii lachrymbundi'. The text used is that of 1646: see Martin's edition for another version.

ll. 19–20. See Martin p. 433 and also Dronke, *Medieval Lyric*, p. 55.
l. 80. *Tagus*   river in Spain.

161. A HYMN OF THE NATIVITY. . . . Based on the text of 1646: see Martin for
another version.
l. 41. *officious*   careful.
l. 78. *Maia*   ancient Italian goddes to whom sacrifices were offered in May.
163. NEW YEAR'S DAY. Based on 1652 text: see Martin for another version.
164. IN THE GLORIOUS EPIPHANY OF OUR LORD . . .
l. 3. *officious*   see above.
l. 17. *Meridian*   pertaining to midday.
l. 25. *indifferent*   disinterested.
l. 35. *Sordidly*   menially.
l. 53. *specious*   deceitful.
l. 69. *Aurora*   the dawn goddess.
ll. 96–7. *Osiris*   Egyptian god, incarnated as a bull; the cow is his sister/
wife Isis
l. 100. *Mithra*   Mithras is the Persian god of light.
l. 116. *deliquium*   eclipse.
l. 191. *areopagite*   the Areopagus was the hill at Athens where the highest
judicial court sat. Strictly, an areopagite is a member of that court, but by
association can mean a member of any secret tribunal or body. Here the
meaning may be 'mystic' or a reference to the pseudo-Areopagite, Dionysius.
l. 250. *index*   finger.
l. 252. *Hyperion*   here, the sun.

170. CHARITAS NIMIA: OR THE DEAR BARGAIN. l. 24. *dominations*   in the
generally accepted hierarchy of Dionysius the dominations are the fourth of
the nine angelic orders.

171. IN THE GLORIOUS ASSUMPTION OF OUR BLESSED LADY. Text based on that of
1652: see Martin for another version.

173. ON A PRAYER BOOK SENT TO MRS M. R. Mrs M. R. has not been identified.
Text of 1646: see Martin for another version. ll. 5–8. this is often cited in
the renaissance as an example of scholastic absurdity, but is now generally
regarded as a renaissance invention.
l. 44. *gad*   wander fecklessly.
l. 45. *god of flies*   Satan.
l. 61. *Effectual*   true.
l. 110. *roseal*   rosy.
ll. 112–13. No explanation of this lacuna is known.

176. IN MEMORY OF THE VIRTUOUS AND LEARNÈD LADY MADRE DE TERESA. Text
based on that of 1646: see Martin for another version.
l. 32. *nonage*   infancy.
l. 71. *race*   raze, tear open.
ll. 123–5. The reference is to the Virgin Mary and her train of virgins (see
Rev. 13:3–4).
l. 172. *zone*   girdle.
l. 175. *score*   tally.
180. AN APOLOGY FOR THE PRECEDENT HYMN. l. 29. *enow*   enough.
l. 40. *wine-press*   see Isa. 63:3.

181. ON HOPE. . . . Text based on that of 1646: see Martin for another version.
l. 12. *entity*   essential being.
l. 50. See above, p. 254, 'The Progress of Learning', l. 168n.

184. TO THE NOBLEST AND BEST OF LADIES. . . . Susan, Countess of Denbigh, was

the daughter of Sir George Villiers and seems finally to have become a Roman Catholic. The collection (*Carmen Deo Nostro*, 1652) from which this poem comes is dedicated to her. See Martin for another version.

185. TO THE NAME ABOVE EVERY NAME. . . . l. 30. These are the concentric spheres of the Ptolemaic astronomy.

l. 211. *transpire*   exhale.

ABRAHAM COWLEY

191. THE REQUEST. l. 36. *Venus*   goddess of love.   *Diana*   goddess of hunting.

192. THE THRALDOM. l. 1. A witty variation of the famous tag 'Veni, vidi, vici' ('I came, I saw, I conquered').
l. 10. See Mark 5 : 8–9 ; Luke 8 : 28f.

193. THE GIVEN LOVE. l. 29. *jointure*   marriage-settlement.
l. 32. See Gen. 2 : 21f.
l. 42. Zeus visited Danae in a shower of gold.
ll. 59–60. According to the Roman Catholic doctrine of indulgences, merit may be acquired by money payments to offset the soul's residence in purgatory.
l. 69. *assize*   the final judgement.

195. THE SPRING. ll. 23–4. Apollo wooed Daphne who fled from his advances and was changed into a tree to save her from rape.
ll. 26–8. *Orpheus*   (see above, p. 253) was from Thrace.
ll. 33–40. The idea that the mistress trancends nature is a renaissance commonplace.

196. WRITTEN IN JUICE OF LEMON. l. 23. Testing innocence by fire (e.g. by holding a red-hot ploughshare) was abolished in England under Henry III.

198. NOT FAIR. l. 2. *idea*   see above, p. 257, 'Wishes to . . .', l. 11n.
l. 14. *succubus*   a female demon (the cleft foot was traditionally a betraying mark of the devil or a demon).

199. PLATONIC LOVE Many seventeenth-century poets treat this theme: Edward Herbert, for example, has three pieces called 'Platonic Love'.
l. 20. *Narcissus*   see above, p. 246, 'Upon Ben Johnson', l. 17n.

200. ANSWER TO THE PLATONICS. l. 15. *the thunderer*   Zeus, who brought Pallas forth from his forehead.
l. 22. *lambent*   gleaming.
l. 29. *Pygmalion*   King of Crete, who fell in love with a statue.
l. 30. *hot youth*   Paris, who abducted Helen.

201. THE WISH. l. 33. *embracing, die*   including the sexual sense of climax.

203. THE THIEF. l. 18. *points*   full stops.
ll. 20–1. *Midas*   semi-legendary King of Phrygia, who was granted his wish that everything he touched should turn to gold.

203. THE BARGAIN. ll. 13–14. The idea that the sun generated gold is common (see, for example, Pope, 'Windsor Forest', l. 396; Marlow, 'Hero and Leander', III, ll. 24f. ; Browne's remark in *Religio Medici* about the 'solary and celestial nature' of 'that mystical metal of Gold').
l. 20. Magus, king of Phrygia, was given a wish by Silenus and wished that everything he touched should become gold.

l. 22. *simony*   strictly, the buying and selling of church benefices.

205. RESOLVED TO BE BELOVED. l. 5. *Canaan*   the Jews' promised lanp (see Gen. 17:8).   *fatal*   destined.
l. 18. *competency*   adequate amount to live on.

207. AGAINST FRUITION. There are a number of seventeenth-century poems on this topic—e.g. Suckling's two poems 'Against Fruition' and King's 'Paradox that fruition destroys love'.
l. 13. *Pellaean*   Alexander the Great of Macedonia—Pella was his capital.

209. THE PROPHET. l. 4. *stews*   brothels.
l. 19. *receipt*   recipe.

210. WOMEN'S SUPERSTITION. l. 3. *contexture*   that which unites things.
l. 15. *Ashtaroth*   Semitic fertility god; Baal's female counterpart.

210. THE SOUL. l. 3. *informed*   dwelt in.

214. THE USURPATION. l. 12. *drav'st*   drive.
l. 31. *basilisk*   fabulous creature whose breath or look was fatal.

215. MAIDENHEAD. l. 31. *charge*   weight of labour or trouble.

216. WEEPING. l. 20. *limbeck*   vessel used in chemistry for distillation (alembic).
l. 24. *admire*   wonder.

219. THE INCURABLE. l. 3. *receipts*   recipes.
l. 20. *clinch*   pun (regarded as a feeble rhetorical device).

221. DIALOGUE. l. 28. *triumph*   ceremonial procession granted to Romans who had achieved a major military victory.

223. OF WIT. l. 12. *Zeuxis*   Greek painter of the fifth century B.C., from Heraclea. There is a story that his painting of a bunch of grapes was so lifelike that birds came to peck it.
l. 20. *tit'lar bishops*   bishops in title only, having no duties.
ll. 29–30. See above, p. 247, 'At Penshurst', l. 17n.
l. 50. *Bajazet*   the Emperor of Turkey in Marlowe's *Tamburlaine*.
l. 52. *Seneca*   (*c.* 4 B.C.–A.D. 65) whose tragedies influenced Elizabethan drama.
ll. 61ff. The idea is that everything exists *in potentia* in the mind of God.

225. UPON HIS MAJESTY'S RESTORATION AND RETURN. From *Aeneid* IX, 6–7: 'See, the passage of time has brought of its own accord a wish which no god would have dared promise you.'
l. 6. *Plenipotentiary*   ambassador with full negotiating powers.
l. 10. The reference is to the seven brightest stars in Ursa Major. The stars are known as Charles's wain—a corruption of O.E. 'carles waēn' ('farmer's wagon')—and were associated with both Charles I and II.
ll. 11f. A bright star was seen on Charles's birth day at noon: as one might expect the event is mentioned by several other poets, including Jonson, Herrick and Corbet.
l. 40. *Halcyon*   see above, p. 245, 'Puerperium', l. 16n
l. 45. *candid*   shining white.
l. 50. The sixth labour of Hercules was to clean the stables of Augeas, King of Elis.
ll. 52–4. John Bradshaw presided at Charles's trial, being President of the High Court of Justice.
l. 72. *sacred four*   James of York, Henry of Gloucester, Mary, Henriette-Anne.

l. 105. *triumvirate*   strictly a union of three men; more loosely, any trinity.
ll. 116f. See Matt, 27:25. The town is Jerusalem, the 'greater blood' Christ's.
ll. 149–50. See above, l. 72n.
l. 157. See Dan. 3.
l. 158. See Exod. 14.
l. 169. *entailed*   bequeathed.
l. 174. *the martyr*   Peter.
l. 203. *foolish lights   ignes fatui.*
l. 210. *his son*   Richard Cromwell, who briefly followed Oliver as Protector.
l. 227. *resuscitation*   resurrection.
l. 237. *doubt*   suspect.
l. 251. *triarian*   third (strictly, referring to the third rank of soldiers).
l. 278. *pious Trojan*   Aeneas ('pius Aeneas').   *prudent Greek*   Ulysses.
ll. 280–1. Referring to the sons of Ge who vainly rebelled against Zeus.
l. 293. *fatal*   destined.
l. 312. *Worcester*   Charles's defeat at Worcester (1651) firmly established Parliament's victory in the Civil War.
l. 319. See Dan. 3.
l. 340. *two bright creatures*   Mary, Henriette-Anne.
l. 341. *the royal three*   Charles, James, Henry.
l. 342. See above, p. 259, 'Written in Juice of Lemon', n.; and Dan. 3.
l. 350. See Dan. 3:25, 28.
l. 378. *the royal mother*   Henrietta Maria.
l. 397. *heroic person*   George Monk (see above, p. 255).
l. 404. *Zerubbabel*   see Hag. and Zech. 4:6f.
l. 440. The Long Parliament sat from 1640 to 1653 and thus through the war and Charles's execution.

236. AGE. l. 2. *Anacreon*   sixth-century Greek poet who specialized in witty, light songs of love and wine.
l. 11. *stake*   here, last section of life.

236. THE ACCOUNT. l. 13. *Chios*   island off the coast of Asia Minor (so also Lesbos at l. 14).
l. 18. *Ionian*   Ionia is part of the west coast of Asia Minor.
l. 19. *Carian*   Caria was a country in S.W. Asia Minor.
l. 29. *Xerxes*   succeeded Darius as Persian king and invaded Greece.

237. THE GRASSHOPPER. l. 8. *Ganymed*   Ganymede was the beautiful Trojan prince who was seized and taken to be Zeus' cupbearer.

239. THE CHRONICLE. l. 74. *Matchavil*   Machiavelli, as symbolic of trickery.
l. 78. *Holinshed*   Ralph Holinshed (?1528–?1580), 'author' of *Chronicles* (1577, revised 1586).   *Stow*   John Stow (1525–1605), author of the *Annals of England* (1560).

241. TO THE BISHOP OF LINCOLN. . . . This Bishop of Lincoln is John Wilson, who was in the Tower 1637–41. When Laud fell from power Wilson, a more moderate man, was appointed Archbishop of York.
l. 17. *Tully*   Marcus Tullius Cicero, who was banished in 58 B.C. and returned in 57.

243. THE TREE OF KNOWLEDGE. . . . l. 4. The reference is to the neo-Platonist Porphyry, a follower of Plotinus.

243. REASON. . . . ll. 21f. See I Sam. 28:7f.
l. 33. *eighth sphere*   in the Ptolemaic system the eighth sphere was that of the fixed stars.
ll. 45–6. See Deut. 34:4.

Index of First Lines